CONTENTS

THE GOOD, THE BAD AND THE UGLY
OF LEEDS UNITED!
Leeds United in the 1980s

First Publishied in Great Britain in 2015 by DB Publishing, an imprint of JMD Media Ltd

ISBN 978-1-78091-368-1

Printed and bound in the UK by Copytech (UK) Ltd Peterborough

THE GOOD, THE BAD AND THE UGLY
OF LEEDS UNITED!
Leeds United in the 1980s

Andrew Dalton & Heidi Haigh

DB PUBLISHING

DEDICATIONS

Andrew's Dedication

I would like to dedicate this book to a very good friend of mine, Michael Walter, who was taken from us this summer. Mike would be one of the first people I would see in the Bremner Suite at home matches and also be the first I would moan to at half-time and full-time! We shared many a conversation over the last five years and he will be sadly missed by all that knew him.

Heidi's Dedication

I would like to dedicate this book to all the Leeds United fans who are no longer with us. Timmy Deighton and Martin Knowles from Snaith, Gadge, Mick Thompson and Bob Vasey from Leeds, Mark Belshaw from Wellingborough, Marion Fudge from London, Brian Austin from Halifax, Christopher Loftus and Kevin Speight to name a few. There are many thousands more sharing memories with Don Revie, Les Cocker, Billy Bremner and Gary Speed and looking down onto the great Leeds support.

They will always be in our hearts. Marching on Together!

FOREWORD

MICKY ADAMS

When I wasn't getting regular match time at Coventry in the old First Division, I got a call from the then Leeds United manager Billy Bremner, asking if I would be interested in joining Leeds? It was a no brainer; being a Sheffield lad and when I wasn't watching the Blades as a kid, I used to watch the Whites at Elland Road. I didn't realise how big the club was, even when they were playing in the old Second Division! The fans would come from all over the country; there were big expectations even back in the 1980s. You had to have a big match mentality to play at Elland Road.

Playing in an FA Cup semi-final in 1987 against my old club, was a nerve racking experience. The Leeds fans were brilliant that day, the Leppings Lane end was packed and it was a fantastic atmosphere. It was a match we really should have won having gone in front thanks to a David Rennie header. We were 14 minutes away from Wembley, when Brendan Ormsby tried to shepherd a ball out and got caught. I still remind him of it to this day! To make matters worse, I was living in Coventry at the time and it was surreal going back after the match as all the pubs were packed! It was strange playing against my old friends!

Playing in the Play-off Final against Charlton, we had players such as Mark Aizlewood and Bobby McDonald available, who we didn't have in the FA Cup semi-final as they were cup tied. Yet again the fans were magnificent that night at St Andrews. Peter Shirtliff, who hadn't scored all season, scored two as we switched off and it felt heartbreaking and we all felt sorry for Billy.

There is always a great debate as to who has the best fans, but the Leeds fans take some beating! They have had to put up with a lot, especially in the 1980s as it was tough for them. We thought we would give them a taste of glory with the FA Cup run and coming so close in the Play-offs. The fans were vociferous and they would always back you, providing we gave it our all.

Playing for someone like Billy Bremner was great. He would tell us that we were Leeds United and should go out and play. We needed to be more organised when we could have been, but he liked players to enjoy training, which was pretty basic. It was great fun working with him every day. He was a fantastic bloke who we had great banter with, especially on the bus when we were playing cards. Howard Wilkinson on the other hand, was everything Billy wasn't. He was meticulous, organised, had team meetings most days, everybody knew their roles and responsibilities, he was a fitness fanatic and training picked up.

Captaining the Whites was one of the greatest honours of my career. This was especially so when I was asked to lead the side out by Billy Bremner the most successful captain in the club's history, as well as scoring one of the goals away at Wigan in the FA Cup quarter-final.

Micky Adams

PROLOGUE

ANDREW'S REASONS FOR WRITING THIS BOOK

Having been a supporter of Leeds United football club since the 1991–92 season (I am not a glory supporter before you ask!) and seen many ups and downs of the great football club, I wanted to explore the forgotten decade of Leeds United, the 1980s. Having seen all the ups and downs over the last 24 years, including seeing us winning the title in 1992, the European runs under David O'Leary, relegation from both the Premier League and the Championship and promotion under Simon Grayson in 2010, the 1980s was an era that time forgot.

Having had a huge thirst for statistics since I was seven years old and having appeared on the *Alvin Blossom Sports Show* at Christmas 1993 on BBC Radio Leeds, I wanted to explore a decade that I hadn't had much prior knowledge about. For the last six seasons, I have been in a very fortunate position to have a lot of my work published in the Leeds United match day programme and will continue to do so for the forthcoming campaign. I also prepare a "stats pack" on the official club website for every match and thoroughly enjoy doing so, looking over past matches involving that week's opposition. As well as having one book published titled *Leeds United All White*, which was co-authored by Jon Howe, I felt that the 1980s, *The Good, The Bad and The Ugly of Leeds United* would be the next period that I would like to look back at.

I first approached Heidi a year or so ago, having seen that she has already had two books published. I felt that with her wonderful memories of supporting Leeds United and the numerous contacts she has with many Leeds supporters far and wide, that this would be the perfect combination to write a book on Leeds United in the 1980s.

Having produced the statistics for my previous book, it was great fun looking back at all the players that have played for this wonderful one city club during the 1980s. From players who made only a handful of appearances such as Roger Eli, to players such as Gordon Strachan who made a significant contribution to the club, every player who wore the white shirt is mentioned in the book. As well as looking back at every player that played for the side in the 1980s, every result is included from season 1980–81 to the end of the 1989–90 season. Who can forget the drubbings at Stoke when Mervyn Day once said, "we won't concede six again," only to go and concede seven, to the euphoria that occurred on 5 May 1990 on the South Coast at Bournemouth and all that went with it.

Having only been born in 1985, I felt that the time was right to produce a book and bring back some of the memories that many supporters may have forgotten. Heidi has been in contact with many supporters to get their views and we both hope that you enjoy reliving all the memories from the 1980s.

It is perhaps fitting that the decade ended with Leeds United winning promotion from the old Second Division and this book will take you on a rollercoaster of what it was like to support the

Whites over the decade. No fan would have ever imagined that having played in the European Cup Final in 1975, that seven years later the club would be playing its football in the second tier for the first time since 1964. Added to that, no one could have ever imagined that it would take eight seasons, three managers and numerous players to get out of the Second Division and back into the First Division!

I then contacted *True Colours* editor John Devlin and was delighted when he responded that he would be more than happy to provide a chapter on the kits that Leeds United wore in the 1980s, as it gives the book that little bit extra and brings back all the memories!

I have, like Heidi, thoroughly enjoyed researching an era that I knew very little about, having only seen small snippets on TV and in the match day programmes. I have also now become a fully-fledged programme collector with every Leeds United programme home and away since the start of the 1973–74 season and my knowledge is increasing on a daily basis.

If you choose to do so, you can follow me on twitter @lufcstats with my daily ramblings! I am shocked to have over 7,000 followers! We both hope you enjoy reading about the 1980s and it brings back all those memories you may have forgotten about. The back end of the decade under Sgt. Wilko really did set Leeds on the way to future success and let's hope that current incumbent Uwe Rösler can have the same affect over the up and coming months:

Happy reading and keep Marching on Together!

HEIDI'S REASONS

I have known Andrew for a number of years and when he asked me to help him with this book, I agreed immediately. He wanted to write about the '80s as he felt that so much happened through this decade, especially the violence on the terraces and he wanted to find out more about what had happened. He loves doing his stats so wanted them to be recorded in the book. As with the two previous books I have written; *Follow Me and Leeds United* and *Once a Leeds fan, always a Leeds fan*, the words "man utd" are written this way for the purpose of this book.

Although I didn't travel to away matches for the first two seasons in the '80s due to having my first two children, I still attended all the home matches. I was still in touch with friends who did go though, so normally would end up chatting to them and they would always talk about what had happened to them. After Leeds were relegated in 1982, I found that I still had the bug of going to matches, regardless of us being in the Second Division. I attended our first match in the Second Division away at Grimsby with my sister Erica, two weeks after giving birth to my daughter Michelle. My sister Karin babysat for me as my dad dropped us both off at Thorne to catch the Griffin coach from Leeds. I then started going back to a few away matches and in 1983, went to the pre-season friendly at Falkirk with both my children, Jamie (aged two) and Michelle (aged 11 months). A friend Mike had offered to take us up to Scotland in his car, which made

Selby Whites Dinner Dance photo courtesy Heidi Haigh

Selby Whites Dinner Dance Russell Doig, Peter Swan and Ronnie Sinclair photo Heidi Haigh

LUSC Selby Branch with David Batty photo Heidi Haigh

it easier for us to go. The away matches I attended were quite sporadic ones to begin with, but it didn't take long for me to want to start going to more and more though.

Abbey Coachways the local coach company always supplied travel to all the home matches and some near away matches. If they were not running, my friend Sue and I would travel by York Pullman coaches. Neither company would travel to the South Coast though, which is how we started to travel by Wallace Arnold coaches. Travelling to away matches during the '70s involved me travelling the 30 miles to Leeds from Carlton, near Goole either by car (with the help of my dad), or train. I would then travel from Leeds to the match with my friends by Wallace Arnold coaches, later National coaches and then with Fullerton Park Supporters Club. When coaches stopped running for a while, I travelled by train.

I have always been a member of the Leeds United Supporters Club, originally starting out in the Postal Branch. When the Selby Branch of the Leeds United Supporters Club was formed in 1985, I made a vow that it didn't matter how many members wanted to go to away matches, I would ensure they would have the transport to do so. After initially travelling with the Selby Branch by mini bus to the matches with me driving, it was nice to eventually be picked up on my doorstep by Ben driving our Voyager International coach. When I volunteered to become secretary of the branch to enable it to get off the ground, I then had another seven years of not missing a match home or away. This time all the matches were in this country and it is because of Don Revie and his great side in the '60s and '70s, that has made me the Leeds fan I still am today having supported them for 50 years.

I also feel that the role of the Supporters Club Branches in helping to stem the violence at matches during the 1980s should not be underestimated. At a personal cost for many branch personnel and the all ticket policy, they all played a part in reducing the violence at matches. Culminating with often over the top policing, this policy carried on into later years as it all settled down. It was only when Ken Bates took over at Leeds United and decided in his infinite wisdom to 'fight' the Supporters Club and made everyone join his Members Club instead, that this deteriorated in my opinion. After having kept a lid on things for many years, it was a free for

Selby Whites Dinner Dance Neil Aspin photo courtesy Heidi Haigh

Halifax Whites penalty competition on Fullerton Park photo Heidi Haigh

all, which saw violence once again appear at Elland Road. This undid all the hard work that had been done over the many years since the all ticket policy at matches came into existence. It also meant that the loyal Leeds United support ended up with division amongst the supporters in his divide and conquer rule!

I have recently been reminded by Charlie from Knaresborough, about me taking part in the Leeds United Supporters Club penalty competition first round. To be honest I couldn't remember it, so it is nice to be reminded of playing the Knaresborough branch on 1 November 1986 before the Shrewsbury Town match. The Selby Whites played them on the Elland Road pitch at the Kop end with me being in goal. It looks like I wasn't very good as Knaresborough won the tie! Leeds won their match 1–0 though with Neil Aspin scoring the goal with an attendance of 14,966.

Despite all the violence and flashpoints that happened at lots of places in the '80s, the thing that stands out in my mind of that time was the fact that Leeds fans had started to stick together. Although there were some fans who did go looking for trouble and enjoyed it, there were many others who if they were attacked, would stand up for themselves and fight back and would never start any trouble. Many others like me just wanted to follow Leeds without any issues. The camaraderie amongst the fans is still something that I treasure to this day, with thousands of loyal fans who have stuck with them regardless. Another thing that stands out for me was that Leeds fans would look after each other too. The atmosphere at Elland Road was electric and very intimidating for opposition teams who came there, with Leeds fans being both in the

Kop and behind the goal in the South Stand. WACCOE – We are the Champions, Champions of Europe rang out with first one side singing – We are the Champions and all putting their arms in the air as a salute, then the other side singing Champions of Europe and doing the same salute. It was absolutely awesome in action and having seen Leeds fans in the South Stand doing this recently on a YouTube clip, it was fantastic to see. They are great memories to have and just made following Leeds special. This was recreated on our recent pre-season tour to Austria and I am hoping to see this catch on with our fans this season. There has been a clapping and waving your scarves version and although the latter looks great, you can't hear what is being sung. Glynn Snodin also started doing the Leeds salute, which was reciprocated by us all and he still does it to this day. Putting your fist to your heart three times whilst chanting Leeds, Leeds, Leeds is something I do automatically at corners, whenever I see another Leeds fan or see stickers in cars! Despite attendances dipping, it was a great time to be a Leeds fan, as Leeds ended the era getting promoted back to League Division One. Two years later we also won the First Division Title under Howard Wilkinson's guidance.

I am still a home season ticket holder with my two youngest daughters Danielle and Emily and I have an away season ticket this year too. After not getting a ticket for Rotherham through official channels last season, it was harder to get tickets unless they used the loyalty scheme. I

Heidi and Phillip with Vinnie Jones

Selby Whites - Sherburn in Elmet lads pub stop in Doncaster photo courtesy Dave Morris

would rather be guaranteed my ticket if at all possible and regardless of all the things still going on in the background at Elland Road, I am looking forward to this forthcoming season. First I am lucky to have had an early birthday present with a trip to the pre-season matches in Austria and Oslo, Norway. It has been great catching up with all our fans and as usual I have taken lots of photos and shared them on my website www.followmeandleedsunited.co.uk and my Facebook page Follow me and Leeds United. I can also be followed on Twitter @FollowMeAndLUFC.

THANK YOU AND ACKNOWLEDGEMENTS!

Andrew and I would like to extend our grateful thanks to the following Leeds United fans for their contributions to this book; as ever, everyone has so many different stories to tell together with their own individual memories that we feel should be shared with others.

Pam Freer, Sean Caden, Tricky Dicky, Andy Johnson, Ray Ashworth, Billy Leeds, Daisy, Andy Peterson, Chris Payne, Dan Toronczak, Darren Aveyard, Graham Watson, Kay Fox, Keith Ingham, Martin Taylor, Paul Blann, Peter Dillon, Phil Mason, Soren Trapp, James Lyons, Ian Halmshaw, Nick Connor, G from South Leeds, Popeye, Mark Dovey and KBEES.

Thank you also to Craig Gill, Dave Morris, Steve Waterhouse, Mark Dovey, Brian Austin, Pam Freer and Heidi Haigh for sharing their photos for the book.

A big thank you also, to Micky Adams for doing the Foreword for this book and John Devlin – www.truecoloursfootballkits.com for his contribution.

Marching on Together!

SEASON 1980–81

The Whites started the first full season of the decade, with manager Jimmy Adamson still coming under mounting pressure. The main piece of transfer news involved Argentinian striker Alex Sabella coming in from Yorkshire rivals Sheffield United for £400,000. Leaving the club were Peter Hampton who went to Stoke City for £175,000 and Wayne Entwistle who joined Blackpool on a free transfer.

Having finished the previous season in 11th place, the pressure was on straight away and Leeds got off to a poor start, losing at home to Aston Villa (2–1) and away at Middlesbrough (3–0). They recovered to win at Norwich City by the odd goal in five, but further defeats in the next two League matches, at home to Leicester (2–1) and 3–0 away at Stoke, coupled with an early exit from the League Cup to Aston Villa, saw Adamson resign.

Maurice Lindley took over as caretaker manager once again, over-seeing a goalless draw at home to Tottenham, before FA Cup Final winning hero Allan Clarke, was handed the reins. He took over a team that was one place off the bottom of the League, but received an outstanding ovation in his first match at home to man utd, which ended 0–0. It was a small step in the right direction. Writing in his programme notes Clarke said, "I have told the players that they will be given the opportunity in the next few weeks to show me what they can do and I think they realise what I expect from them in terms in attitude, not only on Saturday afternoons but throughout the week in training".

One of his first jobs was to switch Eddie Gray to left-back in place of Byron Stevenson, with Brian Greenhoff taking the number two shirt and the right-back slot, in place of Kevin Hird. Captain Trevor Cherry would partner Paul Hart at the centre of defence. Despite a 4–1 defeat away at Sunderland, slowly but surely, results improved. Consecutive 1–0 home victories against Manchester City and Everton, with Alan Curtis and Terry Connor scoring the goals, moved the Whites up to 16th and away from the relegation zone.

A disastrous 5–0 home defeat against Arsenal dropped the Whites to 19th and it was a match that saw the end of a wonderful career of Leeds stalwart Paul Madeley. 'Rolls Royce' as he was known made over 700 appearances for the club, in a career which lasted 18 years. He won both the First and Second Division as a Leeds United player, as well as the League Cup, FA Cup and the Fairs Cup twice. He was named in the First Division team of the year in three consecutive seasons. He was named Leeds United player of the year in 1975–76. He also captained the Whites, for the first and only time in his career. Manager Don Revie handed him the armband in the UEFA Cup first round, first leg tie away at Stromsgodset in September 1973, when both Billy Bremner and Cherry were missing. He also had the unique distinction of wearing every shirt number from 2–11 as well as the number 12 shirt! He would retire at the season's end. It left just Eddie Gray and Cherry as the only former players still going from the Revie Era.

Following the Arsenal drubbing, results improved with only one defeat in the next nine matches, which moved the side up to 16th in the League by the end of the year. Coventry ended any hopes of an FA Cup run by winning a third round replay at Highfield Road, which left the Whites solely with the League to focus on.

A 3–0 away defeat on the South Coast at Southampton, didn't help matters, but back to back victories away at Leicester (1–0) and at home to Norwich also 1–0, moved Leeds up to 14th but defeat at Stoke on St Valentine's day, slipped the club back to 15th. It would be the lowest League position the club would find themselves in for the remainder of the season. Following the defeat at Stoke, Leeds found their best form of the season; winning six out of the next seven League matches. A Carl Harris goal defeated Sunderland at Elland Road, which was then followed up by a result everyone inside Elland Road wanted, a 1–0 away win at Old Trafford, thanks to a goal from Brian Flynn. Everton were then beaten away 2–1 at Goodison Park, with goals coming from Derek Parlane and Carl Harris. Despite Wolves ending the winning run, three more victories followed, 1–0 away at Crystal Palace and two 3–0 wins at home to Ipswich Town and Coventry City respectively.

A sign of improvement came at Highbury as Leeds reversed a 5–0 drubbing earlier in the season, to draw 0–0 in mid-April. Liverpool were held 0–0, before Leeds won at St Andrews 2–0, thanks to strikes from Parlane and a penalty from Kevin Hird. The last away trip of the season, saw a disappointing 2–0 defeat and third goalless draw in five at home to West Bromwich Albion (WBA), which saw the Whites end the season in a respectable 9th place.

Having arrived in mid-September, with the side struggling at the wrong end of the table, Clarke could be satisfied with a top half finish. The final 16 matches of the season saw the side win nine, draw three and lose only four matches. Carl Harris ended the season as top scorer with 10 goals from 33 matches and John Lukic was the only ever present player. Of the outfield players, Trevor Cherry and Brian Flynn only missed one match each, whilst striker Arthur Graham missed only two League matches all season.

The challenge now for Clarke and his management team of Martin Wilkinson and Barry Murphy, was to return the side to the top of the table and challenge for honours.

ANDREW'S BEST AND WORST MATCHES THIS SEASON

Best: man utd (A) 1–0 Flynn, 28 February 1981 – Need I say more!

Worst: Arsenal (H) 0–5, 8 November 1980 – Does it get any worse? –John Lukic had a nightmare!

DIVISION ONE TABLE 1980–81							
	P	W	D	L	F	A	PTS
1. ASTON VILLA **C**	42	26	8	8	72	40	60
2. IPSWICH TOWN	42	23	10	9	77	43	56
3. ARSENAL	42	19	15	8	61	45	53
4. WEST BROMWICH ALBION	42	20	12	10	60	42	52
5. LIVERPOOL	42	17	17	8	62	42	51
6. SOUTHAMPTON	42	29	10	12	76	56	50
7. NOTTINGHAM FOREST	42	19	12	11	62	44	50
8. man utd	42	15	18	9	51	36	48
9. LEEDS UNITED	42	17	10	15	39	47	44
10. TOTTENHAM HOTSPUR	42	14	15	13	70	68	43
11. STOKE CITY	42	12	18	12	51	60	42
12. MANCHESTER CITY	42	14	11	17	56	59	39
13. BIRMINGHAM CITY	42	13	12	17	50	61	38
14. MIDDLESBROUGH	42	16	5	21	53	61	37
15. EVERTON	42	13	10	19	55	58	36
16. COVENTRY CITY	42	13	10	19	48	68	36
17. SUNDERLAND	42	14	7	21	52	53	35
18. WOLVERHAMPTON WANDERERS	42	13	9	20	43	55	35
19. BRIGHTON & HOVE ALBION	42	14	7	21	54	67	35
20. NORWICH CITY **R**	42	13	7	22	49	73	33
21. LEICESTER CITY **R**	42	13	6	23	40	67	32
22. CRYSTAL PALACE **R**	42	6	7	29	47	83	19

DATE	OPPOSITION	VENUE	COMPETITION	SCORE	ATT	SCORERS
16/08/1980	ASTON VILLA	ELLAND ROAD	DIVISION ONE	1–2	23,401	STEVENSON (P)
19/08/1980	MIDDLESBROUGH	AYRESOME PARK	DIVISION ONE	0–3	19,470	
23/08/1980	NORWICH CITY	CARROW ROAD	DIVISION ONE	3–2	17,890	HART, GRAHAM, CONNOR
27/08/1980	ASTON VILLA	VILLA PARK	LEAGUE CUP 2ND ROUND 1ST LEG	0–1	24,238	
30/08/1980	LEICESTER CITY	ELLAND ROAD	DIVISION ONE	1–2	18,530	HART
03/09/1980	ASTON VILLA	ELLAND ROAD	LEAGUE CUP 2ND ROUND 2ND LEG	1–3	12,236	GRAHAM
06/09/1980	STOKE CITY	VICTORIA GROUND	DIVISION ONE	0–3	12,279	
13/09/1980	TOTTENHAM HOTSPUR	ELLAND ROAD	DIVISION ONE	0–0	21,947	
20/09/1980	man utd	ELLAND ROAD	DIVISION ONE	0–0	32,539	
27/09/1980	SUNDERLAND	ROKER PARK	DIVISION ONE	1–4	29,619	PARLANE
04/10/1980	IPSWICH TOWN	PORTMAN ROAD	DIVISION ONE	1–1	24,087	SABELLA
08/10/1980	MANCHESTER CITY	ELLAND ROAD	DIVISION ONE	1–0	19,134	HARRIS
11/10/1980	EVERTON	ELLAND ROAD	DIVISION ONE	1–0	25,601	CURTIS
18/10/1980	WOLVERHAMPTON WANDERERS	MOLINEUX	DIVISION ONE	1–2	20,699	CONNOR
22/10/1980	NOTTINGHAM FOREST	CITY GROUND	DIVISION ONE	1–2	25,033	HARRIS
25/10/1980	CRYSTAL PALACE	ELLAND ROAD	DIVISION ONE	1–0	19,208	CONNOR
01/11/1980	COVENTRY CITY	HIGHFIELD ROAD	DIVISION ONE	1–2	13,970	CONNOR
08/11/1980	ARSENAL	ELLAND ROAD	DIVISION ONE	0–5	20,855	
12/11/1980	MIDDLESBROUGH	ELLAND ROAD	DIVISION ONE	2–1	17,382	HIRD 2 (1P)
15/11/1980	ASTON VILLA	VILLA PARK	DIVISION ONE	1–1	29,106	SABELLA
22/11/1980	SOUTHAMPTON	THE DELL	DIVISION ONE	1–2	20,278	GRAHAM
29/11/1980	BRIGHTON & HOVE ALBION	ELLAND ROAD	DIVISION ONE	1–0	14,333	HARRIS
06/12/1980	WEST BROMWICH ALBION	THE HAWTHORNS	DIVISION ONE	2–1	17,771	HARRIS, GRAHAM
13/12/1980	NOTTINGHAM FOREST	ELLAND ROAD	DIVISION ONE	1–0	21,822	GREENHOFF
20/12/1980	MANCHESTER CITY	MAINE ROAD	DIVISION ONE	0–1	31,866	
26/12/1980	BIRMINGHAM CITY	ELLAND ROAD	DIVISION ONE	0–0	19,214	
27/12/1980	LIVERPOOL	ANFIELD	DIVISION ONE	0–0	44,086	
03/01/1981	COVENTRY CITY	ELLAND ROAD	FA CUP 3RD ROUND	1–1	24,523	HIRD
06/01/1981	COVENTRY CITY	HIGHFIELD ROAD	FA CUP 3RD ROUND REPLAY	0–1	22,057	
10/01/1981	SOUTHAMPTON	ELLAND ROAD	DIVISION ONE	0–3	21,077	

17/01/1981	LEICESTER CITY	FILBERT STREET	DIVISION ONE	1–0	16,094	HART
31/01/1981	NORWICH CITY	ELLAND ROAD	DIVISION ONE	1–0	15,836	HARRIS
07/02/1981	TOTTENHAM HOTSPUR	WHITE HART LANE	DIVISION ONE	1–1	32,372	HARRIS
14/02/1981	STOKE CITY	ELLAND ROAD	DIVISION ONE	1–3	16,530	FLYNN
21/02/1981	SUNDERLAND	ELLAND ROAD	DIVISION ONE	1–0	23,236	HARRIS
28/02/1981	man utd	OLD TRAFFORD	DIVISION ONE	1–0	45,733	FLYNN
14/03/1981	EVERTON	GOODISON PARK	DIVISION ONE	2–1	23,014	PARLANE, HARRIS
21/03/1981	WOLVERHAMPTON WANDERERS	ELLAND ROAD	DIVISION ONE	1–3	19,252	HARRIS
28/03/1981	CRYSTAL PALACE	SELHURST PARK	DIVISION ONE	1–0	15,053	PARLANE
31/03/1981	IPSWICH TOWN	ELLAND ROAD	DIVISION ONE	3–0	26,462	HIRD (P), HARRIS, HART
04/04/1981	COVENTRY CITY	ELLAND ROAD	DIVISION ONE	3–0	15,882	STEVENSON, PARLANE, FLYNN
11/04/1981	ARSENAL	HIGHBURY	DIVISION ONE	0–0	29,339	
18/04/1981	LIVERPOOL	ELLAND ROAD	DIVISION ONE	0–0	39,206	
21/04/1981	BIRMINGHAM CITY	ST ANDREWS	DIVISION ONE	2–0	14,505	PARLANE, HIRD (P)
02/05/1981	BRIGHTON & HOVE ALBION	GOLDSTONE GROUND	DIVISION ONE	0–2	27,577	
06/05/1981	WEST BROMWICH ALBION	ELLAND ROAD	DIVISION ONE	0–0	17,218	

APPEARANCES				
PLAYERS	LEAGUE	FA CUP	LEAGUE CUP	TOTAL
AIDAN BUTTERWORTH	0 (1)			0 (1)
JEFF CHANDLER	8 (1)	1	1	10 (1)
TREVOR CHERRY	41	2	2	45
TERRY CONNOR	25 (2)	1	2	28 (2)
ALAN CURTIS	6			6
MARTIN DICKINSON	0 (1)			0 (1)
NEIL FIRM	5 (1)			5 (1)
BRIAN FLYNN	41	2	2	45
ARTHUR GRAHAM	40	2	2	44
EDDIE GRAY	38	2		40
BRIAN GREENHOFF	36	1	2	39
GARY HAMSON	7 (4)	1 (1)	1	9 (5)
CARL HARRIS	33 (4)		0 (1)	33 (5)
PAUL HART	38	2	2	42

KEVIN HIRD	32 (1)	2		34 (1)
JOHN LUKIC	42	2	2	46
PAUL MADELEY	6		2	8
KEITH PARKINSON	3			3
DEREK PARLANE	22 (4)	2	1	25 (4)
ALEX SABELLA	22 (1)	2	2	26 (1)
BYRON STEVENSON	17 (1)			17 (1)
GWYN THOMAS	0 (2)		1	1 (2)

GOALS	LEAGUE	FA CUP	LEAGUE CUP	TOTAL
CARL HARRIS	10			10
KEVIN HIRD	4	1		5
DEREK PARLANE	5			5
TERRY CONNOR	4			4
ARTHUR GRAHAM	3		1	4
PAUL HART	4			4
BRIAN FLYNN	3			3
ALEX SABELLA	2			2
BYRON STEVENSON	2			2
ALAN CURTIS	1			1
BRIAN GREENHOFF	1			1

SEASON 1981–82

Having steadied the ship the previous season, manager Clarke set about making changes to his side. The board of directors backed him as they splashed out a club record £930,000 to secure the transfer of Peter Barnes from Manchester City. Frank Gray rejoined from Nottingham Forest for £300,000 whilst Alex Sabella ended his one-year stay at the club, by returning to his native Argentina to join Estudiantes for £120,000. Jeff Chandler went to Bolton Wanderers for £40,000.

Hopes were high as Leeds travelled to the Vetch Field to face the Division newcomers Swansea City on day one, but these were evaporated as the Whites fell to an embarrassing 5–1 score line. To make matters worse, highlights of the match were shown on *Match of the Day* later on that evening. Leeds did bounce back taking four points from their next two matches (this was the first season of three points for a win), drawing 1–1 at home to Everton and defeating Wolves 3–0 at Elland Road, with Scotsman Arthur Graham scoring all four goals. It proved to be a false dawn for Leeds, as only one point was picked up in the next five matches, sending the club to the bottom of the table.

Steve Balcombe made a scoring debut in a 1–1 draw in the next match at home to Aston Villa, but another defeat, this time 3–0 away at Liverpool, kept Leeds at the bottom of the pile. Changes needed to be made, especially in defence, as the Whites had conceded 21 goals in just 10 League matches and Clarke spent £400,000 on Nottingham Forest defender Kenny Burns. It meant that Trevor Cherry moved to right-back and Paul Hart partnered Burns in defence. It had an instant effect as West Bromwich Albion were beaten 3–1 at Elland Road, thanks to goals from Graham, Cherry and Terry Connor. Just like the Swansea match, the highlights were shown on *Match of the Day* only this time, the Leeds fans could enjoy their Saturday night. The West Bromwich Albion victory moved the side up to 20th and it also saw Burns handed the captain's armband and he would keep the job for the remainder of the season. The Albion victory was followed by another win, this time at home to Sunderland with Eddie Gray scoring the lone goal.

Burns made an unhappy return to his former club Forest, in a 2–1 defeat, but rivals Notts County were then defeated thanks to a goal from local lad Aidan Butterworth, who was making only his third appearance in a Leeds shirt. By the end of 1981, (Leeds playing their last match on 12 December due to several postponements and bad weather), Leeds were in 17th place, three points above the dreaded bottom three.

The cup competitions came and went as first Ipswich Town knocked the side out in the second round of the League Cup, winning 4–0 on aggregate and Tottenham defeated Leeds 1–0 in the 4th round of the FA Cup at White Hart Lane.

The New Year saw a much-needed win, 2–0 at home to Swansea and it lifted the side up to 14th, their highest position since the start of September. However, five defeats in their next six matches left the Whites in 19th position, level on points with 20th place Wolverhampton Wanderers, but having played three matches less. With no goals in the last six, Clarke needed to pep up his attack and did just that by swooping for Birmingham City's Frank Worthington with Byron Stevenson going the other way.

Worthington made his debut in the last of those six matches and scored his first goal for the side in a morale boosting 1–0 away win at Sunderland. That pushed Leeds up a place, but two defeats in their next three matches, away at Wolves (1–0) and Notts County (2–1) left Leeds in 19th place. Two goalless draws followed at home to arch rivals man utd and away at Middlesbrough, which kept Leeds above water by one point and a maximum haul was achieved away at Birmingham thanks to a vital goal from defender Paul Hart. Leeds were in 18th place, with 10 matches to go and crucially still had three matches in hand over Wolves.

A 1–1 draw at home to Middlesbrough kept Leeds in 18th, but a 3–1 home defeat against Southampton dropped the side back to19th. Suddenly Wolves were in front of the Whites and it was now Birmingham City who held the last relegation spot. More importantly, Leeds only had one more match in hand. On 24 April, Leeds lost by the odd goal in seven at West Ham which found them back in the relegation zone for the first time since November. The only blessing from the trip to East London was that they still had three matches in hand over Wolves. Leeds then produced their best performance of the season, winning 4–1 at European Cup Finalists Aston Villa with Arthur Graham, that man Worthington with two and Connor scoring the goals. This win shot Leeds up to 17th place in the First Division, crucially a point clear of the relegation zone and still with two matches in hand.

The next three matches saw the Whites only pick up one point, 0–0 at home to Stoke. A 1–0 defeat at Everton and 2–1 away loss at Tottenham dropped the club into the bottom three with only three matches to go and to compound matters, West Bromwich Albion who were in 19th place had a match in hand. Leeds knew they had to beat relegation rivals Birmingham at Elland Road in their next match, but six goals were shared, leaving Leeds on the brink of relegation to the second tier of English football for the first time since 1963–64. In their penultimate match of the season at home to Brighton, Leeds trailed the Seagulls but late goals by Gary Hamson and Kevin Hird kept Leeds with their heads above water, but only just.

Leeds travelled to the Hawthorns to face West Bromwich Albion for their last match of the season, knowing a win would guarantee survival. Sadly a 2–0 defeat meant Leeds hopes lay with the hosts when they entertained Stoke City at the Victoria Ground two days later. The West Bromwich Albion match was marred by ugly scenes that the club could do without and their fate was sealed as Stoke won 3–0, 48 hours later.

Relegation meant the axe for Clarke and his assistant Martin Wilkinson with Eddie Gray replacing him. Goalkeeper John Lukic was the only ever present in the side, not missing a match all season. The Whites would start the following campaign in the Second Division. The last time the side was relegated from the top tier, it took four seasons to return, how long it would take this time around, would be anyone's guess!

ANDREW'S BEST AND WORST MATCHES THIS SEASON

Best: Brighton & Hove Albion (H) 2–1, Hamson, Hird, 15 May 1982 – Everyone thought we would be staying up!

Worst: WBA (A) 0–2, 18 May 1982, Relegation.

DIVISION ONE TABLE 1981–82							
	P	W	D	L	F	A	PTS
1. LIVERPOOL **C**	42	26	9	7	80	32	87
2. IPSWICH TOWN	42	26	5	11	75	53	83
3. man utd	42	22	12	8	59	29	78
4. TOTTENHAM HOTSPUR	42	20	11	11	67	48	71
5. ARSENAL	42	20	11	11	48	37	71
6. SWANSEA CITY	42	21	6	15	58	51	69
7. SOUTHAMPTON	42	19	9	14	72	67	66
8. EVERTON	42	17	13	12	56	50	64
9. WEST HAM UNITED	42	14	16	12	66	57	58
10. MANCHESTER CITY	42	15	13	14	49	50	58
11. ASTON VILLA	42	15	12	15	55	53	57
12. NOTTINGHAM FOREST	42	15	12	15	42	48	57
13. BRIGHTON & HOVE ALBION	42	13	13	16	43	52	52
14. COVENTRY CITY	42	13	11	18	56	62	50
15. NOTTS COUNTY	42	13	8	21	61	69	47
16. BIRMINGHAM CITY	42	10	14	18	53	61	44
17. WEST BROMWICH ALBION	42	11	11	20	46	57	44
18. STOKE CITY	42	12	8	22	44	63	44
19. SUNDERLAND	42	11	11	20	38	58	44
20. LEEDS UNITED **R**	42	10	12	20	39	61	42
21. WOLVERHAMPTON WANDERERS **R**	42	10	10	22	32	63	40
22. MIDDLESBROUGH **R**	42	8	15	19	34	52	39

DATE	OPPOSITION	VENUE	COMPETITION	SCORE	ATT	SCORERS
29/08/1981	SWANSEA CITY	VETCH FIELD	DIVISION ONE	1–5	23,489	PARLANE
02/09/1981	EVERTON	ELLAND ROAD	DIVISION ONE	1–1	26,502	GRAHAM
05/09/1981	WOLVERHAMPTON WANDERERS	ELLAND ROAD	DIVISION ONE	3–0	20,216	GRAHAM 3
12/09/1981	COVENTRY CITY	HIGHFIELD ROAD	DIVISION ONE	0–4	13,065	
19/09/1981	ARSENAL	ELLAND ROAD	DIVISION ONE	0–0	20,410	
23/09/1981	MANCHESTER CITY	MAINE ROAD	DIVISION ONE	0–4	35,077	
26/09/1981	IPSWICH TOWN	PORTMAN ROAD	DIVISION ONE	1–2	22,319	BARNES
30/09/1981	man utd	OLD TRAFFORD	DIVISION ONE	0–1	47,019	
03/10/1981	ASTON VILLA	ELLAND ROAD	DIVISION ONE	1–1	21,065	BALCOMBE
07/10/1981	IPSWICH TOWN	ELLAND ROAD	LEAGUE CUP 2ND ROUND 1ST LEG	0–1	16,994	
10/10/1981	LIVERPOOL	ANFIELD	DIVISION ONE	0–3	35,840	
17/10/1981	WEST BROMWICH ALBION	ELLAND ROAD	DIVISION ONE	3–1	19,164	GRAHAM, CHERRY, CONNOR
24/10/1981	SUNDERLAND	ELLAND ROAD	DIVISION ONE	1–0	25,220	E GRAY
27/10/1981	IPSWICH TOWN	PORTMAN ROAD	LEAGUE CUP 2ND ROUND 2ND LEG	0–3	16,464	
31/10/1981	NOTTINGHAM FOREST	CITY GROUND	DIVISION ONE	1–2	25,272	BUTTERWORTH
07/11/1981	NOTTS COUNTY	ELLAND ROAD	DIVISION ONE	1–0	19,552	BUTTERWORTH
21/11/1981	SOUTHAMPTON	THE DELL	DIVISION ONE	0–4	21,127	
28/11/1981	WEST HAM UNITED	ELLAND ROAD	DIVISION ONE	3–3	25,637	GRAHAM, HIRD (P), CHERRY
05/12/1981	STOKE CITY	VICTORIA GROUND	DIVISION ONE	2–1	13,901	GRAHAM, HAMSON
12/12/1981	TOTTENHAM HOTSPUR	ELLAND ROAD	DIVISION ONE	0–0	28,780	
02/01/1982	WOLVERHAMPTON WANDERERS	MOLINEUX	FA CUP 3RD ROUND	3–1	20,923	HAMSON, HIRD, E GRAY
16/01/1982	SWANSEA CITY	ELLAND ROAD	DIVISION ONE	2–0	18,700	STEVENSON, BUTTERWORTH
28/01/1982	TOTTENHAM HOTSPUR	WHITE HART LANE	FA CUP 4TH ROUND	0–1	46,126	
30/01/1982	ARSENAL	HIGHBURY	DIVISION ONE	0–1	22,408	
06/02/1982	COVENTRY CITY	ELLAND ROAD	DIVISION ONE	0–0	16,385	
20/02/1982	IPSWICH TOWN	ELLAND ROAD	DIVISION ONE	0–2	20,287	
27/02/1982	LIVERPOOL	ELLAND ROAD	DIVISION ONE	0–2	33,689	

02/03/1982	BRIGHTON & HOVE ALBION	GOLDSTONE GROUND	DIVISION ONE	0-1	12,857	
10/03/1982	MANCHESTER CITY	ELLAND ROAD	DIVISION ONE	0-1	20,797	
13/03/1982	SUNDERLAND	ROKER PARK	DIVISION ONE	1-0	20,285	WORTHINGTON
16/03/1982	WOLVERHAMPTON WANDERERS	MOLINEUX	DIVISION ONE	0-1	11,729	
20/03/1982	NOTTINGHAM FOREST	ELLAND ROAD	DIVISION ONE	1-1	18,036	WORTHINGTON (P)
27/03/1982	NOTTS COUNTY	MEADOW LANE	DIVISION ONE	1-2	13,316	WORTHINGTON
03/04/1982	man utd	ELLAND ROAD	DIVISION ONE	0-0	31,118	
06/04/1982	MIDDLESBROUGH	AYRESOME PARK	DIVISION ONE	0-0	15,494	
10/04/1982	BIRMINGHAM CITY	ST ANDREWS	DIVISION ONE	1-0	14,497	HART
13/04/1982	MIDDLESBROUGH	ELLAND ROAD	DIVISION ONE	1-1	20,458	PARLANE
17/04/1982	SOUTHAMPTON	ELLAND ROAD	DIVISION ONE	1-3	21,353	WORTHINGTON
24/04/1982	WEST HAM UNITED	UPTON PARK	DIVISION ONE	3-4	24,748	CONNOR, GRAHAM, FLYNN
28/04/1982	ASTON VILLA	VILLA PARK	DIVISION ONE	4-1	20,566	GRAHAM, WORTHINGTON 2, CONNOR
01/05/1982	STOKE CITY	ELLAND ROAD	DIVISION ONE	0-0	17,775	
04/05/1982	EVERTON	GOODISON PARK	DIVISION ONE	0-1	17,137	
08/05/1982	TOTTENHAM HOTSPUR	WHITE HART LANE	DIVISION ONE	1-2	35,020	WORTHINGTON
12/05/1982	BIRMINGHAM CITY	ELLAND ROAD	DIVISION ONE	3-3	18,583	WORTHINGTON 2 (1P), CONNOR
15/05/1982	BRIGHTON & HOVE ALBION	ELLAND ROAD	DIVISION ONE	2-1	19,831	HAMSON, HIRD
18/05/1982	WEST BROMWICH ALBION	THE HAWTHORNS	DIVISION ONE	0-2	23,118	

APPEARANCES				
PLAYERS	LEAGUE	FA CUP	LEAGUE CUP	TOTAL
TONY ARINS	0 (1)			0 (1)
NEIL ASPIN	1			1
STEVE BALCOMBE	1		1	2
PETER BARNES	31		2	33
KENNY BURNS	22 (1)	2		24 (1)
AIDAN BUTTERWORTH	13 (1)	2		15 (1)

TREVOR CHERRY	38	2	1	41
TERRY CONNOR	23 (4)		1	24 (4)
NEIL FIRM	3			3
BRIAN FLYNN	16 (1)	0 (1)		16 (2)
ARTHUR GRAHAM	38	2	2	42
EDDIE GRAY	31	2	2	35
FRANK GRAY	34	2	2	38
BRIAN GREENHOFF	10 (2)		1	11 (2)
GARY HAMSON	17 (1)	2	1	20 (1)
CARL HARRIS	15 (3)		2	17 (3)
PAUL HART	32	2	2	36
KEVIN HIRD	35 (3)	2	2	39 (3)
JOHN LUKIC	42	2	2	46
DEREK PARLANE	12			12
BYRON STEVENSON	18 (1)	2	1 (1)	21 (2)
GWYN THOMAS	13 (2)			13 (2)
FRANK WORTHINGTON	17			17

GOALS	LEAGUE	FA CUP	LEAGUE CUP	TOTAL
ARTHUR GRAHAM	9			9
FRANK WORTHINGTON	9			9
TERRY CONNOR	4			4
AIDAN BUTTERWORTH	3			3
GARY HAMSON	2	1		3
KEVIN HIRD	2	1		3
TREVOR CHERRY	2			2
EDDIE GRAY	1	1		2
DEREK PARLANE	2			2
STEVE BALCOMBE	1			1
PETER BARNES	1			1
BRIAN FLYNN	1			1
PAUL HART	1			1
BYRON STEVENSON	1			1

SEASON 1982–83

Leeds United started their first season out of the top flight since 1963–64 and with a new man in charge. Eddie Gray had taken the reins from Allan Clarke following relegation and the remit was to get back to the First Division as soon as possible. The problem was that crowds were down and the debt was reported to be £1.5million. Gray had to wheel and deal as best as he could and there weren't any incomings, but the club reduced the wage bill by loaning Peter Barnes to Real Betis for the season for £130,000 and Welsh international winger Carl Harris joined Charlton Athletic for £100,000. Gray brought in Jimmy Lumsden as his assistant and Syd Owen rejoined as chief scout.

The scene was set as Leeds travelled to Blundell Park to face Grimsby Town on the opening day of the new season. Despite an impressive performance in a match that finished 1–1 thanks to a goal from Leeds born Terry Connor, the match yet again was remembered for all the wrong reasons. The Leeds fans caused damaged to the stadium despite having hit the headlines for the disgraceful end to the season at the Hawthorns. There were warnings of fines and a possible ground closure, which would be financially disastrous for the club. Sadly the fans took no notice and despite a 3–1 win at home to Newcastle at the end of October, a ball bearing was thrown from the Kop that hit Kevin Keegan. The referee took the players off the pitch as a precaution. After a while they were all brought back on to resume the match.

The board acted swiftly and the front page of the programme at the next home match against Charlton read, 'The future of Leeds United Association Football Club hangs in the balance. This in no way exaggerates the position and must not be taken as an idle threat. Despite repeated pleas and warnings, the mindless actions of a minority of the club's so-called followers last Saturday have placed an enormous degree of uncertainty over this great club. We know from comments received in the last few days that many true supporters deplore what took place at the Newcastle match. And we would ask for the help and co-operation of everyone who have Leeds United at heart – and we appreciate that this is the majority of our supporters – to help rid the club of the "scab" element who, although small in numbers, have caused the club so many problems and whose loathsome actions now place the very existence of Leeds United in jeopardy'. The FA also intervened and announced that the terraces had to be closed for the next two home matches and that the rest of the stadium would be all ticket. The first of the two matches saw only 11,528 turn up against Queens Park Rangers and even less 8,741 watched the match against Shrewsbury Town in mid-December.

On the pitch, Leeds had a reasonable start winning four of their opening seven matches, finding them in a respectable sixth position. The Milk Cup saw Leeds produce one of their best performances of the season. Having lost the first leg at Elland Road against Newcastle, they travelled to St James' Park, knowing they had a job on to turn their fortunes around. This was made doubly difficult when only 90 seconds into the match, home defender Jeff Clarke made it 2–0 on aggregate. Leeds playing some lovely free flowing attacking football, pulled one back through an own goal from Wes Saunders and took the match into extra-time when Frank Worthington scored with a diving header. Twenty-year-old Aidan Butterworth made it 3–1 to Leeds in extra time and Connor finished off the job. Disappointingly for the Whites, West Yorkshire rivals Huddersfield Town knocked them out in the next round at Elland Road. League form was inconsistent and despite a first League goal for another youngster Mark Gavin away at Rotherham, Leeds were stuck in eighth place heading into the New Year.

The FA Cup produced a titanic struggle against First Division Arsenal. Having dispatched Preston North End 3–0 at Elland Road in round three, the Gunners were next up at Highbury in a repeat of the 1972 Final. An own goal from Peter Nicholas, gave the visitors a shock lead, but Alan Sunderland who scored in the 1979 Final, ensured a replay four days later. Leeds looked set to knock their esteemed visitors out of the competition as Butterworth poked the ball home, following good work from Connor in the last minute of extra-time. However, Graham Rix bent a free-kick round John Lukic almost immediately and we were set for a third match in seven days. Back at Highbury again, this time Arsenal made no mistake taking the lead from Tony Woodcock, but Leeds fought back through Connor. However that man Rix, finally finished off the Whites cup exploits for another season.

The focus was now back on League form, but yet again the fans made the headlines following trouble at the Baseball Ground and both Derby County and Leeds were found guilty of 'failing to exercise proper control over their supporters'. Thankfully the rest of the season passed without any more serious incidents or trouble involving the Leeds fans.

During the season, there had been a change in personnel as Frank Worthington joined Sunderland for £50,000 whilst long time skipper Trevor Cherry joined Bradford City as player manager for £10,000. In March, Connor was sold to Brighton for £50,000 with Andy Ritchie coming to Leeds at a cost of £150.000 and another £10,000 was also spent for Dumbarton midfielder John Donnelly. Defender Neil Firm joined Peterborough for £15,000 and Brian Flynn who will never be forgotten by Leeds fans for his winner at Old Trafford two years earlier, returned to Burnley. There was also a change in goal mid-way through the season as John Lukic handed in a transfer request, bringing an end to a record 146 consecutive League matches. David Harvey was brought back from Vancouver Whitecaps to replace him, for his second spell at the club.

Ritchie made a scoring debut at home to Crystal Palace following a 2–1 win away at Bolton and Leeds were fifth, but eight points off the promotion picture. In the end, the side only managed one more win in their final eight matches of the season and finished in eighth position, 10 points off third place Leicester. Butterworth finished top scorer with 13 in all competitions and Frank Gray with 48 made the most appearances.

ANDREW'S BEST AND WORST MATCHES THIS SEASON

Best: Newcastle United (A) Milk Cup second round second leg 4-1, 27 October 1982 – Saunders og, Worthington, Butterworth, Connor – Fantastic performance from 1–0 down to go through 4-2 on aggregate!

Worst: Arsenal (H) FA Cup fourth round first replay 1–1, Connor, 2 February 1983 – To come so close to beating them in extra-time, before Graham Rix equalised for the Gunners!

DIVISION TWO TABLE 1982–83							
	P	W	D	L	F	A	PTS
1. QUEENS PARK RANGERS **C**	42	26	7	9	77	36	85
2. WOLVERHAMPTON WANDERERS **P**	42	20	15	7	68	44	75
3. LEICESTER CITY **P**	42	20	10	12	72	44	70
4. FULHAM	42	20	9	13	64	47	69
5. NEWCASTLE UNITED	42	18	13	11	75	53	67
6. SHEFFIELD WEDNESDAY	42	16	15	11	60	47	63
7. OLDHAM ATHLETIC	42	14	19	9	64	47	61
8. LEEDS UNITED	42	13	21	8	51	46	60
9. SHREWSBURY TOWN	42	15	14	13	48	48	59
10. BARNSLEY	42	14	15	13	57	55	57
11. BLACKBURN ROVERS	42	15	12	15	58	58	57
12. CAMBRIDGE UNITED	42	13	12	17	42	60	51
13. DERBY COUNTY	42	10	19	13	49	58	49
14. CARLISLE UNITED	42	12	12	18	68	70	48
15. CRYSTAL PALACE	42	12	12	18	43	52	48
16. MIDDLESBROUGH	42	11	15	16	46	67	48
17. CHARLTON ATHLETIC	42	13	9	20	63	86	48
18. CHELSEA	42	11	14	17	51	61	47
19. GRIMSBY TOWN	42	12	11	19	45	70	47
20. ROTHERHAM UNITED **R**	42	10	15	17	45	68	45
21. BURNLEY **R**	42	12	8	22	56	66	44
22. BOLTON WANDERERS **R**	42	11	11	20	42	61	44

DATE	OPPOSITION	VENUE	COMPETITION	SCORE	ATT	SCORERS
28/08/1982	GRIMSBY TOWN	BLUNDELL PARK	DIVISION TWO	1–1	16,137	CONNOR
04/09/1982	WOLVERHAMPTON WANDERERS	ELLAND ROAD	DIVISION TWO	0–0	16,462	
08/09/1982	LEICESTER CITY	FILBERT STREET	DIVISION TWO	1–0	12,963	BUTTERWORTH
11/09/1982	SHEFFIELD WEDNESDAY	HILLSBOROUGH	DIVISION TWO	3–2	29,050	WORTHINGTON 2, BUTTERWORTH
18/09/1982	DERBY COUNTY	ELLAND ROAD	DIVISION TWO	2–1	16,889	F GRAY, WORTHINGTON
25/09/1982	FULHAM	CRAVEN COTTAGE	DIVISION TWO	2–3	12,798	THOMAS, GRAHAM
02/10/1982	CAMBRIDGE UNITED	ELLAND ROAD	DIVISION TWO	2–1	14,910	BUTTERWORTH, HIRD
06/10/1982	NEWCASTLE UNITED	ELLAND ROAD	MILK CUP 2ND ROUND 1ST LEG	0–1	24,012	
09/10/1982	CHELSEA	STAMFORD BRIDGE	DIVISION TWO	0–0	25,358	
16/10/1982	CARLISLE UNITED	ELLAND ROAD	DIVISION TWO	1–1	14,141	HART
20/10/1982	BURNLEY	ELLAND ROAD	DIVISION TWO	3–1	13,827	WORTHINGTON, BUTTERWORTH, HIRD
23/10/1982	BLACKBURN ROVERS	EWOOD PARK	DIVISION TWO	0–0	12,040	
27/10/1982	NEWCASTLE UNITED	ST JAMES' PARK	MILK CUP 2ND ROUND 2ND LEG	4–1	24,173	SAUNDERS OG, WORTHINGTON, BUTTERWORTH, CONNOR
30/10/1982	NEWCASTLE UNITED	ELLAND ROAD	DIVISION TWO	3–1	26,570	WORTHINGTON, BURNS, BUTTERWORTH
06/11/1982	CHARLTON ATHLETIC	ELLAND ROAD	DIVISION TWO	1–2	15,148	CONNOR
10/11/1982	HUDDERSFIELD TOWN	ELLAND ROAD	MILK CUP 3RD ROUND	0–1	24,215	
13/11/1982	CRYSTAL PALACE	SELHURST PARK	DIVISION TWO	1–1	11,673	CONNOR
20/11/1982	MIDDLESBROUGH	ELLAND ROAD	DIVISION TWO	0–0	18,482	
27/11/1982	BARNSLEY	OAKWELL	DIVISION TWO	1–2	21,530	BUTTERWORTH
04/12/1982	QUEENS PARK RANGERS	ELLAND ROAD	DIVISION TWO	0–1	11,528	
11/12/1982	ROTHERHAM UNITED	MILLMOOR	DIVISION TWO	1–0	13,034	GAVIN
18/12/1982	SHREWSBURY TOWN	ELLAND ROAD	DIVISION TWO	1–1	8,741	HIRD
26/12/1982	OLDHAM ATHLETIC	BOUNDARY PARK	DIVISION TWO	2–2	15,658	BURNS, SHERIDAN
28/12/1982	BOLTON WANDERERS	ELLAND ROAD	DIVISION TWO	1–1	16,180	GRAHAM
01/01/1983	MIDDLESBROUGH	AYRESOME PARK	DIVISION TWO	0–0	17,000	

03/01/1983	WOLVERHAMPTON WANDERERS	MOLINEUX	DIVISION TWO	0–3	22,567	
08/01/1983	PRESTON NORTH END	ELLAND ROAD	FA CUP 3RD ROUND	3–0	16,816	SHERIDAN, CONNOR, GRAHAM
15/01/1983	GRIMSBY TOWN	ELLAND ROAD	DIVISION TWO	1–0	13,583	BUTTERWORTH
22/01/1983	DERBY COUNTY	BASEBALL GROUND	DIVISION TWO	3–3	17,005	GRAHAM 2, HART
29/01/1983	ARSENAL	HIGHBURY	FA CUP 4TH ROUND	1–1	33,930	NICHOLAS OG
02/02/1983	ARSENAL	ELLAND ROAD	FA CUP 4TH ROUND REPLAY	1–1	24,140	BUTTERWORTH
09/02/1983	ARSENAL	HIGHBURY	FA CUP 4TH ROUND 2ND REPLAY	1–2	26,802	CONNOR
12/02/1983	CAMBRIDGE UNITED	ABBEY STADIUM	DIVISION TWO	0–0	6,909	
19/02/1983	CHELSEA	ELLAND ROAD	DIVISION TWO	3–3	19,365	BUTTERWORTH, F GRAY (P), GRAHAM
26/02/1983	CARLISLE UNITED	BRUNTON PARK	DIVISION TWO	2–2	6,419	CONNOR, BUTTERWORTH
05/03/1983	BLACKBURN ROVERS	ELLAND ROAD	DIVISION TWO	2–1	12,280	F GRAY (P), HIRD
12/03/1983	NEWCASTLE UNITED	ST JAMES' PARK	DIVISION TWO	1–2	24,580	CONNOR
19/03/1983	CHARLTON ATHLETIC	THE VALLEY	DIVISION TWO	1–0	8,229	SHERIDAN
26/03/1983	CRYSTAL PALACE	ELLAND ROAD	DIVISION TWO	2–1	13,973	RITCHIE, F GRAY (P)
02/04/1983	BOLTON WANDERERS	BURNDEN PARK	DIVISION TWO	2–1	10,784	BUTTERWORTH, HART
05/04/1983	OLDHAM ATHLETIC	ELLAND ROAD	DIVISION TWO	0–0	18,442	
09/04/1983	BURNLEY	TURF MOOR	DIVISION TWO	2–1	12,149	RITCHIE, SCOTT OG
16/04/1983	FULHAM	ELLAND ROAD	DIVISION TWO	1–1	24,328	WRIGHT
23/04/1983	QUEENS PARK RANGERS	LOFTUS ROAD	DIVISION TWO	0–1	19,573	
27/04/1983	SHEFFIELD WEDNESDAY	ELLAND ROAD	DIVISION TWO	1–2	16,591	RITCHIE
30/04/1983	BARNSLEY	ELLAND ROAD	DIVISION TWO	0–0	15,344	
02/05/1983	LEICESTER CITY	ELLAND ROAD	DIVISION TWO	2–2	14,442	O'NEILL OG, F GRAY (P)
07/05/1983	SHREWSBURY TOWN	GAY MEADOW	DIVISION TWO	0–0	6,052	
14/05/1983	ROTHERHAM UNITED	ELLAND ROAD	DIVISION TWO	2–2	14,958	BUTTERWORTH, DONNELLY

APPEARANCES				
PLAYERS	LEAGUE	FA CUP	LEAGUE CUP	TOTAL
NEIL ASPIN	14 (1)	4		18 (1)
TONY BROWN	1			1
KENNY BURNS	19 (1)	1	3	23 (1)
AIDAN BUTTERWORTH	37 (1)	4	4	44 (1)
TREVOR CHERRY	15 (1)		3	18 (1)
TERRY CONNOR	15 (4)	4	1 (2)	20 (6)
MARTIN DICKINSON	31	3		34
JOHN DONNELLY	13 (1)			13 (1)
BRIAN FLYNN	2			2
MARK GAVIN	3 (4)			3 (4)
ARTHUR GRAHAM	39	4	3	46
EDDIE GRAY	20 (1)	4	3	27 (1)
GARY HAMSON		1		1
DAVID HARVEY	13			13
PAUL HART	39	4	3	46
KEVIN HIRD	30 (9)	1 (2)	2 (1)	33 (12)
JOHN LUKIC	29	4	3	36
NEIL MCNAB	5	1		6
DEREK PARLANE	0 (1)			0 (1)
ANDY RITCHIE	10			10
SCOTT SELLARS	1			1
JOHN SHERIDAN	27	2		29
GWYN THOMAS	39	4	3	46
TOMMY WRIGHT	3 (1)			3 (1)
FRANK WORTHINGTON	15		3	18
GOALS	LEAGUE	FA CUP	LEAGUE CUP	TOTAL
AIDAN BUTTERWORTH	11	1	1	13
TERRY CONNOR	5	2	1	8
ARTHUR GRAHAM	5	1		6
FRANK WORTHINGTON	5		1	6
FRANK GRAY	5			5
KEVIN HIRD	4			4
PAUL HART	3			3
ANDY RITCHIE	3			3

JOHN SHERIDAN	2	1		3
KENNY BURNS	2			2
JOHN DONNELLY	1			1
MARK GAVIN	1			1
GWYN THOMAS	1			1
TOMMY WRIGHT	1			1
OWN GOALS	2	1	1	4

SEASON 1983–84

The summer of 1983 was a busy one for manager Eddie Gray as Arthur Graham departed for man utd for £50,000; Paul Hart joined Nottingham Forest for £40,000 whilst Kenny Burns went to Derby County and Brian Greenhoff joined Rochdale on free transfers. This allowed Gray to invest in the squad bringing in Celtic striker George McCluskey for £161,000, £60,000 was spent on midfielder Andy Watson from Aberdeen. Peter Barnes also re-joined the United squad following a loan spell in Spain.

It proved to be a false dawn for Leeds, as they only won one of their opening four League matches, which left the Whites floundering in 14th position. Worse was to follow with three consecutive defeats, including an embarrassing 5–1 away loss at Cambridge. This result saw Leeds in 19th position, their lowest League position since relegation in 1982. An embarrassing first leg, Milk Cup second round home defeat to Chester who were 92nd out of 92 Football League clubs followed, as did a Yorkshire derby defeat away at Sheffield Wednesday. A first win since August at home to Cambridge, was a welcome return to winning ways and Chester were then beaten 4–1 in the second leg of the Milk Cup, thus preventing a repeat of 1974, when Chester knocked the First Division champions out of the League Cup. Barnsley and Portsmouth both went away from Elland Road with nothing to show for it and Leeds crept up to 12th position. The Barnsley defeat was marred when talented midfielder John Sheridan broke his leg and wouldn't play again all season.

Three straight 1–1 draws followed before Oxford knocked the Whites out of the Milk Cup, in a 4–1 replay at the Manor Ground, before 20,000 fans turned up for the visit of Chelsea. A McCluskey goal ensured a share of the spoils. Sadly, form took a nosedive and four consecutive defeats left the Whites in 19th place, four points above the dreaded relegation zone. A 4–1 victory at home to Middlesbrough, with goals coming from Scott Sellars, two from McCluskey and one from Tommy Wright, was just what was needed and this was followed by a draw away at Manchester City.

The FA Cup came and went although it did take Allan Clarke's Third Division Scunthorpe United three matches to knock the Whites out. Results had to improve and they did quickly as the side put together a run of five straight League wins. First off, Fulham were defeated at Elland Road thanks to a strike from Watson and he was on the score sheet again as revenge was taken in a 3–0 home win against Shrewsbury. A victory away at Cardiff thanks to a solitary strike from McCluskey and then Welsh neighbours Swansea were sent the same way as the returning Peter Lorimer scored his first goal back in his second spell at the club. It was a strike that took 'hot shot' past John Charles's all time League mark. Finally Portsmouth were beaten by the odd goal in five and Leeds were in 10th place, well clear of the relegation zone but too far out to make the promotion places.

Yorkshire neighbours Barnsley ended the winning run, but spirits were then lifted by back-to-back victories at home to Blackburn (1–0) and Grimsby Town (2–1) respectively. This left Leeds in a season highest League position of ninth. Consecutive defeats away at Brighton and Newcastle left Leeds with little to play for heading into the last nine matches of the season. However this didn't stop over 25,000 fans turning up for the Yorkshire derby at home to Sheffield Wednesday. Andy Ritchie 'headed' home the equaliser with what looked to be his hand. Three more draws, two away at Cambridge and Derby and at home to Huddersfield, kept Leeds in tenth place.

A 5–0 away defeat at Chelsea came at the end of April, again in a match, which the supporters made the headlines for all the wrong reasons. The rivalry between the two sides was still a volatile one and the Leeds supporters took their anger out on then chairman Ken Bates's scoreboard, completely destroying it. It left Bates wanting to kick Leeds United out of football and saying that the fans were the scum of the earth. In the end, this did not prevail and 21 years later Bates was the new chairman of the Whites! Funny old game is football! As for Leeds, they finished the season by taking seven points from the remaining three matches, to finish in 10th place with a respectable 60 points. After all the problems that had faced the Whites and with a possible relegation on the cards at Christmas, a mid table finish could be somewhat described as a success.

Goalkeeper David Harvey tops the appearance charts for the season, with 47 in all and Tommy Wright's strike on the last day of the season at home to Charlton meant that he edged ahead of the scoring charts over Andy Ritchie with 11 goals. The main plus points for the side was that Denis Irwin had established himself as first choice at right-back, as had Neil Aspin in central defence. Scott Sellars had done the same on the left side of midfield as had striker Tommy Wright. If Gray could keep his youngsters fit and at the club, there was real hope that a promotion push could happen next season. Leslie Silver also replaced Manny Cussins as chairman.

The end of the season saw one more major change as manager Eddie Gray retired as a player after 579 appearances and 69 goals for the club. In a career that had seen the likeable Scotsman make a goal scoring debut on New Year's Day 1966 at home to Sheffield Wednesday. In a playing career that lasted 18 years, Gray won the First Division twice in 1969 and 1974, the League and FA Cup once in 1968 and 1972 and the Charity Shield in 1969. He was also named Leeds United player of the year at the end of the 1981–82 season. He could now concentrate solely on restoring the Whites to their former glories.

Andrew's best and worst matches this season

Best: Cardiff City (A) 1–0 McCluskey, 2 February 1984, Always great to win at Cardiff! Amazing that it's our last win down there!

Worst: Chelsea (A) 0–5, 28 April 1984 – Chelsea celebrating promotion, Leeds fans ripping down the scoreboard!

DIVISION TWO TABLE 1983–84							
	P	W	D	L	F	A	PTS
1. CHELSEA **C**	42	25	13	4	90	40	88
2. SHEFFIELD WEDNESDAY **P**	42	26	10	6	72	34	88
3. NEWCASTLE UNITED **P**	42	24	8	10	85	53	80
4. MANCHESTER CITY	42	20	10	12	66	48	70
5. GRIMSBY TOWN	42	19	13	10	60	47	70
6. BLACKBURN ROVERS	42	17	16	9	57	46	67
7. CARLISLE UNITED	42	16	16	10	48	41	64
8. SHREWSBURY TOWN	42	17	10	15	49	53	61
9. BRIGHTON & HOVE ALBION	42	17	9	16	69	60	60
10. LEEDS UNITED	42	16	12	14	55	56	60
11. FULHAM	42	15	12	15	60	53	57
12. HUDDERSFIELD TOWN	42	14	15	13	56	49	57
13. CHARLTON ATHLETIC	42	16	9	17	53	64	57
14. BARNSLEY	42	15	7	20	57	53	52
15. CARDIFF CITY	42	15	6	21	53	66	51
16. PORTSMOUTH	42	14	7	21	73	64	49
17. MIDDLESBROUGH	42	12	13	17	41	47	49
18. CRYSTAL PALACE	42	12	11	19	42	52	47
19. OLDHAM ATHLETIC	42	13	8	21	47	73	47
20. DERBY COUNTY **R**	42	11	9	22	36	72	42
21. SWANSEA CITY **R**	42	7	8	27	36	85	29
22. CAMBRIDGE UNITED **R**	42	4	12	26	28	27	24

DATE	OPPOSITION	VENUE	COMPETITION	SCORE	ATT	SCORERS
27/08/1983	NEWCASTLE UNITED	ELLAND ROAD	DIVISION TWO	0–1	30,086	
29/08/1983	BRIGHTON & HOVE ALBION	ELLAND ROAD	DIVISION TWO	3–2	13,303	WATSON, F. GRAY, SHERIDAN
03/09/1983	MIDDLESBROUGH	AYRESOME PARK	DIVISION TWO	2–2	12,793	F. GRAY (P), MCCLUSKEY
06/09/1983	GRIMSBY TOWN	BLUNDELL PARK	DIVISION TWO	0–2	8,000	
10/09/1983	CARDIFF CITY	ELLAND ROAD	DIVISION TWO	1–0	12,336	MCCLUSKEY
17/09/1983	FULHAM	CRAVEN COTTAGE	DIVISION TWO	1–2	10,005	RITCHIE
24/09/1983	MANCHESTER CITY	ELLAND ROAD	DIVISION TWO	1–2	21,918	RITCHIE
01/10/1983	SHREWSBURY TOWN	GAY MEADOW	DIVISION TWO	1–5	6,289	RITCHIE

05/10/1983	CHESTER CITY	ELLAND ROAD	MILK CUP 2ND ROUND 1ST LEG	0-1	8,106	
08/10/1983	SHEFFIELD WEDNESDAY	HILLSBOROUGH	DIVISION TWO	1-3	26,814	F. GRAY (P)
14/10/1983	CAMBRIDGE UNITED	ELLAND ROAD	DIVISION TWO	3-1	9,923	HIRD, WATSON, DONNELLY
22/10/1983	BARNSLEY	OAKWELL	DIVISION TWO	2-0	18,236	DONNELLY, BARNES
26/10/1983	CHESTER CITY	SEALAND ROAD	MILK CUP 2ND ROUND 2ND LEG	4-1	8,004	RITCHIE 2, BURNS, BARNES
29/10/1983	PORTSMOUTH	ELLAND ROAD	DIVISION TWO	2-1	16,254	WATSON, BURNS
05/11/1983	CRYSTAL PALACE	ELLAND ROAD	DIVISION TWO	1-1	14,847	MCCLUSKEY
09/11/1983	OXFORD UNITED	ELLAND ROAD	MILK CUP 3RD ROUND	1-1	13,349	MCCLUSKEY
12/11/1983	BLACKBURN ROVERS	EWOOD PARK	DIVISION TWO	1-1	9,556	DONNELLY
19/11/1983	DERBY COUNTY	BASEBALL GROUND	DIVISION TWO	1-1	16,726	RITCHIE
23/11/1983	OXFORD UNITED	MANOR GROUND	MILK CUP 3RD ROUND REPLAY	1-4	13,389	BURNS
26/11/1983	CHELSEA	ELLAND ROAD	DIVISION TWO	1-1	20,680	MCCLUSKEY
03/12/1983	CARLISLE UNITED	BRUNTON PARK	DIVISION TWO	0-1	6,845	
15/12/1983	CHARLTON ATHLETIC	THE VALLEY	DIVISION TWO	0-2	6,285	
26/12/1983	HUDDERSFIELD TOWN	ELLAND ROAD	DIVISION TWO	1-2	23,791	WRIGHT
27/12/1983	OLDHAM ATHLETIC	BOUNDARY PARK	DIVISION TWO	2-3	8,393	WRIGHT, F GRAY
31/12/1983	MIDDLESBROUGH	ELLAND ROAD	DIVISION TWO	4-1	14,215	SELLARS, MCCLUSKEY 2, WRIGHT
02/01/1984	MANCHESTER CITY	MAINE ROAD	DIVISION TWO	1-1	34,441	BOND OG
07/01/1984	SCUNTHORPE UNITED	ELLAND ROAD	FA CUP 3RD ROUND	1-1	17,130	WRIGHT
10/01/1984	SCUNTHORPE UNITED	OLD SHOWGROUND	FA CUP 3RD ROUND REPLAY	1-1	13,129	WRIGHT
16/01/1984	SCUNTHORPE UNITED	OLD SHOWGROUND	FA CUP 3RD ROUND 2ND REPLAY	2-4	13,312	WRIGHT, RITCHIE
21/01/1984	FULHAM	ELLAND ROAD	DIVISION TWO	1-0	11,421	WATSON
04/02/1984	SHREWSBURY TOWN	ELLAND ROAD	DIVISION TWO	3-0	10,628	WATSON 2, BROWN
11/02/1984	CARDIFF CITY	NINIAN PARK	DIVISION TWO	1-0	9,407	MCCLUSKEY
15/02/1984	SWANSEA CITY	ELLAND ROAD	DIVISION TWO	1-0	10,031	LORIMER
18/02/1984	PORTSMOUTH	FRATTON PARK	DIVISION TWO	3-2	13,911	WRIGHT, WATSON, LORIMER (P)
25/02/1984	BARNSLEY	ELLAND ROAD	DIVISION TWO	1-2	19,138	WRIGHT
03/03/1984	CRYSTAL PALACE	SELHURST PARK	DIVISION TWO	0-0	8,077	

10/03/1984	BLACKBURN ROVERS	ELLAND ROAD	DIVISION TWO	1–0	12,857	BUTTERWORTH
17/03/1984	GRIMSBY TOWN	ELLAND ROAD	DIVISION TWO	2–1	14,412	ASPIN, SELLARS
24/03/1984	BRIGHTON & HOVE ALBION	GOLDSTONE GROUND	DIVISION TWO	0–3	12,605	
28/03/1984	NEWCASTLE UNITED	ST JAMES' PARK	DIVISION TWO	0–1	30,877	
31/03/1984	SHEFFIELD WEDNESDAY	ELLAND ROAD	DIVISION TWO	1–1	25,343	RITCHIE
07/04/1984	CAMBRIDGE UNITED	ABBEY STADIUM	DIVISION TWO	2–2	4,700	BARNES, SELLARS
14/04/1984	DERBY COUNTY	ELLAND ROAD	DIVISION TWO	0–0	12,549	
21/04/1984	HUDDERSFIELD TOWN	LEEDS ROAD	DIVISION TWO	2–2	16,270	WRIGHT, BARNES
24/04/1984	OLDHAM ATHLETIC	ELLAND ROAD	DIVISION TWO	2–0	9,576	RITCHIE, LORIMER (P)
28/04/1984	CHELSEA	STAMFORD BRIDGE	DIVISION TWO	0–5	33,447	
05/05/1984	CARLISLE UNITED	ELLAND ROAD	DIVISION TWO	3–0	8,278	GAVIN, RITCHIE, MCCLUSKEY
07/05/1984	SWANSEA CITY	VETCH FIELD	DIVISION TWO	2–2	5,498	WRIGHT, LORIMER
12/05/1984	CHARLTON ATHLETIC	ELLAND ROAD	DIVISION TWO	1–0	13,254	WRIGHT

APPEARANCES				
PLAYERS	LEAGUE	FA CUP	LEAGUE CUP	TOTAL
NEIL ASPIN	21	3	2	26
PETER BARNES	25 (2)	1	3	29 (2)
TONY BROWN	22			22
KENNY BURNS	13		4	17
AIDAN BUTTERWORTH	4 (7)		1	5 (7)
MARTIN DICKINSON	34	2	4	40
JOHN DONNELLY	23 (2)	1	3	27 (2)
MARK GAVIN	10 (2)		1 (1)	11 (3)
EDDIE GRAY	4			4
FRANK GRAY	24	2	4	30
GARY HAMSON	23 (2)	3		26 (2)
DAVID HARVEY	40	3	4	47
KEVIN HIRD	16 (2)		1	17 (2)
PHIL HUGHES	2			2
DENIS IRWIN	12	1		13
PETER LORIMER	20 (2)	2 (1)		22 (3)
GEORGE MCCLUSKEY	24 (8)	3	3 (1)	30 (9)
JOHN MCGOLDRICK	7	3	2	12

ANDY RITCHIE	38	3	4	45
SCOTT SELLARS	19	2		21
JOHN SHERIDAN	11			11
GWYN THOMAS	16 (1)		4	20 (1)
NIGEL THOMPSON	1			1
ANDY WATSON	30 (1)	1	4	35 (1)
TOMMY WRIGHT	23 (2)	3	0 (1)	26 (3)
GOALS	**LEAGUE**	**FA CUP**	**LEAGUE CUP**	**TOTAL**
TOMMY WRIGHT	8	3		11
ANDY RITCHIE	7	1	2	10
GEORGE MCCLUSKEY	8		1	9
ANDY WATSON	7			7
PETER BARNES	4		1	5
FRANK GRAY	4			4
PETER LORIMER	4			4
JOHN DONNELLY	3			3
SCOTT SELLARS	3			3
KENNY BURNS			2	2
NEIL ASPIN	1			1
TONY BROWN	1			1
AIDAN BUTTERWORTH	1			1
MARK GAVIN	1			1
KEVIN HIRD	1			1
JOHN SHERIDAN	1			1
OWN GOALS	1			1

SEASON 1984–85

With very little money to spend, manager Eddie Gray made the best of a bad situation, signing centre-half Andy Linighan from Hartlepool United for £20,000 but did promote John Stiles, Terry Phelan, Peter Swan and Lyndon Simmonds up from the youth ranks. The one main departure was Peter Barnes who joined Coventry City for £65,000. Also moving on were coach Barry Murphy and chief scout Syd Owen.

Leeds made their best start to a season since winning the First Division in 1973–74, by winning their opening four matches and topping the table in the process. First off, Notts County were defeated at Meadow Lane (2–1) thanks to a brace of goals from Tommy Wright. Wright was again on the scoresheet as was George McCluskey in a 2–0 home win against Fulham. Wolves were beaten by the odd goal in five, as that man Wright scored another brace and finally Grimsby Town were beaten at Blundell Park thanks to goals from McCluskey and Peter Lorimer.

Sadly for the Whites following four consecutive wins, three straight defeats followed, 2–1 away at Cardiff, 1–0 at home to Portsmouth and 3–1 away at Crystal Palace. It dropped the Whites to eighth place in the League. Gillingham were dispatched in the Milk Cup and then Oldham Athletic were hammered 6–0 at Elland Road, in which was the club's best result in the League since beating Arsenal 6–1 at Elland Road at the end of the 1972–73 season. Scorers that September day were Tommy Wright, a hat-trick from striker Andy Ritchie and one each from John Sheridan and Andy Linighan. It moved Leeds up to fourth place in the League table. Sadly back-to-back defeats away at Yorkshire rivals Barnsley and Huddersfield slipped Leeds to 11th, although this would be their lowest position of the season. To make a promotion push, Leeds knew that they would need to show consistency, but results were up and down.

First Division Watford showed the gulf in class as they strolled to a 4–0 win in the Milk Cup at Elland Road. At the back end of November, Leeds travelled to Oxford in fifth place, in a match featured on BBC *Match of the Day*. Sadly for the Whites, the match was remembered for a red card for Leeds legend Peter Lorimer and for the fans trying to rip down a TV gantry in the away end. As for matters on the field, Leeds lost the match 5–2, with goals coming from Wright and Lorimer. The side did bounce back, defeating Wimbledon by the same score line, with another hat-trick from Ritchie.

Leading up to the busy Christmas spell, Leeds found themselves in fifth position getting victories away at Shrewsbury 3–2 and Wolves 2–0. The festive period proved a disappointing one though with Leeds taking only two points from a possible nine. This wasn't the best build up for a Friday night live televised FA Cup third round tie against holders Everton at Elland Road. In front of a crowd of 21,211, Leeds were beaten 2–0, which left the Whites with just the League programme to concentrate on. With 19 League matches left, Leeds were sixth, although they were nine points away from Manchester City who held the final promotion place in third. Leeds had to show Championship form if they were going to make a conservative effort to return to the First Division. There was no FA Cup hangover as second bottom Notts County were demolished 5–0 with Tommy Wright scoring a hat-trick, a John Sheridan goal and a first ever strike in a Leeds shirt for right back Denis Irwin. By the time Leeds visited Oldham for their next match, there was a change in goal as Mervyn Day was brought in from Aston Villa for £30,000. This allowed veteran and popular 'keeper David Harvey to join Bradford City.

The Whites failure to turn draws into wins in February kept Leeds out of the promotion slots, lying in fifth place at the end of month, four points off Oxford in third. Again Gray dipped into the transfer market, bringing in striker Ian Baird from Southampton for £75,000. Leaving the club and both going north of the border were Andy Watson to Heart of Midlothian for £75,000 and John Donnelly to Partick Thistle for £15,000. Baird made his debut away at former rivals Portsmouth, in a match the Whites needed to win to stay in the promotion mix. However a 3–1 defeat, despite a strike from Sheridan, dropped Leeds to seventh, five points off the promotion picture. Yet again they responded with a 2–0 home win over Barnsley to move up a place to sixth. Baird scored his first goal in a Leeds shirt in a morale boosting 2–1 win at Maine Road over second place Manchester City and kept Leeds's faint hopes alive with Sellars scoring the other goal. Leeds followed this up with a 4–1 win at home to Crystal Palace in which Baird scored again and the gap was closed to just four points. An away draw at Brighton, dented the Whites hopes, but leaders Oxford were then defeated by a wonderful individual strike from that man Baird. It left the Whites five points off with just three matches to play. Leeds travelled to Plough Lane to face Wimbledon, knowing anything but a win would just about kill off any hopes they had. Despite two more from Baird, a point was the best Leeds could muster and promotion looked to have faded.

A 1–0 win over Shrewsbury in the last home match of the season, meant that Leeds headed to St Andrews, knowing a win, coupled with defeats for Manchester City at home to Charlton and Portsmouth away at Huddersfield would send Leeds up. Tragically the match was remembered for all the wrong reasons, as once Martin Kuhl had put the hosts 1–0 up in the first half, a group of Birmingham fans at the Clock End invaded the pitch and there were fights breaking out on the playing surface at either end of the pitch. The sides were taken off as mounted police were called in to clear the supporters from the pitch. Despite a 30-minute delay, the match was completed, albeit in a very tense atmosphere. As the match finished a wall collapsed under the pressure of fans and crushed a teenage boy. The match was known as the 'Battle of St Andrews' and will be touched upon later on in the book in more detail. It felt like Leeds were back to square one, following previous incidents at Oxford, Huddersfield and Barnsley. On the pitch it had been a hugely encouraging campaign for Leeds, having just missed out on promotion, off it though, work had to be done to restore a now damaged reputation.

Andrew's best and worst matches this season

Best: Oldham Athletic (H) 6–0 Wright, Ritchie 3 (1P), Sheridan, Linighan, 29 September 1984, Eddie Gray's kids come of age!

Worst: Birmingham City (A) 0-1, 11 May 1985 – All hell breaks loose at St Andrews, on the same day as the Bradford City fire tragedy.

DIVISION TWO TABLE 1984–85							
	P	W	D	L	F	A	PTS
1. OXFORD UNITED **C**	42	25	9	8	84	36	84
2. BIRMINGHAM CITY **P**	42	25	7	10	59	33	82
3. MANCHESTER CITY **P**	42	21	11	10	66	40	74
4. PORTSMOUTH	42	20	14	8	69	50	74
5. BLACKBURN ROVERS	42	21	10	11	66	41	73
6. BRIGHTON & HOVE ALBION	42	20	12	10	54	34	72
7. LEEDS UNITED	42	19	12	11	66	43	69
8. SHREWSBURY TOWN	42	18	11	13	66	53	65
9. FULHAM	42	19	8	15	68	64	65
10. GRIMSBY TOWN	42	18	8	16	72	64	62
11. BARNSLEY	42	14	16	12	42	42	58
12. WIMBLEDON	42	16	10	16	71	75	58
13. HUDDERSFIELD TOWN	42	15	10	17	52	64	55
14. OLDHAM ATHLETIC	42	15	8	19	49	67	53
15. CRYSTAL PALACE	42	12	12	18	46	65	48
16. CARLISLE UNITED	42	13	8	21	50	67	47
17. CHARLTON ATHLETIC	42	11	12	19	51	63	45
18. SHEFFIELD UNITED	42	10	14	18	54	66	44
19. MIDDLESBROUGH	42	10	10	22	41	57	40
20. NOTTS COUNTY **R**	42	10	7	25	45	73	37
21. CARDIFF CITY **R**	42	9	8	25	47	79	35
22. WOLVERHAMPTON WANDERERS **R**	42	8	9	25	37	79	33

DATE	OPPOSITION	VENUE	COMPETITION	SCORE	ATT	SCORERS
25/08/1984	NOTTS COUNTY	MEADOW LANE	DIVISION TWO	2-1	12,196	WRIGHT 2
27/08/1984	FULHAM	ELLAND ROAD	DIVISION TWO	2-0	14,207	MCCLUSKEY, WRIGHT
01/09/1984	WOLVERHAMPTON WANDERERS	ELLAND ROAD	DIVISION TWO	3-2	17,843	WRIGHT 2, LORIMER
08/09/1984	GRIMSBY TOWN	BLUNDELL PARK	DIVISION TWO	2-0	13,290	MCCLUSKEY, LORIMER

12/09/1984	CARDIFF CITY	NINIAN PARK	DIVISION TWO	1–2	6,893	SELLARS
15/09/1984	PORTSMOUTH	ELLAND ROAD	DIVISION TWO	0–1	19,438	
22/09/1984	CRYSTAL PALACE	SELHURST PARK	DIVISION TWO	1–3	19,460	SELLARS
25/09/1984	GILLINGHAM	PRIESTFIELD STADIUM	MILK CUP 2ND ROUND 1ST LEG	2–1	8,881	WRIGHT, RITCHIE
29/09/1984	OLDHAM ATHLETIC	ELLAND ROAD	DIVISION TWO	6–0	14,290	WRIGHT, RITCHIE 3 (1P), SHERIDAN, LINIGHAN
06/10/1984	SHEFFIELD UNITED	ELLAND ROAD	DIVISION TWO	1–1	25,547	LORIMER (P)
10/10/1984	GILLINGHAM	ELLAND ROAD	MILK CUP 2ND ROUND 2ND LEG	3–2	11,109	GAVIN, SELLARS, LORIMER
13/10/1984	BARNSLEY	OAKWELL	DIVISION TWO	0–1	16,199	
20/10/1984	HUDDERSFIELD TOWN	LEEDS ROAD	DIVISION TWO	0–1	15,257	
27/10/1984	MIDDLESBROUGH	ELLAND ROAD	DIVISION TWO	2–0	14,838	LORIMER (P), RITCHIE
31/10/1984	WATFORD	ELLAND ROAD	MILK CUP 3RD ROUND	0–4	21,221	
03/11/1984	CHARLTON ATHLETIC	THE VALLEY	DIVISION TWO	3–2	6,950	SHERIDAN, MCCLUSKEY, GAVIN
10/11/1984	CARLISLE UNITED	ELLAND ROAD	DIVISION TWO	1–1	13,327	DICKINSON
17/11/1984	BRGHTON & HOVE ALBION	ELLAND ROAD	DIVISION TWO	1–0	13,127	RITCHIE
24/11/1984	OXFORD UNITED	MANOR GROUND	DIVISION TWO	2–5	12,192	WRIGHT, LORIMER
01/12/1984	WIMBLEDON	ELLAND ROAD	DIVISION TWO	5–2	10,899	WRIGHT, RITCHIE 3, SELLARS
08/12/1984	SHREWSBURY TOWN	GAY MEADOW	DIVISION TWO	3–2	6,358	RITCHIE 2, LINIGHAN
15/12/1984	BIRMINGHAM CITY	ELLAND ROAD	DIVISION TWO	0–1	15,854	
22/12/1984	WOLVERHAMPTON WANDERERS	MOLINEUX	DIVISION TWO	2–0	9,259	F. GRAY, MCCLUSKEY
26/12/1984	BLACKBURN ROVERS	EWOOD PARK	DIVISION TWO	1–2	20,149	MCCLUSKEY
29/12/1984	CARDIFF CITY	ELLAND ROAD	DIVISION TWO	1–1	11,798	LORIMER (P)
01/01/1985	MANCHESTER CITY	ELLAND ROAD	DIVISION TWO	1–1	22,626	RITCHIE
04/01/1985	EVERTON	ELLAND ROAD	FA CUP 3RD ROUND	0–2	21,211	
19/01/1985	NOTTS COUNTY	ELLAND ROAD	DIVISION TWO	5–0	11,369	SHERIDAN, WRIGHT 3, IRWIN
02/02/1985	OLDHAM ATHLETIC	BOUNDARY PARK	DIVISION TWO	1–1	8,824	LORIMER (P)
09/02/1985	GRIMSBY TOWN	ELLAND ROAD	DIVISION TWO	0–0	12,517	
23/02/1985	CHARLTON ATHLETIC	ELLAND ROAD	DIVISION TWO	1–0	10,644	LORIMER
26/02/1985	CARLISLE UNITED	BRUNTON PARK	DIVISION TWO	2–2	5,484	WRIGHT, ASPIN
02/03/1985	MIDDLESBROUGH	AYRESOME PARK	DIVISION TWO	0–0	8,781	

09/03/1985	HUDDERSFIELD TOWN	ELLAND ROAD	DIVISION TWO	0–0	18,607	
12/03/1985	PORTSMOUTH	FRATTON PARK	DIVISION TWO	1–3	16,208	SHERIDAN
16/03/1985	BARNSLEY	ELLAND ROAD	DIVISION TWO	2–0	13,091	LORIMER, SELLARS
23/03/1985	SHEFFIELD UNITED	BRAMALL LANE	DIVISION TWO	1–2	21,468	RITCHIE
30/03/1985	FULHAM	CRAVEN COTTAGE	DIVISION TWO	2–0	7,901	WRIGHT 2
06/04/1985	BLACKBURN ROVERS	ELLAND ROAD	DIVISION TWO	0–0	15,829	
08/04/1985	MANCHESTER CITY	MAINE ROAD	DIVISION TWO	2–1	33,553	BAIRD, SELLARS
13/04/1985	CRYSTAL PALACE	ELLAND ROAD	DIVISION TWO	4–1	12,286	BAIRD, SELLARS, SHERIDAN 2
20/04/1985	BRGHTON & HOVE ALBION	GOLDSTONE GROUND	DIVISION TWO	1–1	17,279	SELLARS
27/04/1985	OXFORD UNITED	ELLAND ROAD	DIVISION TWO	1–0	17,992	BAIRD
04/05/1985	WIMBLEDON	PLOUGH LANE	DIVISION TWO	2–2	6,638	BAIRD 2
06/05/1985	SHREWSBURY TOWN	ELLAND ROAD	DIVISION TWO	1–0	12,423	BAIRD
11/05/1985	BIRMINGHAM CITY	ST ANDREWS	DIVISION TWO	0–1	24,487	

APPEARANCES				
PLAYERS	LEAGUE	FA CUP	LEAGUE CUP	TOTAL
NEIL ASPIN	32	1		33
IAN BAIRD	10			10
TONY BROWN	1			1
MERVYN DAY	18			18
MARTIN DICKINSON	12		3	15
JOHN DONNELLY	0 (1)			0 (1)
ROGER ELI	0 (1)			0 (1)
MARK GAVIN	7 (4)	0 (1)	3	10 (5)
FRANK GRAY	39	1	3	43
GARY HAMSON	31	1		32
DAVID HARVEY	20		3	23
PHIL HUGHES	4	1		5
DENIS IRWIN	41	1	3	45
ANDY LINIGHAN	42	1	3	46
PETER LORIMER	40	1	3	44
GEORGE MCCLUSKEY	13 (6)	1	0 (1)	14 (7)
ANDY RITCHIE	22 (6)		3	25 (6)

SCOTT SELLARS	39	1	3	43
JOHN SHERIDAN	42	1	3	46
LYNDON SIMMONDS	0 (1)			0 (1)
JOHN STILES	1			1
ANDY WATSON	7			7
TOMMY WRIGHT	41 (1)	1	3	45 (1)
GOALS	LEAGUE	FA CUP	LEAGUE CUP	TOTAL
TOMMY WRIGHT	14		1	15
ANDY RITCHIE	12		1	13
PETER LORIMER	9		1	10
SCOTT SELLARS	7		1	8
IAN BAIRD	6			6
JOHN SHERIDAN	6			6
GEORGE MCCLUSKEY	5			5
MARK GAVIN	1		1	2
ANDY LINIGHAN	2			2
NEIL ASPIN	1			1
MARTIN DICKINSON	1			1
FRANK GRAY	1			1
DENIS IRWIN	1			1

SEASON 1985–86

Following the horrific scenes at St Andrews, the Whites were hit with a £5,000 fine and their away fixtures were made all ticket. As for the on field matters, Frank Gray left to join Sunderland for £110,000 and Ian Snodin joined from Doncaster Rovers. The start of the season was a complete disaster for the Whites, losing three of their opening five matches, including a horrendous 6–2 defeat away at Stoke City. Leeds found themselves in 20th position and manager Eddie was under mounting pressure.

Thankfully a run of eight matches brought only one defeat and it looked like the Whites had turned their dreadful start around. Despite a 3–0 win in the Milk Cup away at Walsall, manager Eddie Gray and his assistant Jimmy Lumsden were sacked on a split decision by the board. Fans and players alike were stunned by the news and at the next home match to Middlesbrough, supporters chanted for the re-instatement of Gray, who had been part of the furniture at Elland Road for the last 22 years. Coach Peter Gunby was put in as caretaker manager and during his spell; the Whites took four points from two League matches and were knocked out of the newly introduced Full Members Cup.

With one legend departing the club, another returned as former captain Billy Bremner left Doncaster Rovers to take over the reins at Elland Road. His first job was to strip former teammate Peter Lorimer of the captaincy and hand it to his former player Snodin. In the end Lorimer would only play one match under Bremner's stewardship in a 3–0 defeat away at Barnsley. Lorimer made 677 starts, 28 substitute appearances and scoring a club record 268 goals in two spells for Leeds.

With money at a premium at Elland Road, the ground was sold to Leeds City Council for £2.5 million in exchange for a 125-year lease. Gray had left the Whites in 14th place and under Bremner results were hit and miss. His first win came in his third match in charge, a 2–1 victory over Portsmouth in which Lyndon Simmonds scored a brace. Sadly hooliganism was back in the news as four policemen were injured in the next away match at Millwall and the authorities decided that all Leeds fans should be banned from away matches. In the end the decision lasted only two matches but the original all ticket ban remained.

Amazingly Leeds won their next two away matches at Carlisle 2–1 thanks to goals from the two Andy's, Linighan and Ritchie and at Plough Lane, Wimbledon 3–0, with strikes from Snodin, Ian Baird and Martin Dickinson. United's form was very hit and miss and they struggled to find any consistency and by the time the year was out, they were in 14th place, 13 points off the promotion spots. Manager Bremner sold central defender Linighan to Oldham Athletic for £55,000 whilst Dickinson also followed him out of Elland Road, joining West Bromwich Albion for £40,000. Coming into the club were defenders Brendan Ormsby from Aston Villa for £65,000 and David Rennie from Leicester City for £50,000. Ronnie Robinson was picked up from Ipswich

Town for a free transfer and Bremner also raided his former club for Brian Caswell for £30,000 and David Harle for £5,000. He would also promote from within, handing debuts to John Stiles, Peter Swan and Bob Taylor before the season was out.

The start of the New Year summed the Whites season up perfectly. A New Year's day win at home to Oldham Athletic moved the side up two places to 12th, but this was soon followed by an embarrassing FA Cup third round exit away at Fourth Division Peterborough United. Two more away defeats at Sunderland and Charlton meant that at the end of January Leeds were in 16th position, their lowest League placing since Bremner took over at the end of October. Youngsters Stiles, Swan with two together with Baird, all scored to help the Whites to a season best 4–0 win at home to Stoke City, but yet again the side couldn't string together back to back wins. Defeats at Grimsby and at home to Barnsley meant Leeds had little to play for at the start of March. With the pressure seemingly off, the results started to improve, firstly goals from Ormsby his first for the club and captain Snodin saw off Huddersfield at Elland Road in front of nearly 15,000 fans and Ormsby's new central defensive partner Rennie netted in draws away at Middlesbrough and at home to Shrewsbury. Oldham gained revenge for the New Year's Day defeat with a 3–1 win at Boundary Park, in which Ritchie netted the lone goal for the visitors. Ritchie then netted three in the next matches, one a 1–1 draw at home to Blackburn and hitting a brace in a morale boosting victory at Portsmouth. It was the Whites first away victory since Wimbledon some ten matches ago.

For the first time all season, the Whites managed to record back-to-back victories following the win at Portsmouth, as Bradford City were defeated at Odsal thanks to a very rare goal from right-back Neil Aspin. Suddenly from nowhere, back-to-back wins turned into nine points from nine, as Millwall were defeated 3–1 at Elland Road thanks to goals from Scott Sellars, Peter Swan and Andy Ritchie. It didn't last and back-to-back defeats away at Crystal Palace and Sheffield United soon followed. 13,868 loyal fans turned up for the last home match of the season and that man Ritchie sent the fans home happy by scoring a brace in a 2–0 win taking his total for the season to 11. It wasn't enough to finish top scorer though as that honour went to Baird with 12. The Whites ended their disappointing season away at Champions Norwich and the gulf in class told as the Canaries celebrated in style with a 4–0 victory. Leeds finished the campaign in 14th place with goalkeeper Mervyn Day missing only two matches all season. Bremner knew hard work had to be done to turn the Whites into serious promotion contenders the following season.

ANDREW'S BEST AND WORST MATCHES THIS SEASON

Best: Stoke City (H) 4–0 Stiles, Baird 2, Swan, 1 February 1986 – A Season's best performance at Elland Road.

Worst: Norwich City (A) 0–4, 3 May 1986 – Norwich celebrate promotion, Leeds go out with a whimper at Carrow Road.

DIVISION TWO TABLE 1985–86							
	P	W	D	L	F	A	PTS
1. NORWICH CITY **C**	42	25	9	8	84	37	84
2. CHARLTON ATHLETIC **P**	42	22	11	9	78	45	77
3. WIMBLEDON **P**	42	21	13	8	58	37	76
4. PORTSMOUTH	42	22	7	13	69	41	73
5. CRYSTAL PALACE	42	19	9	14	57	52	66
6. HULL CITY	42	17	13	12	65	55	64
7. SHEFFIELD UNITED	42	17	11	14	64	63	62
8. OLDHAM ATHLETIC	42	17	9	16	62	61	60
9. MILLWALL	42	17	8	17	64	65	59
10, STOKE CITY	42	14	15	13	48	50	57
11. BRIGHTON & HOVE ALBION	42	16	8	18	64	64	56
12. BARNSLEY	42	14	14	14	47	50	56
13. BRADFORD CITY	42	16	6	20	51	63	54
14. LEEDS UNITED	42	15	8	19	56	72	53
15. GRIMSBY TOWN	42	14	10	18	58	62	52
16. HUDDERSFIELD TOWN	42	14	10	18	51	67	52
17. SHREWSBURY TOWN	42	14	9	19	52	64	51
18. SUNDERLAND	42	13	11	18	47	61	50
19. BLACKBURN ROVERS	42	12	13	17	53	62	49
20. CARLISLE UNITED **R**	42	13	7	22	47	71	46
21. MIDDLESBROUGH **R**	42	12	9	21	44	53	45
22. FULHAM **R**	42	10	6	26	45	69	36

DATE	OPPOSITION	VENUE	COMPETITION	SCORE	ATT	SCORERS
17/08/1985	FULHAM	CRAVEN COTTAGE	DIVISION TWO	1–3	5,772	LORIMER
21/08/1985	WIMBLEDON	ELLAND ROAD	DIVISION TWO	0–0	12,426	
24/08/1985	HULL CITY	ELLAND ROAD	DIVISION TWO	1–1	16,689	BAIRD
26/08/1985	STOKE CITY	VICTORIA GROUND	DIVISION TWO	2–6	7,047	ASPIN, SNODIN
31/08/1985	CHARLTON ATHLETIC	ELLAND ROAD	DIVISION TWO	1–2	10,860	LORIMER (P)
04/09/1985	BRIGHTON & HOVE ALBION	GOLDSTONE GROUND	DIVISION TWO	1–0	9,798	MCCLUSKEY
07/09/1985	SHREWSBURY TOWN	GAY MEADOW	DIVISION TWO	3–1	4,168	WRIGHT, MCCLUSKEY, BAIRD
14/09/1985	SUNDERLAND	ELLAND ROAD	DIVISION TWO	1–1	19,693	SHERIDAN

Date	Opponent	Venue	Competition	Score	Attendance	Scorers
21/09/1985	BRADFORD CITY	ELLAND ROAD	DIVISION TWO	2–1	21,104	LORIMER, SELLARS
25/09/1985	WALSALL	ELLAND ROAD	MILK CUP 2ND ROUND 1ST LEG	0–0	8,869	
28/09/1985	SHEFFIELD UINITED	ELLAND ROAD	DIVISION TWO	1–1	15,622	BAIRD
05/10/1985	HUDDERSFIELD TOWN	LEEDS ROAD	DIVISION TWO	1–3	9,983	BAIRD
08/10/1985	WALSALL	FELLOWS PARK	MILK CUP 2ND ROUND 2ND LEG	3–0	7,085	LINIGHAN, SNODIN 2
12/10/1985	MIDDLESBROUGH	ELLAND ROAD	DIVISION TWO	1–0	14,117	LORIMER (P)
14/10/1985	MANCHESTER CITY	MAINE ROAD	FULL MEMBERS CUP NORTHERN SECTION GROUP 1	1–6	4,029	LORIMER (P)
16/10/1985	SHEFFIELD UNITED	ELLAND ROAD	FULL MEMBERS CUP NORTHERN SECTION GROUP 1	1–1	2,274	SELLARS
19/10/1985	GRIMSBY TOWN	ELLAND ROAD	DIVISION TWO	1–1	11,244	BAIRD
27/10/1985	BARNSLEY	OAKWELL	DIVISION TWO	0–3	8,302	
30/10/1985	ASTON VILLA	ELLAND ROAD	MILK CUP 3RD ROUND	0–3	15,444	
02/11/1985	PORTSMOUTH	ELLAND ROAD	DIVISION TWO	2–1	15,672	SIMMONDS 2 (1P)
09/11/1985	MILLWALL	THE DEN	DIVISION TWO	1–3	9,158	RITCHIE
16/11/1985	CRYSTAL PALACE	ELLAND ROAD	DIVISION TWO	1–3	10,378	MCCLUSKEY
23/11/1985	CARLISLE UNITED	BRUNTON PARK	DIVISION TWO	2–1	3,504	LINIGHAN, RITCHIE
30/11/1985	NORWICH CITY	ELLAND ROAD	DIVISION TWO	0–2	11,480	
07/12/1985	WIMBLEDON	PLOUGH LANE	DIVISION TWO	3–0	3,492	SNODIN, BAIRD, DICKINSON
14/12/1985	FULHAM	ELLAND ROAD	DIVISION TWO	1–0	9,998	SHERIDAN
22/12/1985	HULL CITY	BOOTHFERRY PARK	DIVISION TWO	1–2	11,852	SHERIDAN
26/12/1985	BLACKBURN ROVERS	EWOOD PARK	DIVISION TWO	0–2	8,666	
28/12/1985	BRIGHTON & HOVE ALBION	ELLAND ROAD	DIVISION TWO	2–3	13,110	BAIRD, SNODIN
01/01/1986	OLDHAM ATHLETIC	ELLAND ROAD	DIVISION TWO	3–1	10,830	BAIRD 2, RITCHIE
04/01/1986	PETERBOROUGH UNITED	LONDON ROAD	FA CUP 3RD ROUND	0–1	10,137	
11/01/1986	SUNDERLAND	ROKER PARK	DIVISION TWO	2–4	15,139	BAIRD, SHERIDAN
18/01/1986	CHARLTON ATHLETIC	SELHURST PARK	DIVISION TWO	0–4	4,333	
01/02/1986	STOKE CITY	ELLAND ROAD	DIVISION TWO	4–0	10,425	STILES, BAIRD, SWAN 2
08/02/1986	GRIMSBY TOWN	BLUNDELL PARK	DIVISION TWO	0–1	6,382	

15/02/1986	BARNSLEY	ELLAND ROAD	DIVISION TWO	0–2	11,765	
08/03/1986	HUDDERSFIELD TOWN	ELLAND ROAD	DIVISION TWO	2–0	14,667	ORMSBY, SNODIN
15/03/1986	MIDDLESBROUGH	AYRESOME PARK	DIVISION TWO	2–2	6,889	SIMMONDS, RENNIE
22/03/1986	SHREWSBURY TOWN	ELLAND ROAD	DIVISION TWO	1–1	9,641	RENNIE
28/03/1986	OLDHAM ATHLETIC	BOUNDARY PARK	DIVISION TWO	1–3	4,937	RITCHIE
31/03/1986	BLACKBURN ROVERS	ELLAND ROAD	DIVISION TWO	1–1	9,919	RITCHIE
05/04/1986	PORTSMOUTH	FRATTON PARK	DIVISION TWO	3–2	14,430	RITCHIE 2, BAIRD
09/04/1986	BRADFORD CITY	ODSAL	DIVISION TWO	1–0	10,751	ASPIN
12/04/1986	MILLWALL	ELLAND ROAD	DIVISION TWO	3–1	15,067	SELLARS, SWAN, RITCHIE
19/04/1986	CRYSTAL PALACE	SELHURST PARK	DIVISION TWO	0–3	6,285	
22/04/1986	SHEFFIELD UNITED	BRAMALL LANE	DIVISION TWO	2–3	9,158	RITCHIE, SNODIN
26/04/1986	CARLISLE UNITED	ELLAND ROAD	DIVISION TWO	2–0	13,868	RITCHIE 2
03/05/1986	NORWICH CITY	CARROW ROAD	DIVISION TWO	0–4	17,942	

APPEARANCES					
PLAYERS	LEAGUE	FA CUP	MILK CUP	F M CUP	TOTAL
NEIL ASPIN	38	1	1	2	42
IAN BAIRD	34 (1)	1	3	2	40 (1)
BRIAN CASWELL	8				8
MERVYN DAY	40	1	3	2	46
MARTIN DICKINSON	17 (2)	1	3		21 (2)
ROGER ELI	1				1
GARY HAMSON	30	1	2	1	34
DAVID HARLE	3				3
DENIS IRWIN	19	1	2	2	24
ANDY LINIGHAN	24	1	3	2	30
PETER LORIMER	14		2	2	18
GEORGE MCCLUSKEY	20 (2)		2 (1)	1	23 (3)
JOHN MCGREGOR	5				5
BRENDAN ORMSBY	12				12
TERRY PHELAN	12 (2)		3	2	17 (2)
DAVID RENNIE	16				16
ANDY RITCHIE	28 (1)	1	2		31 (1)
RONNIE ROBINSON	16				16

SCOTT SELLARS	13 (4)	1	1	2	17 (4)
JOHN SHERIDAN	31 (1)	0 (1)	3	2	36 (2)
LYNDON SIMMONDS	6 (2)			1 (1)	7 (3)
IAN SNODIN	37	1	3		41
JOHN STILES	11 (1)			0 (1)	11 (2)
PETER SWAN	16	1		0 (2)	17 (2)
TREVOR SWINBURNE	2				2
BOB TAYLOR	2				2
NIGEL THOMPSON	1			1	2
TOMMY WRIGHT	6 (4)			0 (1)	6 (5)
GOALS	**LEAGUE**	**FA CUP**	**MILK CUP**	**F M CUP**	**TOTAL**
IAN BAIRD	12				12
ANDY RITCHIE	11				11
IAN SNODIN	5		2		7
PETER LORIMER	4			1	5
JOHN SHERIDAN	4				4
GEORGE MCCLUSKEY	3				3
LYNDON SIMMONDS	3				3
PETER SWAN	3				3
NEIL ASPIN	2				2
DAVID RENNIE	2				2
SCOTT SELLARS	2			1	3
ANDY LINIGHAN	1	1			2
MARTIN DICKINSON	1				1
BRENDAN ORMSBY	1				1
JOHN STILES	1				1
TOMMY WRIGHT	1				1

SEASON 1986–87

In his first full season in charge of the Whites, Bremner set about his task of turning Leeds into promotion contenders. In came striker Keith Edwards from Sheffield United for £125,000, defender Peter Haddock from Newcastle United for £40,000 and another defender Jack Ashurst from Carlisle United for £35,000. Winger John Buckley joined from the manager's old club Doncaster for £40,000 and completing the jigsaw were keeper Ronnie Sinclair from Nottingham Forest for £10,000 and right-winger Russell Doig from Scottish side East Stirlingshire for £15,000. Going out of the club were Denis Irwin and Tommy Wright both to Oldham, Scott Sellars to Blackburn Rovers, Terry Phelan to Swansea, George McCluskey to Hibernian, Gary Hamson to Bristol City and finally David Harle to Bristol City.

Early signs were encouraging as after the opening seven matches of the season, Leeds found themselves in fifth position, having taken 10 points from their opening seven matches. Included in that run was a 3–2 victory over Reading at Elland Road, in which the Whites came from 2–0 down to win thanks to goals from Edwards, Andy Ritchie and Brendan Ormsby. Sadly the trip to Odsal, to face Yorkshire rivals Bradford City, was remembered for all the wrong reasons. At the time the FA had lifted the away ticket ban after noting good behaviour from the Leeds supporters, but this was soon forgotten as hooligans brought shame on the club and a fish and chip van was overturned and set alight. The match was held up for 20 minutes and fans were told that the match would not be abandoned. Although many fans had left the ground, the match was eventually completed. Due to this, the Whites requested that the all ticket restrictions be re-introduced.

Back to matters on the field and there was real hope that Leeds could make a surge to the newly introduced play-off system. Following back-to-back home victories against Crystal Palace (3–0) and Portsmouth (3–1), Leeds found themselves in second position, their highest position since topping the table at the start of the 1984–85 season. Sadly only one win in their next seven matches left the Whites in eighth place, but just three points away from Plymouth Argyle in that all important fifth place. One result that would live in memory of all Leeds fans was a 7–2 drubbing away at mid-table Stoke City in mid-December. Following the defeat away in the Potteries, Bremner made changes to his side selling Captain Ian Snodin to Everton for a club record £800,000. He used the money wisely bringing in full backs Micky Adams from Coventry City for £110,000, Bobby McDonald from Oxford United for £25,000 and he raided First Division side Charlton Athletic for defender Mark Aizlewood for £72,000 and beanpole striker John Pearson for £200,000. The message was clear, that it was Play-offs at all cost.

The Littlewoods and Full Members cup saw early exits against Oldham and Bradford respectively, which left Leeds to concentrate on both the League programme and the FA Cup.

The FA Cup started in inauspicious circumstances, as the Whites had come out of the hat with non-League Telford United. The match was moved to the Hawthorns as there was real fear that Telford's ground could not cope with the influx of Leeds fans. In the end, Leeds survived and went through to the fourth round 2–1, thanks to two goals from Ian Baird and a trip to the County Ground to face Swindon Town. Sandwiched in between the FA Cup matches was a goalless draw at home to Blackburn which saw the side drop to ninth in the League. Swindon were dispatched by the same score as Telford and 31,324 fans turned up for the visit of First Division Queens Park Rangers in the fifth round at Elland Road. Leeds turned in one of their best performances of the season in another 2–1 win, thanks to headed goals from Baird and new club captain Brendan Ormsby.

Leeds were in the quarter-finals for the first time in 10 years and got the dream draw away at Wigan Athletic! Before the trip to Springfield Park in mid-March, Leeds had to get their faltering League form back on track and they did exactly that, taking seven points from their next three moving them up to sixth place, leaving Leeds just two points outside the Play-offs. Leeds travelled to Lancashire to face Wigan brimming with confidence and despite a shaky start played in a swirling wind, second half goals from John Stiles and Adams, booked Leeds a place in the last four of the competition and a showdown with First Division Coventry City at Hillsborough in mid-April. Leeds warmed up for the semi-final with two wins, 4–0 at home to Plymouth, 2–0 at home to Millwall, one defeat 1–0 away at Crystal Palace and a goalless draw away at Hull City. The FA Cup semi-final, 12 April 1987, was the date that Leeds had hoped would go down in history, sadly it proved to be heartbreaking for the Whites. Despite taking an early lead thanks to a David Rennie goal and equalising thanks to a header from Keith Edwards, Dave Bennett sent the Sky Blues to Wembley in extra-time.

Leeds had no time to lick their wounds and set about qualifying for the Play-offs and did it in style, winning four of the next seven matches and the 3–2 home win against West Bromwich Albion, sealed the deal. It would be Oldham first up in the semi-final who Leeds had actually finished seven points behind in the League table. In what was a tense affair in the first leg at Elland Road, Leeds held a slender advantage thanks to a last minute goal through super sub Keith Edwards. In the return leg at Boundary Park, it looked all over as Gary Williams and Mike Cecere gave the home side an aggregate lead, but that man Edwards did the trick once more in normal time and Leeds held out in extra-time to go through on the away goals rule. First Division side Charlton Athletic was all that stood between Leeds and a place back amongst England's elite. A Jim Melrose goal gave the home side a 1–0 victory in the first leg held at Crystal Palace's ground where Charlton had been playing their home matches. Back at Elland Road, it was captain Brendan Ormsby who got the final touch to a Bob Taylor shot, which meant a third match at St Andrews four days later. This match ended 0–0 after normal time and Leeds looked to be heading for the promised land as John Sheridan curled in a wonderful free-kick in the first half of extra-time. Unfortunately two goals from Peter Shirtliff meant it was heartbreak yet again for the second time in eight weeks. Leeds had given everything and were so close from both Wembley and a place back in the First Division. To make matters worse captain Ormsby was stretchered off in the match at St Andrews and would miss the following season. A sad end to a season that had promised so much!

Andrew's best and worst matches this season

Best: QPR (H) 2–1 FA Cup fifth round – Baird, Ormsby, 21 February 1987 – Leeds upset the odds in the FA Cup fifth round to make it through the last eight of the competition!

Worst: Charlton Athletic (St Andrews) 1–2 Play off final replay – Sheridan, 29 May 1987 – Promotion cruelly snatched away by the Addicks.

DIVISION TWO TABLE 1986–87							
	P	W	D	L	F	A	PTS
1. DERBY COUNTY **C**	42	25	9	8	64	38	84
2. PORTSMOUTH **P**	42	23	9	10	53	28	78
3. OLDHAM ATHLETIC **PL**	42	22	9	11	65	44	75
4. LEEDS UNITED **PL**	42	19	11	12	58	44	68
5. IPSWICH TOWN **PL**	42	17	13	12	59	43	64
6. CRYSTAL PALACE	42	19	5	18	51	53	62
7. PLYMOUTH ARGYLE	42	16	13	13	62	57	61
8. STOKE CITY	42	16	10	16	63	53	58
9. SHEFFIELD UNITED	42	15	13	14	50	49	58
10. BRADFORD CITY	42	15	10	17	62	62	55
11. BARNSLEY	42	14	13	15	49	52	55
12. BLACKBURN ROVERS	42	15	10	17	45	55	55
13. READING	42	14	11	17	52	59	53
14. HULL CITY	42	13	14	15	41	55	53
15. WEST BROMWICH ALBION	42	13	12	17	51	49	51
16. MILLWALL	42	14	9	19	39	45	51
17. HUDDERSFIELD TOWN	42	13	12	17	54	61	51
18. SHREWSBURY TOWN	42	15	6	21	41	53	51
19. BIRMINGHAM CITY	42	11	17	14	47	59	50
20. SUNDERLAND **R**	42	12	12	18	49	59	48
21. GRIMSBY TOWN **R**	42	10	14	18	39	59	44
22. BRIGHTON & HOVE ALBION **R**	42	9	12	21	37	54	39

DATE	OPPOSITION	VENUE	COMPETITION	SCORE	ATT	SCORERS
23/08/1986	BLACKBURN ROVERS	EWOOD PARK	DIVISION TWO	1–2	8,346	RITCHIE
25/08/1986	STOKE CITY	ELLAND ROAD	DIVISION TWO	2–1	13,334	SHERIDAN, BAIRD
30/08/1986	SHEFFIELD UNITED	ELLAND ROAD	DIVISION TWO	0–1	18,294	
02/09/1986	BARNSLEY	OAKWELL	DIVISION TWO	1–0	6,839	BAIRD
06/09/1986	HUDDERSFIELD TOWN	LEEDS ROAD	DIVISION TWO	1–1	9,306	SHERIDAN
13/09/1986	READING	ELLAND ROAD	DIVISION TWO	3–2	12,248	EDWARDS, RITCHIE, BUCKLEY
20/09/1986	BRADFORD CITY	ODSAL	DIVISION TWO	0–2	13,525	
23/09/1986	OLDHAM ATHLETIC	BOUNDARY PARK	LITTLEWOODS CUP 2ND ROUND 1ST LEG	2–3	5,569	ASPIN, TAYLOR
27/09/1986	HULL CITY	ELLAND ROAD	DIVISION TWO	3–0	13,551	RITCHIE (P), BAIRD, ORMSBY
01/10/1986	BRADFORD CITY	ELLAND ROAD	FULL MEMBERS CUP 1ST ROUND	0–1	3,960	
04/10/1986	PLYMOUTH ARGYLE	HOME PARK	DIVISION TWO	1–1	11,923	BAIRD
08/10/1986	OLDHAM ATHLETIC	ELLAND ROAD	LITTLEWOODS CUP 2ND ROUND 2ND LEG	0–1	11,449	
11/10/1986	CRYSTAL PALACE	ELLAND ROAD	DIVISION TWO	3–0	14,316	SHERIDAN (P), ORSMBY, EDWARDS
18/10/1986	PORTSMOUTH	ELLAND ROAD	DIVISION TWO	3–1	21,361	SHERIDAN (P), RITCHIE, BAIRD
25/10/1986	GRIMSBY TOWN	BLUNDELL PARK	DIVISION TWO	0–0	7,223	
01/11/1986	SHREWSBURY TOWN	ELLAND ROAD	DIVISION TWO	1–0	14,966	ASPIN
08/11/1986	MILLWALL	THE DEN	DIVISION TWO	0–1	6,869	
15/11/1986	OLDHAM ATHLETIC	ELLAND ROAD	DIVISION TWO	0–2	21,052	
21/11/1986	BIRMINGHAM CITY	ST ANDREWS	DIVISION TWO	1–2	7,836	SHERIDAN
29/11/1986	DERBY COUNTY	ELLAND ROAD	DIVISION TWO	2–0	19,129	SHERIDAN, EDWARDS
06/12/1986	WEST BROMWICH ALBION	THE HAWTHORNS	DIVISION TWO	0–3	19,853	
13/12/1986	BRIGHTON & HOVE ALBION	ELLAND ROAD	DIVISION TWO	3–1	12,014	SHERIDAN, SNODIN, BAIRD
21/12/1986	STOKE CITY	VICTORIA GROUND	DIVISION TWO	2–7	12,358	BAIRD, SHERIDAN (P)
26/12/1986	SUNDERLAND	ELLAND ROAD	DIVISION TWO	1–1	21,286	BENNETT OG
27/12/1986	OLDHAM ATHLETIC	BOUNDARY PARK	DIVISION TWO	1–0	8,477	RITCHIE
01/01/1987	IPSWICH TOWN	PORTMAN ROAD	DIVISION TWO	0–2	14,125	
03/01/1987	HUDDERSFIELD TOWN	ELLAND ROAD	DIVISION TWO	1–1	17,983	BAIRD

11/01/1987	TELFORD UNITED	THE HAWTHORNS	FA CUP 3RD ROUND	2–1	6,460	BAIRD 2
24/01/1987	BLACKBURN ROVERS	ELLAND ROAD	DIVISION TWO	0–0	14,452	
03/02/1987	SWINDON TOWN	COUNTY GROUND	FA CUP 4TH ROUND	2–1	14,031	QUINN OG, BAIRD
07/02/1987	SHEFFIELD UNITED	BRAMALL LANE	DIVISION TWO	0–0	12,494	
14/02/1987	BARNSLEY	ELLAND ROAD	DIVISION TWO	2–2	14,216	BAIRD, SHERIDAN
21/02/1987	QUEENS PARK RANGERS	ELLAND ROAD	FA CUP 5TH ROUND	2–1	31,324	BAIRD, ORMSBY
28/02/1987	BRADFORD CITY	ELLAND ROAD	DIVISION TWO	1–0	21,802	EDWARDS
07/03/1987	GRIMSBY TOWN	ELLAND ROAD	DIVISION TWO	2–0	14,270	RITCHIE, SHERIDAN (P)
10/03/1987	PORTSMOUTH	FRATTON PARK	DIVISION TWO	1–1	13,745	ADAMS
15/03/1987	WIGAN ATHLETIC	SPRINGFIELD PARK	FA CUP QUARTER FINAL	2–0	12,479	STILES, ADAMS
21/03/1987	CRYSTAL PALACE	SELHURST PARK	DIVISION TWO	0–1	8,781	
28/03/1987	PLYMOUTH ARGYLE	ELLAND ROAD	DIVISION TWO	4–0	18,618	SHERIDAN (P), BAIRD 3
04/04/1987	MILLWALL	ELLAND ROAD	DIVISION TWO	2–0	18,304	BAIRD, RITCHIE
08/04/1987	HULL CITY	BOOTHFERRY PARK	DIVISION TWO	0–0	9,531	
12/04/1987	COVENTRY CITY	HILLSBOROUGH	FA CUP SEMI-FINAL	2–3	51,372	RENNIE, EDWARDS
14/04/1987	SHREWSBURY TOWN	GAY MEADOW	DIVISION TWO	2–0	4,186	SHERIDAN, PEARSON
18/04/1987	IPSWICH TOWN	ELLAND ROAD	DIVISION TWO	3–2	24,839	MCDONALD, SHERIDAN, ORMSBY
20/04/1987	SUNDERLAND	ROKER PARK	DIVISION TWO	1–1	14,725	PEARSON
22/04/1987	READING	ELM PARK	DIVISION TWO	1–2	7,415	PEARSON
25/04/1987	BIRMINGHAM CITY	ELLAND ROAD	DIVISION TWO	4–0	19,100	SHERIDAN, BAIRD 2, EDWARDS
02/05/1987	DERBY COUNTY	BASEBALL GROUND	DIVISION TWO	1–2	20,087	ASHURST
04/05/1987	WEST BROMWICH ALBION	ELLAND ROAD	DIVISION TWO	3–2	24,688	SHERIDAN (P), PEARSON, ORMSBY
09/05/1987	BRIGHTON & HOVE ALBION	GOLDSTONE GROUND	DIVISION TWO	1–0	8,139	EDWARDS
14/05/1987	OLDHAM ATHLETIC	ELLAND ROAD	DIVISION TWO PLAY OFF SEMI FINAL 1ST LEG	1–0	29,472	EDWARDS
17/05/1987	OLDHAM ATHLETIC	BOUNDARY PARK	DIVISION TWO PLAY OFF SEMI FINAL 2ND LEG	1–2	19,216	EDWARDS
23/05/1987	CHARLTON ATHLETIC	SELHURST PARK	DIVISION TWO PLAY OFF FINAL 1ST LEG	0–1	16,680	
25/05/1987	CHARLTON ATHLETIC	ELLAND ROAD	DIVISION TWO PLAY OFF FINAL 2ND LEG	1–0	31,395	ORMSBY
29/05/1987	CHARLTON ATHLETIC	ST ANDREWS	DIVISION TWO PLAY OFF FINAL REPLAY	1–2	18,000	SHERIDAN

APPEARANCES						
PLAYERS	LEAGUE	PLAY OFFS	FA CUP	LITT CUP	F M CUP	TOTAL
MICKY ADAMS	17	5	4			26
MARK AIZLEWOOD	15	5				20
JACK ASHURST	41	5	5	2	1	54
NEIL ASPIN	41	5	5	2	1	54
IAN BAIRD	40	5	4	1		50
JOHN BUCKLEY	6 (3)		0 (1)			7 (4)
BRIAN CASWELL	1					1
MERVYN DAY	34	5	5	1	1	46
RUSSELL DOIG	2 (2)		1			3 (2)
KEITH EDWARDS	24 (6)	1 (4)	2 (3)	2	1	30 (13)
PETER HADDOCK	10 (1)		0 (1)		1	11 (2)
BOBBY MCDONALD	17	5				22
BRENDAN ORMSBY	33	5	4	1	1	44
JOHN PEARSON	18	4	4			26
DAVID RENNIE	24		5	2	1	32
ANDY RITCHIE	29 (2)	2 (1)	5	2		38 (3)
RONNIE ROBINSON	11					11
JOHN SHERIDAN	40	5	5	2	1	53
IAN SNODIN	14					14
JOHN STILES	26 (3)	2	5	2	1	36 (3)
RONNIE SINCLAIR	8			1		9
PETER SWAN	5 (2)		1	1		7 (2)
BOB TAYLOR	2	1		1 (1)	1	5 (1)
NIGEL THOMPSON	4 (1)		2	0 (1)		6 (2)
TOMMY WRIGHT				0 (1)	0 (1)	0 (1)
GOALS	LEAGUE	PLAY OFFS	FA CUP	LITT CUP	F M CUP	TOTAL
IAN BAIRD	15		4			19
JOHN SHERIDAN	15	1				16
KEITH EDWARDS	6	2	1			9
ANDY RITCHIE	7					7
BRENDAN ORMSBY	4	1	1			6
JOHN PEARSON	4					4
MICKY ADAMS	1		1			2
NEIL ASPIN	1			1		2

JACK ASHURST	1				1
JOHN BUCKLEY	1				1
BOBBY MCDONALD	1				1
DAVID RENNIE			1		1
IAN SNODIN	1				1
JOHN STILES			1		1
BOB TAYLOR				1	1
OWN GOALS	1		1		2

SEASON 1987–88

Having come so close the previous season, there was a real expectation that this time the Whites could finally return to the promised land of First Division football. Manager Bremner brought in full-back/midfielder Glynn Snodin from Sheffield Wednesday, brother of former captain Ian for £150,000, Aston Villa full-back Gary Williams for £230,000 and exiting the club were strikers Ian Baird to promoted Portsmouth for £285,000 and Andy Ritchie who joined Oldham for £50,000. With Brendan Ormsby ruled out for the season with a cartilage injury, suffered in the heartbreaking Play-off Final defeat against Charlton, manager Bremner turned to Mark Aizlewood in his first full season at the club to captain the side.

Sadly expectation gave way to a sense of realism as the Whites got off to a dismal start winning only two of their first nine matches, both with goals thanks to John Sheridan at home to Leicester and Hull respectively. This left Leeds in a somewhat unfamiliar 16th place, well off the pace in the Second Division. With only three League goals scored in the opening nine matches, Bremner brought in Jim Melrose from Charlton for £50,000 to replace Keith Edwards who was subsequently sold to Aberdeen for a paltry £60,000. Midfielder Ken DeMange arrived from Liverpool.

DeMange made a scoring debut in a 2–0 home win against Manchester City, but it proved to be brief respite for Leeds, as it was the only win in the next six matches. Included in that was a shocking 6–3 defeat away at Plymouth Argyle in mid-October. DeMange didn't see out the season at Elland Road, moving onto Hull City having made only 20 appearances for the club. Changes needed to be made to arrest the slide and Bremner turned to youth in the introduction of rookie midfielder David Batty. Batty made his debut in the 4–2 home win against Swindon as did striker Bobby Davison brought in from Derby County for £300,000. The cup competitions came and went as first Oldham gained some revenge for the Play-off semi-final defeat, by beating Leeds 4–2 in the third round replay Littlewoods Cup tie at Boundary Park. Millwall also dispatched the Whites in the much maligned Simod Cup. At the start of December, Leeds found themselves in 13th place knowing they needed to improve their championship form if they were going to gatecrash the Play-offs. Suddenly results improved dramatically and the Whites went on a six match winning run scoring 12 goals and conceding only two. Included in this run, were wins at home to Birmingham (4–1), Yorkshire rivals Huddersfield (3–0) and a Boxing Day win at Manchester City (2–1), in which Batty scored his first goal for the club.

Unlike last season, the FA Cup never really got off the ground as Aston Villa won at Elland Road for the second time in the season and it left the Whites to concentrate on the League. Results were very much hit and miss in the second half of the season and the prime example was in January, when the Whites lost 2–0 at Barnsley, before returning to form in a 4–1 victory away at West Bromwich Albion thanks to goals from John Sheridan, Gary Williams, John Pearson and

Bobby Davison. This left the Whites in eighth place, five points off a Play-off place and real hope they could make the end of season lottery for a second consecutive season.

Victory at home to Ipswich thanks to a John Pearson goal, lifted Leeds up a place, but the next two matches really hit the Whites top five ambitions, as both Leicester 3–2 at Filbert Street and Stoke City 2–1 at the Victoria Ground, took all three points. This left Leeds marooned in seventh place, five points off the chasing pack having played three matches more than Yorkshire rivals Bradford who were in sixth place and one more than Crystal Palace who held that all important fifth place.

Striker Ian Baird returned to the club from an all too brief stay at Portsmouth for a sum of £180,000 which meant Leeds had made a profit of £105,000. He made an instant impact by scoring the winner at home to Plymouth and then League leaders Aston Villa were beaten 2–1 at Villa Park, thanks to goals from Peter Swan and striker Bob Taylor. Leeds couldn't shrug off that seventh place, although the gap had closed to just four points, this time it was Millwall who held that all important final place.

Yorkshire rivals Sheffield United were thumped 5–0 at Elland Road, with goals from Peter Swan, a first hat-trick of the season from John Pearson and one from John Sheridan, closed the gap to two points, but the next three matches extinguished any hopes the Whites had of making the Play-offs. A goalless draw away at Bournemouth was followed by a shocking 1–0 defeat at Shrewsbury, before Millwall won 2–1 at Elland Road. It left the Whites six points behind, with Bradford having two matches in hand over their Yorkshire rivals. With little to play for in the remaining four matches of the season only 13,000 fans turned up for the home matches against Oldham (1–1) and Crystal Palace (1–0). The Crystal Palace match saw the debuts of youngsters Vince Brockie and Peter Maguire. Both players kept their place for the last match of the season away at Birmingham, which was put back to a 7.15 pm kick off, to avoid any repeat of the clashes of three years ago.

The Whites did however return to Wembley for the first time since 1974 in the Mercantile Credit Festival in April, when they were defeated 3–0 by First Division side Nottingham Forest. In the end, Leeds finished in seventh place, eight points off the final Play-off place, with only goalkeeper Mervyn Day playing in every match. Midfielder John Sheridan finished top of the goal scoring charts, with 14 in all competitions. Despite missing out on the Play-offs, the one bright spot of the season, was the emergence of the youngsters who made 26 appearances for the side.

Andrew's best and worst matches this season
Best: Sheffield United (H) 5–0 Swan, Pearson 3, Sheridan, 19 March 1988 – Always nice to get one over your Yorkshire rivals.
Worst: Hull City (H) 0–2, 12 September 1987 – The opposite from the Sheffield United match!

DIVISION TWO TABLE – 1987–88							
	P	W	D	L	F	A	PTS
1. MILLWALL **C**	44	25	7	12	72	52	82
2. ASTON VILLA **P**	44	22	12	10	68	41	78
3. MIDDLESBROUGH **P**	44	22	12	10	63	36	78
4. BRADFORD CITY **PL**	44	22	11	11	74	54	77
5. BLACKBURN ROVERS **PL**	44	21	14	9	68	52	77
6. CRYSTAL PALACE	44	22	9	13	86	59	75
7. LEEDS UNITED	44	19	12	13	61	51	69
8. IPSWICH TOWN	44	19	9	16	61	52	66
9. MANCHESTER CITY	44	19	8	17	80	60	65
10. OLDHAM ATHLETIC	44	18	11	15	72	64	65
11. STOKE CITY	44	17	11	16	50	57	62
12. SWINDON TOWN	44	16	11	17	73	60	59
13. LEICESTER CITY	44	16	11	17	62	61	59
14. BARNSLEY	44	15	12	17	61	62	57
15. HULL CITY	44	14	15	15	54	60	57
16. PLYMOUTH ARGYLE	44	16	8	20	65	67	56
17. BOURNEMOUTH	44	13	10	21	56	68	49
18. SHREWSBURY TOWN	44	11	16	17	42	54	49
19. BIRMINGHAM CITY	44	11	15	18	41	66	48
20. WEST BROMWICH ALBION	44	12	11	21	50	69	47
21. SHEFFIELD UNITED **R**	44	13	7	24	45	74	46
22. READING **R**	44	10	12	22	44	70	42
23. HUDDERSFIELD TOWN **R**	44	6	10	28	41	100	28

DATE	OPPOSITION	VENUE	COMPETITION	SCORE	ATT	SCORERS
16/08/1987	BARNSLEY	OAKWELL	DIVISION TWO	1–1	9,778	TAYLOR
19/08/1987	LEICESTER CITY	ELLAND ROAD	DIVISION TWO	1–0	21,034	SHERIDAN (P)
22/08/1987	READING	ELLAND ROAD	DIVISION TWO	0–0	19,286	
29/08/1987	BRADFORD CITY	VALLEY PARADE	DIVISION TWO	0–0	11,428	
31/08/1987	WEST BROMWICH ALBION	ELLAND ROAD	DIVISION TWO	1–0	19,847	SHERIDAN
05/09/1987	IPSWICH TOWN	PORTMAN ROAD	DIVISION TWO	0–1	11,163	
12/09/1987	HULL CITY	ELLAND ROAD	DIVISION TWO	0–2	18,205	
15/09/1987	HUDDERSFIELD TOWN	LEEDS ROAD	DIVISION TWO	0–0	9,085	
19/09/1987	MIDDLESBROUGH	AYRESOME PARK	DIVISION TWO	0–2	12,051	

23/09/1987	YORK CITY	ELLAND ROAD	LITTLEWOODS CUP 2ND ROUND 1ST LEG	1–1	11,527	SNODIN
26/09/1987	MANCHESTER CITY	ELLAND ROAD	DIVISION TWO	2–0	25,358	DE MANGE, SNODIN
30/09/1987	STOKE CITY	ELLAND ROAD	DIVISION TWO	0–0	17.208	
03/10/1987	BLACKBURN ROVERS	EWOOD PARK	DIVISION TWO	1–1	7,675	TAYLOR
06/10/1987	YORK CITY	BOOTHAM CRESCENT	LITTLEWOODS CUP 2ND ROUND 2ND LEG	4–0	5,996	SHERIDAN 2, TAYLOR, MUMBY
10/10/1987	ASTON VILLA	ELLAND ROAD	DIVISION TWO	1–3	20,741	TAYLOR
17/10/1987	PLYMOUTH ARGYLE	HOME PARK	DIVISION TWO	3–6	9,358	TAYLOR, SNODIN 2
20/10/1987	OLDHAM ATHLETIC	BOUNDARY PARK	DIVISION TWO	1–1	6,312	SWAN
24/10/1987	BOURNEMOUTH	ELLAND ROAD	DIVISION TWO	3–2	15,253	TAYLOR, SWAN, RENNIE
28/10/1987	OLDHAM ATHLETIC	ELLAND ROAD	LITTLEWOODS CUP 3RD ROUND	2–2	15,600	SWAN 2
31/10/1987	SHEFFIELD UNITED	BRAMALL LANE	DIVISION TWO	2–2	12,095	SNODIN, SWAN
04/11/1987	OLDHAM ATHLETIC	BOUNDARY PARK	LITTLEWOODS CUP 3RD ROUND REPLAY	2–4	7,058	SNODIN, TAYLOR
07/11/1987	SHREWSBURY TOWN	ELLAND ROAD	DIVISION TWO	2–1	13,760	STILES, TAYLOR
14/11/1987	MILLWALL	THE DEN	DIVISION TWO	1–3	8,014	MCLEARY OG
21/11/1987	SWINDON TOWN	ELLAND ROAD	DIVISION TWO	4–2	15,457	RENNIE, DAVISON, TAYLOR, HADDOCK
25/11/1987	SHEFFIELD UNITED	ELLAND ROAD	SIMOD CUP 1ST ROUND	3–0	4,425	RENNIE, TAYLOR, NOTEMAN
28/11/1987	CRYSTAL PALACE	SELHURST PARK	DIVISION TWO	0–3	8,749	
05/12/1987	BIRMINGHAM CITY	ELLAND ROAD	DIVISION TWO	4–1	15,977	SHERIDAN (P), DAVISON, SWAN, TAYLOR
08/12/1987	MILLWALL	THE DEN	SIMOD CUP 2ND ROUND	0–2	5,034	
12/12/1987	READING	ELM PARK	DIVISION TWO	1–0	6,505	SHERIDAN (P)
19/12/1987	HUDDERSFIELD TOWN	ELLAND ROAD	DIVISION TWO	3–0	20,111	SHERIDAN 2, DAVISON
26/12/1987	MANCHESTER CITY	MAINE ROAD	DIVISION TWO	2–1	30,153	REDMOND OG, BATTY
28/12/1987	MIDDLESBROUGH	ELLAND ROAD	DIVISION TWO	2–0	34,186	DAVISON, SWAN
01/01/1988	BRADFORD CITY	ELLAND ROAD	DIVISION TWO	2–0	36,004	WIILLIAMS, SNODIN
03/01/1988	HULL CITY	BOOTHFERRY PARK	DIVISION TWO	1–3	14,694	SWAN
09/01/1988	ASTON VILLA	ELLAND ROAD	FA CUP 3RD ROUND	1–2	29,002	DAVISON
16/01/1988	BARNSLEY	OAKWELL	DIVISION TWO	0–2	19,028	

65

30/01/1988	WEST BROMWICH ALBION	THE HAWTHORNS	DIVISION TWO	4–1	9,008	SHERIDAN, WILLIAMS, PEARSON, DAVISON
06/02/1988	IPSWICH TOWN	ELLAND ROAD	DIVISION TWO	1–0	19,564	PEARSON
13/02/1988	LEICESTER CITY	FILBERT STREET	DIVISION TWO	2–3	11,937	WILLIAMS, SHERIDAN (P)
23/02/1988	STOKE CITY	VICTORIA GROUND	DIVISION TWO	1–2	10,129	PEARSON
27/02/1988	BLACKBURN ROVERS	ELLAND ROAD	DIVISION TWO	2–2	23,843	SHERIDAN (P), SNODIN
05/03/1988	PLYMOUTH ARGYLE	ELLAND ROAD	DIVISION TWO	1–0	18,115	BAIRD
12/03/1988	ASTON VILLA	VILLA PARK	DIVISION TWO	2–1	19,677	SWAN, TAYLOR
19/03/1988	SHEFFIELD UNITED	ELLAND ROAD	DIVISION TWO	5–0	22,376	SWAN, PEARSON 3, SHERIDAN
26/03/1988	BOURNEMOUTH	DEAN COURT	DIVISION TWO	0–0	9,147	
02/04/1988	SHREWSBURY TOWN	GAY MEADOW	DIVISION TWO	0–1	7,369	
06/04/1988	MILLWALL	ELLAND ROAD	DIVISION TWO	1–2	24,241	SHERIDAN (P)
23/04/1988	OLDHAM ATHLETIC	ELLAND ROAD	DIVISION TWO	1–1	13,442	SNODIN
30/04/1988	SWINDON TOWN	COUNTY GROUND	DIVISION TWO	2–1	8,299	BAIRD 2
02/05/1988	CRYSTAL PALACE	ELLAND ROAD	DIVISION TWO	1–0	13,217	SHERIDAN (P)
06/05/1988	BIRMINGHAM CITY	ST ANDREWS	DIVISION TWO	0–0	6,024	

APPEARANCES					
PLAYERS	**LEAGUE**	**FA CUP**	**LITT CUP**	**SIMOD CUP**	**TOTAL**
MICKY ADAMS	40	1	3	1	45
MARK AIZLEWOOD	16 (1)				16 (1)
JACK ASHURST	41	1	4	2	48
NEIL ASPIN	25 (1)	1	2	1	29 (1)
IAN BAIRD	10				10
DAVID BATTY	23 (1)	1		2	25 (1)
VINCE BROCKIE	2				2
JOHN BUCKLEY	0 (1)				0 (1)
BOBBY DAVISON	15 (1)	1		2	18 (1)
MERVYN DAY	44	1	4	2	51
KEN DEMANGE	14 (1)		3	2	19 (1)
RUSSELL DOIG	1 (1)		1 (2)		2 (3)
KEITH EDWARDS	4 (4)				4 (4)
SIMON GRAYSON	2			1	3
PETER HADDOCK	38 (2)	1	3	2	44 (2)

BOBBY MCDONALD	1		1		2
PETER MAGUIRE	2				2
JIM MELROSE	3 (1)	0 (1)	0 (1)		3 (3)
PETER MUMBY	3 (2)		0 (2)		3 (4)
KEVIN NOTEMAN	0 (1)			1	1 (1)
JOHN PEARSON	21 (7)		2	0 (1)	23 (8)
DAVID RENNIE	25 (3)		2	1	28 (3)
JOHN SHERIDAN	36 (2)	1	4	1	42 (2)
GLYNN SNODIN	33 (2)	1	4	1	39 (2)
JOHN STILES	7 (6)		2 (2)	0 (1)	9 (9)
PETER SWAN	21 (4)		2	1	24 (4)
BOB TAYLOR	27 (5)	1	4	2	34 (5)
GARY WILLIAMS	31	1	3		35

GOALS	LEAGUE	FA CUP	LITT CUP	SIMOD CUP	TOTAL
JOHN SHERIDAN	12		2		14
BOB TAYLOR	9		2	1	12
PETER SWAN	8		2		10
GLYNN SNODIN	7		2		9
BOBBY DAVISON	5	1			6
JOHN PEARSON	6				6
IAN BAIRD	3				3
DAVID RENNIE	2			1	3
GARY WILLIAMS	3				3
DAVID BATTY	1				1
KEN DEMANGE	1				1
PETER HADDOCK	1				1
PETER MUMBY			1		1
KEVIN NOTEMAN				1	1
JOHN STILES	1				1
OWN GOALS	2				2

SEASON 1988–89

Having finished the previous season in seventh place, hopes were high that manager Billy Bremner could at least finish in a play-off place and end seven years of hurt for Leeds United. Compared to the previous summer, this one was relatively quiet with only Noel Blake on a free and Vince Hilaire for £170,000 who both joined from Portsmouth. The season started in disappointing fashion as only a point was taken at home to Oxford, thanks to a goal from Glynn Snodin. Worse was to follow as Blake, Hilaire and Ian Baird made an unhappy return to Fratton Park in a 4–0 defeat. To make matters worse Baird saw red. Only one win in the next four followed, a midweek win at home to Barnsley, thanks to goals from Bobby Davison and Hilaire, (his first for the club), which left the Whites in 18th position after six matches. Despite a 2–1 win in the first leg of the second round Littlewoods Cup tie at Peterborough, Bremner was sacked the following day. Peter Gunby was put in charge as the caretaker manager and oversaw three straight defeats, 2–1 at Brighton and Sunderland and a 1–0 home reverse against Watford. The Watford defeat was seen as the last resort for many fans as they attacked Chairman Leslie Silver's car in the West Stand car park.

Fourty-eight hours later, United got their man in Sheffield Wednesday manager Howard Wilkinson. It was a move that was a total surprise as Leeds were struggling at the wrong end of the Second Division and the Owls were in the top half of the First Division. He came with a big reputation, he had helped Notts County win promotion to the top flight in 1980–81 as part of the coaching team and in the summer of 1983, he succeeded Leeds United legend Jack Charlton in the Sheffield Wednesday hot seat. It was a move that proved hugely successful there as he won promotion in his first season by finishing runners up in the Second Division, losing six of his 42 League matches.

One of his first jobs at Elland Road was to order the removal of all the past glories from the corridors and then Norman Hunter was axed from the coaching set up when Wilkinson brought in Mick Hennigan from Sheffield Wednesday. His first match in charge was a 3–1 win in the Littlewoods Cup second leg tie at Elland Road, in front of just eight thousand fans. Things needed to improve and slowly but surely they did as an impressive 10 match unbeaten League run began that took Leeds away from the relegation zone. Wilkinson's first League win as Leeds boss, came in a 2–1 Yorkshire derby at home to Hull City. That was followed up by another win away at Ipswich Town thanks to a John Sheridan penalty and was the first time the club had managed back-to-back League wins all season.

His first dip into the transfer market saw winger Andy Williams join from Rotherham United for £170,000 whilst Neil Parsley and Mike Whitlow joined from non-League Witton Albion for a combined fee of £30,000. Going out of the club were FA Cup hero Micky Adams who joined Southampton for £250,000, defender Peter Swan went to Hull City for £200,000 and Jack Ashurst for £10,000 and Vince Brockie for £15,000 both joined Doncaster Rovers. By the time Blackburn

Rovers were defeated 2–0 on Boxing Day in front of 31,622 fans at Elland Road, Leeds had moved up to 11th place and were looking up, rather than looking nervously over their shoulder. Five days later, Plymouth Argyle were beaten and Leeds had only suffered one League defeat in 14, amazingly at home to lowly Shrewsbury in mid-December.

Following a 1–0 home win over Birmingham thanks to Vince Hilaire on 14 January, Leeds climbed to seventh in the table and all the talk was suddenly of a late Play-off push. However, a 3–2 defeat away at Oxford United and an FA Cup fourth round defeat away at Brian Clough's Nottingham Forest seemed to dent the Whites confidence. With the run over and only one win in the next six, this left Leeds in 12th place and thoughts would start to turn to the following campaign.

By the time Portsmouth visited for the return fixture at the end of March, Wilkinson had yet again been busy in the transfer market, securing a player that would play a huge part in the history of Leeds United. Scottish midfielder Gordon Strachan joined from arch rivals man utd for £300,000 in a move, which had the pundits questioning the sense of signing a 32-year-old. Also joining was central defender Chris Fairclough who originally joined on loan from Tottenham Hotspur. Another piece in the jigsaw was the signing of Carl Shutt who joined from Bristol City in a player exchange deal, which saw Bob Taylor go the other way for £200,000 whilst Shutt took the opposite move for £50,000. It was a move that paid immediate dividends as Shutt scored all three goals on his debut at home to Bournemouth.

Leeds season fizzled out with only one win in their next five matches; however this was not without incident. As captain Mark Aizlewood who had been heckled all afternoon scored the only goal in a low-key win at home to Walsall, he celebrated in front of the Kop by giving them a rude gesture. Manager Wilkinson substituted him immediately; he was subsequently stripped of the captaincy and given a fourteen-day ban.

The final match of the season away at Shrewsbury might have had nothing riding on it, but for former captain Brendan Ormsby it was the end of an injury nightmare that had lasted two years. Ormsby had been injured in the Play-off final replay at St Andrews against Charlton in May 1987, where he severely damaged his cartilage. He played the full 90 minutes in an entertaining 3–3 draw, in which Strachan took over as the Whites penalty taker from John Sheridan. In the end the Whites finished 10th and thoughts quickly turned to next season as Wilko looked to mould together a side capable of promotion.

Andrew's best and worst matches this season

Best: Stoke City (H) 4–0 Baird 2, Davison, Sheridan (P), 26 November 1988 – Howard Wilkinson's boys flex their muscles.

Worst: Shrewsbury Town (H) 2–3 Sheridan (P), Davison, 10 December 1988 – The polar opposite from the Stoke home match, losing at home to a side who would eventually be relegated.

DIVISION TWO TABLE 1988–89							
	P	W	D	L	F	A	PTS
1. CHELSEA **C**	46	29	12	5	96	50	99
2. MANCHESTER CITY **P**	46	23	13	10	77	53	82
3. CRYSTAL PALACE **P**	46	23	12	11	71	49	81
4. WATFORD **PL**	46	22	12	12	74	48	78
5. BLACKBURN ROVERS **PL**	46	22	11	13	74	59	77
6. SWINDON TOWN **PL**	46	20	16	10	68	53	76
7. BARNSLEY	46	20	14	12	66	58	74
8. IPSWICH TOWN	46	22	7	17	71	61	73
9. WEST BROMWICH ALBION	46	18	18	10	65	41	72
10. LEEDS UNITED	46	17	16	13	59	50	67
11. SUNDERLAND	46	16	15	15	60	60	63
12. BOURNEMOUTH	46	18	8	20	53	62	62
13. STOKE CITY	46	15	14	17	57	72	59
14. BRADFORD CITY	46	13	17	16	52	59	56
15. LEICESTER CITY	46	13	16	17	56	63	55
16. OLDHAM ATHLETIC	46	11	21	14	75	72	54
17. OXFORD UNITED	46	14	12	20	62	70	54
18. PLYMOUTH ARGYLE	46	14	12	20	55	66	54
19. BRIGHTON & HOVE ALBION	46	14	9	23	57	66	51
20. PORTSMOUTH	46	13	12	21	53	62	51
21. HULL CITY	46	11	14	21	52	68	47
22. SHREWSBURY TOWN **R**	46	8	18	20	40	67	42
23. BIRMINGHAM CITY **R**	46	8	11	27	31	76	35
24. WALSALL **R**	46	5	16	25	41	80	31

DATE	OPPOSITION	VENUE	COMPETITION	SCORE	ATT	SCORERS
27/08/1988	OXFORD UNITED	ELLAND ROAD	DIVISION TWO	1–1	22,038	SNODIN
03/09/1988	PORTSMOUTH	FRATTON PARK	DIVISION TWO	0–4	15,263	
10/09/1988	MANCHESTER CITY	ELLAND ROAD	DIVISION TWO	1–1	23,677	BLAKE
17/09/1988	BOURNEMOUTH	DEAN COURT	DIVISION TWO	0–0	7,922	
21/09/1988	BARNSLEY	ELLAND ROAD	DIVISION TWO	2–0	17,370	DAVISON, HILAIRE
24/09/1988	CHELSEA	ELLAND ROAD	DIVISION TWO	0–2	26,080	
27/09/1988	PETERBOROUGH UNITED	LONDON ROAD	LITTLEWOODS CUP 2ND ROUND 1ST LEG	2–1	4,979	SNODIN, BAIRD

01/10/1988	BRIGHTON & HOVE ALBION	GOLDSTONE GROUND	DIVISION TWO	1–2	7,109	BAIRD
04/10/1988	SUNDERLAND	ROKER PARK	DIVISION TWO	1–2	12,671	DAVISON
08/10/1988	WATFORD	ELLAND ROAD	DIVISION TWO	0–1	15,657	
12/10/1988	PETERBOROUGH UNITED	ELLAND ROAD	LITTLEWOODS CUP 2ND ROUND 2ND LEG	3–1	8,894	DAVISON, HILAIRE, SHERIDAN (P)
16/10/1988	SWINDON TOWN	COUNTY GROUND	DIVISION TWO	0–0	9,234	
22/10/1988	LEICESTER CITY	ELLAND ROAD	DIVISION TWO	1–1	17,263	HILAIRE
26/10/1988	BRADFORD CITY	VALLEY PARADE	DIVISION TWO	1–1	13,048	DAVISON
29/10/1988	HULL CITY	ELLAND ROAD	DIVISION TWO	2–1	17,536	SHERIDAN, BAIRD
02/11/1988	LUTON TOWN	ELLAND ROAD	LITTLEWOODS CUP 3RD ROUND	0–2	19,447	
05/11/1988	IPSWICH TOWN	PORTMAN ROAD	DIVISION TWO	1–0	11,750	SHERIDAN (P)
09/11/1988	SHREWSBURY TOWN	ELLAND ROAD	SIMOD CUP 1ST ROUND	3–1	3,220	DAVISON 2, AIZLEWOOD
12/11/1988	WEST BROMWICH ALBION	ELLAND ROAD	DIVISION TWO	2–1	20,442	AIZLEWOOD, BAIRD
19/11/1988	OLDHAM ATHLETIC	BOUNDARY PARK	DIVISION TWO	2–2	8,824	DAVISON 2
22/11/1988	BIRMINGHAM CITY	ST ANDREWS	DIVISION TWO	0–0	6,168	
26/11/1988	STOKE CITY	ELLAND ROAD	DIVISION TWO	4–0	19,933	BAIRD 2, DAVISON, SHERIDAN (P)
29/11/1988	MILLWALL	THE DEN	SIMOD CUP 2ND ROUND	0–2	4,242	
03/12/1988	WALSALL	FELLOWS PARK	DIVISION TWO	3–0	6,885	DAVISON 2, WHITLOW
10/12/1988	SHREWSBURY TOWN	ELLAND ROAD	DIVISION TWO	2–3	19,967	SHERIDAN (P), DAVISON
17/12/1988	CRYSTAL PALACE	SELHURST PARK	DIVISION TWO	0–0	9,847	
26/12/1988	BLACKBURN ROVERS	ELLAND ROAD	DIVISION TWO	2–0	31,622	BAIRD, DAVISON
31/12/1988	PLYMOUTH ARGYLE	ELLAND ROAD	DIVISION TWO	2–0	24,043	BAIRD, SNODIN
02/01/1989	MANCHESTER CITY	MAINE ROAD	DIVISION TWO	0–0	33,034	
07/01/1989	BRIGHTON & HOVE ALBION	GOLDSTONE GROUND	FA CUP 3RD ROUND	2–1	10,900	BAIRD 2
14/01/1989	BIRMINGHAM CITY	ELLAND ROAD	DIVISION TWO	1–0	21,937	HILAIRE
21/01/1989	OXFORD UNITED	MANOR GROUND	DIVISION TWO	2–3	7,928	BLAKE, HILAIRE
28/01/1989	NOTTINGHAM FOREST	CITY GROUND	FA CUP 4TH ROUND	0–2	28,107	
04/02/1989	SUNDERLAND	ELLAND ROAD	DIVISION TWO	2–0	31,985	DAVISON, SHERIDAN (P)
11/02/1989	WATFORD	VICARAGE ROAD	DIVISION TWO	1–1	13,439	PEARSON
18/02/1989	LEICESTER CITY	FILBERT STREET	DIVISION TWO	2–1	14,151	DAVISON, SNODIN
25/02/1989	SWINDON TOWN	ELLAND ROAD	DIVISION TWO	0–0	22,651	
01/03/1989	BRADFORD CITY	ELLAND ROAD	DIVISION TWO	3–3	33,325	BLAKE, HILAIRE, BAIRD

05/03/1989	WEST BROMWICH ALBION	THE HAWTHORNS	DIVISION TWO	1–2	15,914	ADAMS
11/03/1989	IPSWICH TOWN	ELLAND ROAD	DIVISION TWO	2–4	19,639	HILAIRE, BLAKE
14/03/1989	HULL CITY	BOOTHFERRY PARK	DIVISION TWO	2–1	8,887	BAIRD, DAVISON
19/03/1989	BARNSLEY	OAKWELL	DIVISION TWO	2–2	11,578	AIZLEWOOD, SHERIDAN (P)
25/03/1989	PORTSMOUTH	ELLAND ROAD	DIVISION TWO	1–0	27,049	BAIRD
27/03/1989	BLACKBURN ROVERS	EWOOD PARK	DIVISION TWO	0–2	11,533	
01/04/1989	BOURNEMOUTH	ELLAND ROAD	DIVISION TWO	3–0	21,095	SHUTT 3
05/04/1989	CRYSTAL PALACE	ELLAND ROAD	DIVISION TWO	1–2	25,604	SHUTT
09/04/1989	PLYMOUTH ARGYLE	HOME PARK	DIVISION TWO	0–1	9,365	
15/04/1989	BRIGHTON & HOVE ALBION	ELLAND ROAD	DIVISION TWO	1–0	14,915	A WILLIAMS
22/04/1989	CHELSEA	STAMFORD BRIDGE	DIVISION TWO	0–1	30,337	
29/04/1989	STOKE CITY	VICTORIA GROUND	DIVISION TWO	3–2	9,051	SHERIDAN (P), DAVISON, STRACHAN
01/05/1989	WALSALL	ELLAND ROAD	DIVISION TWO	1–0	13,208	AIZLEWOOD
06/05/1989	OLDHAM ATHLETIC	ELLAND ROAD	DIVISION TWO	0–0	14,459	
13/05/1989	SHREWSBURY TOWN	GAY MEADOW	DIVISION TWO	3–3	4,693	STRACHAN 2 (1P), RENNIE

APPEARANCES					
PLAYERS	LEAGUE	FA CUP	LITT CUP	SIMOD CUP	TOTAL
MICKY ADAMS	15 (1)	1	1		17 (1)
MARK AIZLEWOOD	34 (4)	1	3	2	40 (4)
IAN ANDREWS	1				1
JACK ASHURST	6 (1)				6 (1)
NEIL ASPIN	31 (2)	2	2	2	37 (2)
IAN BAIRD	43	2	3	2	50
DAVID BATTY	25 (5)	1	3	1	30 (5)
NOEL BLAKE	44	2	3	2	51
BOBBY DAVISON	37 (2)	1 (1)	2	2	42 (3)
MERVYN DAY	45	2	3	2	52
CHRIS FAIRCLOUGH	11				11
PETER HADDOCK	8 (4)	0 (1)	0 (1)		8 (6)
VINCE HILAIRE	42	2	3	2	49
DYLAN KERR	1 (2)				1 (2)
PETER MUMBY	0 (1)				0 (1)
BRENDAN ORMSBY	1				1
JOHN PEARSON	6 (27)	0 (1)	1 (1)	0 (1)	7 (30)
DAVID RENNIE	30 (3)	2	3	2	37 (3)

JOHN SHERIDAN	38 (2)	2	2	2	44 (2)
CARL SHUTT	3				3
GLYNN SNODIN	33 (2)	2	3	1	39 (2)
GARY SPEED	1				1
JOHN STILES	4 (6)				4 (6)
GORDON STRACHAN	11				11
PETER SWAN	1	1			2
BOB TAYLOR	2 (4)			0 (1)	2 (5)
MICHAEL WHITLOW	18 (2)			2	20 (2)
ANDY WILLIAMS	7 (11)	1			8 (11)
GARY WILLIAMS	8	0 (1)	1		9 (1)

GOALS	LEAGUE	FA CUP	LITT CUP	SIMOD CUP	TOTAL
BOBBY DAVISON	14		1	2	17
IAN BAIRD	10	2	1		13
JOHN SHERIDAN	7		1		8
VINCE HILAIRE	6		1		7
MARK AIZLEWOOD	3			1	4
NOEL BLAKE	4				4
CARL SHUTT	4				4
GLYNN SNODIN	3		1		4
GORDON STRACHAN	3				3
MICKY ADAMS	1				1
JOHN PEARSON	1				1
DAVID RENNIE	1				1
MICHAEL WHITLOW	1				1
ANDY WILLIAMS	1				1

SEASON 1989-90

Following a 10th place finish the previous season, hopes were high that the Whites could finally end their eight year exile in the Second Division, with promotion back to the First Division. Manager Howard Wilkinson made many changes during the summer months, bringing in Vinnie Jones from Wimbledon, John Hendrie from Bradford City, Mel Sterland from Rangers, John McClelland from Watford, Mickey Thomas from Shrewsbury, Chris O'Donnell from Ipswich and Jim Beglin from Liverpool. They were dubbed 'the magnificent seven' whilst John Sheridan, former captain Mark Aizlewood, Neil Aspin, David Rennie and FA Cup hero John Stiles all departed.

The first job for Sgt Wilko was to name his new captain and what a masterstroke it proved to be! Gordon Strachan who was signed from arch rivals man utd the previous March was handed the armband ahead of the new season and a trip to relegated Newcastle United. Expectations were high and after taking a 2–1 half time lead thanks to goals from Bobby Davison and Ian Baird, things looked good for the Whites. However, they were quickly dashed and Micky Quinn scored four goals in the second half and Leeds lost their opening day fixture 5–2. However, the smiles were soon back on the fans faces, thanks to a freak own goal by Middlesbrough defender Gary Parkinson which saw Leeds snatch three points in a 2–1 win at home to the Teessiders. The match also saw the debut of new signing Vinnie Jones. The victory saw the Whites embark on a 15 match unbeaten run in Division Two. Consecutive wins at Hull City (1–0), a 4–0 home rout thanks to a Strachan hat-trick against Swindon and a hard fought mid-week win over Oxford saw the Whites handily placed in fourth position after eight matches.

Despite being knocked out of the Littlewoods Cup by annual cup opponents Oldham Athletic, this did nothing to derail Wilkinson's men as they kept the unbeaten run going with six wins in seven. This took them to second place in the League, their highest League position in the last eight years! The run had to come to an end and it did in an eventful match at Filbert Street against Leicester City. Despite goals from Baird, Andy Williams and another from Strachan, Leeds lost out to the odd goal in seven and worse was to come as 'keeper Mervyn Day was stretchered off as Leicester scored their winning goal. Leeds did bounce back a week later with a 2–1 home win against Watford with Williams scoring the winning goal, but West Bromwich Albion exposed their defensive frailties with a 2–1 win at the Hawthorns. However, Newcastle were defeated thanks to a flying Ian Baird header. When Middlesbrough were beaten 2–0 at Ayresome Park thanks to goals from Carl Shutt making his first start in place of the injured Davison and Chris Fairclough on the second Saturday in December, Leeds finally hit top spot for the first time in the season. John Hendrie who had missed part of the season having been injured in the win at home to Swindon, inspired a comfortable 3–0 win at home to Brighton and kept Leeds in top spot ahead of their Boxing Day showdown with second placed Sheffield United. A 2–2 draw kept Leeds top, but they finished 1989 with a 1–0 defeat away at Oakwell.

Following a 1–1 draw at home to Oldham, Wilkinson dipped into the transfer market, signing prolific striker Lee Chapman from Nottingham Forest for £400,000. Ian Baird made way by joining Middlesbrough for £500,000. Baird would still have a major role to play in the Division Two title race. The signing of Chapman proved dividends straight away as the Lincolnshire born striker scored the equaliser on his debut away at Blackburn. Captain marvel Strachan had the final word with his goal, although there was a scare in the last minute as David May saw his penalty blaze over the crossbar.

By this time Ipswich Town had put paid to Leeds FA Cup hopes in the third Round and Aston Villa had done the same in the Northern Area semi-final in the much maligned Zenith Data Systems Cup. It left the Whites with no distractions and the way ahead was clear. Following another defeat this time 3–2 away at Swindon Town, Sgt Wilko yet again moved into the transfer market by acquiring Imre Varadi from Sheffield Wednesday for £50,000 and Chris Kamara from Stoke City for £150,000. Both players made their debuts in the thrilling 4–3 win at home to Hull City, in a match that also saw Chris O'Donnell finally don the famous white shirt for the first time.

Suddenly though the Whites form started to dip, with only three points from a possible 12 before the visit to Oxford United. With the Whites 2–0 down at half time and looking down the barrel of another defeat, Leeds turned it all around, with the help of youngster Gary Speed, winning 4–2. Three more important victories followed at home to both West Ham and Portsmouth and away at Sunderland, which left the Whites 10 points clear of their nearest challengers but more importantly 12 points clear of third place Swindon with only nine matches to go.

Suddenly nerves seemed to hit the Leeds players, as another four matches without a win set them up for the Easter Monday showdown against nearest and local rivals Sheffield United. The gap was down to three points and the Whites knew that a victory over Dave Bassett's side would go a long way to securing promotion back to the 'big time'. In front of a crowd of 32,727, Leeds produced their best performance of the season and blew Sheffield United away with a 4–0 win thanks to goals from Strachan 2 (1P), Chapman his 11th since joining from Nottingham Forest and a solo goal from Gary Speed, ensured that Leeds opened up a six point gap at the top of the table. With the finishing line in sight, Leeds yet again made it hard for themselves, following a 2–2 draw away at Brighton and a shock home defeat to Barnsley, this left them needing six points from the final two matches to be ensured of promotion and a return to the First Division.

The first of them was at home to Leicester in front of 32,597 fans. Mel Sterland gave Leeds the lead before Gary McAllister scored with a long range effort to level matters, but with six minutes left on the clock, Gordon Strachan thumped in his 16th League goal and 18th of the season, to send the home fans wild. However the win did not ensure promotion, but it did leave their fate in their own hands going into the last day decider away at Bournemouth. Heading into the last day of the season, Leeds were top on 82 points, with Sheffield United just behind on goal difference and Newcastle in third place on 80 points. Leeds knew that victory would take them back up to the First Division. Sadly the match was remembered for what happened off the field rather than on the field.

A lot has been written about the events of Saturday 5 May 1990, some of which will be touched on later on in this book but the main focus of that day was to end eight years of hurt. When Lee Chapman headed in Chris Kamara's cross, the dream had been realised, the Championship had been won and Leeds could now look to the future and hosting the likes of Liverpool, man utd, Arsenal and Everton once again. Ian Baird also had his say, as his two goals helped Middlesbrough defeat North East rivals Newcastle, as well as guaranteeing himself a championship medal.

Andrew's best and worst matches this season

Best: Bournemouth (A) 1–0 Chapman, 5 May 1990 – We are going up!!!

Worst: Barnsley (H) 1–2 Fairclough, 25 April 1990 – Promotion off the cards?

DIVISION TWO TABLE 1989–90							
	P	W	D	L	F	A	PTS
1. LEEDS UNITED **C**	46	24	13	9	79	52	85
2. SHEFFIELD UNITED **P**	46	24	13	9	78	58	85
3. NEWCASTLE UNITED **PL**	46	22	14	10	80	55	80
4. SWINDON TOWN **PL**	46	20	14	12	79	59	74
5. BLACKBURN ROVERS **PL**	46	19	17	10	74	59	74
6. SUNDERLAND **P**	46	20	14	12	70	64	74
7. WEST HAM UNITED	46	20	12	14	80	57	72
8. OLDHAM ATHLETIC	46	19	14	13	70	57	71
9. IPSWICH TOWN	46	19	12	15	67	66	69
10. WOLVERHAMPTON WANDERERS	46	18	13	15	67	60	67
11. PORT VALE	46	15	16	15	62	57	61
12. PORTSMOUTH	46	15	16	15	62	65	61
13. LEICESTER CITY	46	15	14	17	67	79	59
14. HULL CITY	46	14	16	16	58	65	58
15. WATFORD	46	14	15	17	58	60	57
16. PLYMOUTH ARGYLE	46	14	13	19	58	63	55
17. OXFORD UNITED	46	15	9	22	57	66	54

18. BRIGHTON & HOVE ALBION	46	15	9	22	56	72	54
19. BARNSLEY	46	13	15	18	49	71	54
20. WEST BROMWICH ALBION	46	12	15	19	67	61	51
21. MIDDLESBROUGH	46	13	11	22	52	63	50
22. BOURNEMOUTH **R**	46	12	12	22	57	76	48
23. BRADFORD CITY **R**	46	9	14	23	44	68	41
24. STOKE CITY **R**	46	6	19	21	35	63	37

DATE	OPPOSITION	VENUE	COMPETITION	SCORE	ATT	SCORERS
19/08/1989	NEWCASTLE UNITED	ST JAMES' PARK	DIVISION TWO	2–5	24,482	DAVISON, BAIRD
23/08/1989	MIDDLESBROUGH	ELLAND ROAD	DIVISION TWO	2–1	25,004	DAVISON, PARKINSON OG
26/08/1989	BLACKBURN ROVERS	ELLAND ROAD	DIVISION TWO	1–1	25,045	FAIRCLOUGH
02/09/1989	STOKE CITY	VICTORIA GROUND	DIVISION TWO	1–1	10,915	STRACHAN
09/09/1989	IPSWICH TOWN	ELLAND ROAD	DIVISION TWO	1–1	22,972	JONES
16/09/1989	HULL CITY	BOOTHFERRY PARK	DIVISION TWO	1–0	11,620	BAIRD
19/09/1989	OLDHAM ATHLETIC	BOUNDARY PARK	LITTLEWOODS CUP 2ND ROUND 1ST LEG	1–2	8,415	STRACHAN
23/09/1989	SWINDON TOWN	ELLAND ROAD	DIVISION TWO	4–0	21,694	STRACHAN 3 (1P), DAVISON
27/09/1989	OXFORD UNITED	ELLAND ROAD	DIVISION TWO	2–1	24,097	DAVISON, STERLAND
30/09/1989	PORT VALE	VALE PARK	DIVISION TWO	0–0	11,156	
03/10/1989	OLDHAM ATHLETIC	ELLAND ROAD	LITTLEWOODS CUP 2ND ROUND 2ND LEG	1–2	18,092	FAIRCLOUGH
07/10/1989	WEST HAM UNITED	UPTON PARK	DIVISION TWO	1–0	23,539	JONES
14/10/1989	SUNDERLAND	ELLAND ROAD	DIVISION TWO	2–0	27,815	DAVISON, FAIRCLOUGH
17/10/1989	PORTSMOUTH	FRATTON PARK	DIVISION TWO	3–3	10,260	DAVISON, WHITLOW, STERLAND
21/10/1989	WOLVERHAMPTON WANDERERS	ELLAND ROAD	DIVISION TWO	1–0	28,024	DAVISON
28/10/1989	BRADFORD CITY	VALLEY PARADE	DIVISION TWO	1–0	12,527	DAVISON
01/11/1989	PLYMOUTH ARGYLE	ELLAND ROAD	DIVISION TWO	2–1	26,791	STRACHAN (P), DAVISON
04/11/1989	BOURNEMOUTH	ELLAND ROAD	DIVISION TWO	3–0	26,484	BAIRD, STRACHAN (P), FAIRCLOUGH
07/11/1989	BLACKBURN ROVERS	ELLAND ROAD	ZENITH DATA SYSTEMS CUP NORTHERN SECTION 1ST ROUND	1–0	5,070	DAVISON

11/11/1989	LEICESTER CITY	FILBERT STREET	DIVISION TWO	3–4	18,032	BAIRD, WILLIAMS, STRACHAN (P)
18/11/1989	WATFORD	ELLAND ROAD	DIVISION TWO	2–1	26,921	FAIRCLOUGH, WILLIAMS
25/11/1989	WEST BROMWICH ALBION	THE HAWTHORNS	DIVISION TWO	1–2	15,116	FAIRCLOUGH
28/11/1989	BARNSLEY	OAKWELL	ZENITH DATA SYSTEMS CUP NORTHERN SECTION 2ND ROUND	2–1	6,136	STRACHAN (P), WILLIAMS
02/12/1989	NEWCASTLE UNITED	ELLAND ROAD	DIVISION TWO	1–0	31,715	BAIRD
09/12/1989	MIDDLESBROUGH	AYRESOME PARK	DIVISION TWO	2–0	19,686	SHUTT, FAIRCLOUGH
16/12/1989	BRIGHTON & HOVE ALBION	ELLAND ROAD	DIVISION TWO	3–0	24,070	STRACHAN, HENDRIE, JONES
19/12/1989	STOKE CITY	VICTORIA GROUND	ZENITH DATA SYSTEMS CUP NORTHERN SECTION 3RD ROUND	2–2 (5–4 ON PENS)	5,792	SHUTT 2 (PENS SCORED BY STRACHAN, STERLAND, DAY, KERR, JONES)
26/12/1989	SHEFFIELD UNITED	BRAMALL LANE	DIVISION TWO	2–2	31,254	STERLAND, SHUTT
30/12/1989	BARNSLEY	OAKWELL	DIVISION TWO	0–1	14.481	
01/01/1990	OLDHAM ATHLETIC	ELLAND ROAD	DIVISION TWO	1–1	30,217	HENDRIE
06/01/1990	IPSWICH TOWN	ELLAND ROAD	FA CUP 3RD ROUND	0–1	26,766	
13/01/1990	BLACKBURN ROVERS	EWOOD PARK	DIVISION TWO	2–1	14,485	CHAPMAN, STRACHAN
17/01/1990	ASTON VILLA	VILLA PARK	ZENITH DATA SYSTEMS CUP NORTHERN SECTION SEMI FINAL	0–2	17,543	
20/01/1990	STOKE CITY	ELLAND ROAD	DIVISION TWO	2–0	29,318	STRACHAN (P), HENDRIE
04/02/1990	SWINDON TOWN	COUNTY GROUND	DIVISION TWO	2–3	16,208	STRACHAN (P), HENDRIE
10/02/1990	HULL CITY	ELLAND ROAD	DIVISION TWO	4–3	29,977	HENDRIE, JONES, VARADI, STRACHAN
17/02/1990	IPSWICH TOWN	PORTMAN ROAD	DIVISION TWO	2–2	17.102	CHAPMAN 2
24/02/1990	WEST BROMWICH ALBION	ELLAND ROAD	DIVISION TWO	2–2	30,004	KAMARA, CHAPMAN
03/03/1990	WATFORD	VICARAGE ROAD	DIVISION TWO	0–1	13,468	
07/03/1990	PORT VALE	ELLAND ROAD	DIVISION TWO	0–0	28,756	
10/03/1990	OXFORD UNITED	MANOR GROUND	DIVISION TWO	4–2	8,397	CHAPMAN 2, VARADI, FAIRCLOUGH
17/03/1990	WEST HAM UNITED	ELLAND ROAD	DIVISION TWO	3–2	32,536	CHAPMAN 2, STRACHAN

20/03/1990	SUNDERLAND	ROKER PARK	DIVISION TWO	1–0	17.851	STERLAND
24/03/1990	PORTSMOUTH	ELLAND ROAD	DIVISION TWO	2–0	27,600	JONES, CHAPMAN
31/03/1990	WOLVERHAMPTON WANDERERS	MOLINEUX	DIVISION TWO	0–1	22,419	
07/04/1990	BRADFORD CITY	ELLAND ROAD	DIVISION TWO	1–1	32,316	SPEED
10/04/1990	PLYMOUTH ARGYLE	HOME PARK	DIVISION TWO	1–1	11,382	CHAPMAN
13/04/1990	OLDHAM ATHLETIC	BOUNDARY PARK	DIVISION TWO	1–3	16,292	DAVISON
16/04/1990	SHEFFIELD UNITED	ELLAND ROAD	DIVISION TWO	4–0	32,727	STRACHAN 2 (1P), CHAPMAN, SPEED
21/04/1990	BRIGHTON & HOVE ALBION	GOLDSTONE GROUND	DIVISION TWO	2–2	11,359	SPEED, I CHAPMAN OG
25/04/1990	BARNSLEY	ELLAND ROAD	DIVISION TWO	1–2	31,700	FAIRCLOUGH
28/04/1990	LEICESTER CITY	ELLAND ROAD	DIVISION TWO	2–1	32,597	STERLAND, STRACHAN
05/05/1990	BOURNEMOUTH	DEAN COURT	DIVISION TWO	1–0	9,918	CHAPMAN

Leicester photo courtesy
Mark Dovey

Millwall photo courtesy
Craig Gill

APPEARANCES					
PLAYERS	LEAGUE	FA CUP	LITT CUP	ZDS CUP	TOTAL
IAN BAIRD	23 (1)	1	2	4	30 (1)
DAVID BATTY	39 (3)	1	2	4	46 (3)
JIM BEGLIN	18 (1)			1	19 (1)
NOEL BLAKE	7		1 (1)	2	10 (1)
LEE CHAPMAN	21				21
BOBBY DAVISON	25 (4)		2	2	29 (4)
MERVYN DAY	44	1	2	3	50
NEIL EDWARDS				1	1
CHRIS FAIRCLOUGH	42	1	1 (1)	1	45 (1)
PETER HADDOCK	40	1	2	4	47
JOHN HENDRIE	22 (5)	1	1	2	26 (5)
VINCE HILAIRE	0 (2)				0 (2)
VINNIE JONES	43 (2)	1	2	4	50 (2)
CHRIS KAMARA	10 (1)				10 (1)
DYLAN KERR	2 (3)	1		0 (3)	3 (6)
JOHN MCCLELLAND	3				3
CHRIS O'DONNELL	0 (1)				0 (1)
JOHN PEARSON	2 (5)	0 (1)		1 (1)	3 (7)
CARL SHUTT	6 (15)	1		0 (2)	7 (17)
GLYNN SNODIN	3 (1)	0 (1)			3 (2)
GARY SPEED	12 (12)		0 (1)	0 (1)	12 (14)
MEL STERLAND	41 (1)	1	2	3	47 (1)
GORDON STRACHAN	46	1	2	4	53
MICKEY THOMAS	3				3
CHRIS TURNER	2				2
IMRE VARADI	12 (1)				12 (1)
MICHAEL WHITLOW	27 (2)		2	4	33 (2)
ANDY WILLIAMS	13 (3)		1 (1)	2	16 (4)
GOALS	LEAGUE	FA CUP	LITT CUP	ZDS CUP	TOTAL
GORDON STRACHAN	16		1	1	18
LEE CHAPMAN	12				12
BOBBY DAVISON	10			1	11
CHRIS FAIRCLOUGH	8		1		9
IAN BAIRD	5				5

Photos courtesy Craig Gill

JOHN HENDRIE	5				5
VINNIE JONES	5				5
MEL STERLAND	5				5
CARL SHUTT	2			2	4
GARY SPEED	3				3
ANDY WILLIAMS	2			1	3
IMRE VARADI	2				2
CHRIS KAMARA	1				1
MICHAEL WHITLOW	1				1
OWN GOALS	2				2

Oxford photo courtesy Mark Dovey

London Leeds photo courtesy Craig Gill

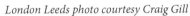

Leeds Holbeck Park photo courtesy Craig Gill

Leeds fans Wellingborough branch photo Craig Gill

Plymouth photo courtesy Mark Dovey

Plymouth photo courtesy Mark Dovey

Selby Whites flag on Voyager coach photo Mark Dovey

Watford photo courtesy Mark Dovey

LEEDS KITS IN THE '80S
COURTESY OF JOHN DEVLIN – WWW.TRUECOLOURSFOOTBALLKITS. COM

Leeds entered the decade still sporting the spoils of their early '70s groundbreaking deal with Admiral that effectively introduced the modern-day replica kit concept to football. By now though, with their logo taping and button up necks, the strips were beginning to look a little dated – the introduction of the 'peacock' badge the only fresh element in the design.

Although the '70s found influence primarily from British designers, the '80s saw a resurgence in continental style kits complete with V-necks, pinstripes and tight-fitting outfits. Umbro's return to Elland Road in 1981, ensured Leeds were bang up to date with a set of fine looking strips. The home design incorporated alternate yellow and blue pinstripes with simple trim on shorts and socks. The '80s saw the rapid rise of another addition to the sacred team kit and one that really upset the purists – sponsorship. Leeds took the plunge in 1981 and signed a deal with local electrical engineers R.F. Winder who opted for an RFW acronym on the team shirts. Subsequent sponsors in the first half of the decade were Systime, WGK and Lion Cabinets (all interrelated computer/electronic companies).

The equivalent away strip retained the familiar all-yellow colourway from the '70s which was now topped off with blue raglan seam piping, V-neck and cuffs. This design lasted (albeit with different sponsors and blue shorts) until 1986.

By 1984 the pinstripes were gone and replaced by elegant shadow stripes – the next major design trend to hit football shirts. The V-neck and cuffs also gained a complex trim of yellow and white bands.

The club's next set of kits were launched in 1986 and took a new, more colourful approach with triangular panels on each side of the shirt which now also featured a wrap over V-neck, centralised badge and an Umbro logo on each sleeve. The away kit mirrored the design, but reversed in yellow and lashings of blue. The concept of 'third kits' began to enter the increasingly replica-driven football kit world around this time and Leeds's first (and only) example of the decade appeared in the 1986–87 season, presumably to counter problems when playing teams who sported blue and white stripes. The all-yellow strip could not have been simpler and featured no contrasting trim whatsoever in a design that bucked the current trends. Interestingly though replicas of this kit were never offered for retail. The team's shirt sponsor by now was the Burton clothing group (of whom Leeds's Director Peter Ridsdale was also Managing Director) who were later to famously promote their 'Top Man' brand on the Leeds's jerseys.

The next home kit featured a tidy button-down collar that worked neatly with a simple round neck. The previous plain white fabric was now adorned with a small chequerboard style jacquard

pattern. New techniques in fabric technology began to influence kit design and increasingly complicated patterns were beginning to emerge on shirts (and sometimes even shorts) during this period. A spear like-blue and yellow trim was included on the shorts.

The previous all-yellow third strip was promoted to first choice away outfit for the 1988–89 season, yet was still not marketed for sale.

The last new Leeds kit of the '80s was the sublime yellow away kit that was introduced in 1989 and lasted until 1992, therefore seeing plenty of action during the club's 1991–92 title winning campaign. Created from a slightly richer shade of yellow, triangular jacquard patterns combined with subtle swirls to create a complex design. The shirt also featured the standard late '80s style button up collar with placket neck. Although the shorts were still, shall we say, a little snug, the shirts were definitely more roomy thanks to the introduction of a new, lightweight fabric.

Looking back through the club kit during the '80s it's clear that they were lucky in avoiding many of the sartorial disasters that cropped up during this and the subsequent decade and in the main sported elegant and distinguished outfits.

PRE-SEASON IN THE '80S, SHEFFIELD UNITED AND CHELSEA SCOREBOARD!

1981 – PRE-SEASON IN DENMARK

At the start of this season, Leeds were invited to take part in a pre-season tournament in Denmark between 21 and 28 July 1981. Other teams taking part were Start Kristiansand from Norway, FC Utrecht from Holland, Ikast FC from Denmark, Widzew Lodz from Poland and Eintracht Braunschweig from West Germany. One Leeds fan travelled alone to the tournament by train and ferry via the Hook of Holland, then Copenhagen before arriving in Ikast. On arrival he thought it looked like a war zone with that many broken bottles and bricks lying all over. It was a lovely place though and eventually he found a campsite, meeting up with other Leeds fans there. He found that someone had borrowed a flagpole from the local police station (it was reclaimed by the police at the end of the week) and hoisted a Leeds flag up it. Someone had a spare tent luckily but everyone was taking the p**s after it was pitched on a slope facing downwards. He had the last laugh though, because when it rained everyone else was washed out! As the week went on, the campsite became home to an increasing number of pushbikes that were borrowed by Leeds fans on their way home. These were all reclaimed at the end of the week also.

Another day they met some Utrecht fans who loved the Leeds fans to bits. They certainly weren't the people to get on the wrong side of though as they opened up the boot of a car to show axes, cheese wire and all sorts of weapons!!!

The local Hell's Angels were causing a lot of problems during the week as they kept riding about (some in a hearse) and picking on lone Leeds fans and beating them up. One evening as some of the Leeds fans all met up together for a drink in a pub, the Hell's Angels decided to attack this particular group but they got more than they

Brod and Kevin Hird fan club Ikast, Denmark 1981 photo courtesy Pam Freer

bargained for! The bikers attacked the Leeds fans with glasses who retaliated by throwing cobblestones at them. The Leeds fans stood and fought back which ended up with them beating the Hell's Angels into submission. Later when back at the campsite some of the lads were told by the security guards there, that the coppers were leaving the Leeds fans to it, as finally there was someone in town who could sort the bikers out!

PAM FREER PRE-SEASON MEMORIES

Ikast 1981 Scouse Steve, Scouse Alan, Carole and Brod photo courtesy Pam Freer

IKAST 1981

The pre-season tour in July 1981 was in Denmark and I travelled with the Griffin branch of the Leeds United Supporters Club. We stayed in a hotel in Aarhus going by coach to the matches with most of the other Leeds fans staying on a campsite near the ground in Ikast. They were having a whale of a time as the Danish girls seemed to be very 'fond' of British men! It was a tournament with Start Kristiansand, FC Utrecht, Ikast FS, Widzew Lodz and Eintract Braunschweig. The Utrecht fans were tooled up (even had guns) but they loved the Leeds fans. Some of our fans were attacked in a pub by some bikers who came off second best. I heard about this, but didn't see it as we were based in Aarhus when it happened. I was with Carole Parkhouse a big Maggie Thatcher fan and she went round pulling down all the anti-Thatcher posters!

Ikast Denmark (Collar, daughter and Brian) photo courtesy Brian Austin

Ikast, Denmark 1981 photo courtesy Brian Austin

Marbella 1984 photo courtesy Pam Freer

MARBELLA 1984

The pre-season tour in July 1984 was to Spain. Mick Hewitt organised the trip but there were so many of us, that we were split between hotels in Fuengirola and Torremolinos. I was in Fuengirola in a hotel a mile away from the resort and the Leeds fans were the majority

of the people staying there. The American navy were in the region too and we got chatting to some of them in a Fuengirola bar. Some of the lads told them I was Wendy Sly who had just won a medal at the Olympics and they believed it! There was just one match but I can't remember who we played.

Menwith Hill 1983 photo courtesy Pam Freer

South Kirkby trip Stockholm October 1984 photo courtesy Pam Freer

STOCKHOLM 1984

This was played during the season in Djurgarden, which is about two hours away from Stockholm where we stayed. The match was indoors. After complaining about the beer prices on the ferry over, we were shocked at the prices in Sweden. I've never seen the fans that went with us as sober as they were on that trip!

SHEFFIELD UNITED 2 V LEEDS UNITED 1 – 23 MARCH 1985
BY SEAN CADEN

This away day was unforgettable on many levels. A Yorkshire derby in Sheffield, local rivals; I could hardly contain my excitement as we set off down the M1 to the Steel City. It seemed like no time and we were there. Game on!

When walking to the ground, there was an atmosphere in the air that I've seldom felt. The best way to describe it was Venomous!!! Seriously, it felt like we were walking into bandit country and it reminded me of the old Moss Side area near Maine Road. One or two unpleasant experiences there but that's another story!! LOL! There were a few handbags at dawn incidents on the way to

Photo courtesy of Craig Gill

the ground, which were a bit tame, but eventually we made it to the street outside the away end of the Lane!

We waited in the queue to get in and were all VERY excited, as this was a big match in our unlikely push for promotion! Suddenly like a scene from Braveheart, a mob of about 60 red and white loonies ran around the corner at the end of the street to our right. It turned into one of those slow motion moments as the seemingly foaming at the mouth mob got closer, some carrying pickaxe handles and I thought, "Ooh, this isn't good!" Whilst being a big lad myself, forgive me, but having just turned 17, I didn't fancy taking on a full-grown man with a pickaxe handle!!

Miraculously when they were about 30 yards away the cavalry arrived!! About 30 coppers blocked their path. Whilst many of the lads in the line were WELL UP for a battle, personally I had NEVER been happier to see the Old Bill in my life! Ha Ha!!

Eventually we got in the ground still alive, which is always good and got into the seats at the back of the away end! The home pen to the left of the away supporters gave us a very warm welcome! Within minutes, I started to hear strange noises, which sounded like a demented xylophone! It didn't take long to realise that there was a hail of coins coming from both sides hitting the metal of the stand, one of which narrowly missed my head!

This being 1985, the Leeds away following were no angels (to say the least!) and you could certainly have bought a VERY good drink picking up the coins that were being launched!! The thought of being lucky sat at the front of the seats was quickly quelled, when the Leeds fans at the back of the seats starting ripping them out to bang and throw. The situation was rapidly turning into a Wild West Saloon situation and I seriously considered leaving at half time! Suddenly things seemed to calm down a bit and football slowly broke out!!

Photo courtesy of Craig Gill

Although we lost the match 2–1 to a Mel Eves thunderbolt, the best memory of the match for me, was an absolute clinical display by the GREAT Peter Lorimer! He was sat in the middle of the park spraying pinpoint 50-yard balls all day! It was truly a sight to behold seeing a master at work! If my memory serves me right, the Sunday papers gave him 10/10! One of the only times I've ever seen this happen. LASH was TRULY brilliant that day!!

Walking back to the car was like a military operation, but luckily there were plenty of police around. There were a few handbags at 10 paces again, but nothing major. As we left the Steel City I thought to myself that it would be a cold day in hell before I'd be back there. Little did I know that two years later at Hillsborough, we would have one of THE BEST days even in defeat!

One thing for sure is that Leeds United have THE BEST and most loyal away following in football and as ALWAYS we will be Marching on Together! FOREVER!! WACCOE! MOT!

CHELSEA V LEEDS 28 APRIL 1984 BY TRICKY DICKY

Back in the good old days of terracing and 3.00 pm kick-offs on Saturdays, me and a few lads from Derby (born and bred there and enjoyed many a victory over them, especially when Clough was in charge), used to travel to virtually every home and away match. I had been fortunate enough to see the great Revie team live in the few years before Don left us and took charge of a bunch of inferior players, but we were now languishing in the old Division Two.

When we had been dumped there (courtesy of F**k Off West Brom... capitulating at Stoke after we had dismantled their away end a few days before), many of us had thought that we just had to turn up in vast numbers (which we did) at away matches and the team would dispatch the minnows. Home matches would be a formality and we would bounce back to Division One

Photo courtesy of Craig Gill

at the first attempt… Even though results weren't quite as expected, the matches especially away matches, were rarely dull, usually as a result of activities not on the pitch.

Away matches in London were particularly memorable (and there seemed to be many each season) as I had quite a few ex Uni mates, some Londoners, others not, scattered around various parts of the capital. As a result, away matches usually included a weekend away with free accommodation. This particular weekend involved four of us enjoying a two-night stay with a fellow Leeds fan (also Derby born and bred) in his Putney (one of the nicer locations) flat. We duly travelled down the M1 on the Friday night and enjoyed, with some other London based mates, many beers and the compulsory curry before retiring to bed.

We were all looking forward to the match as we would surely upset Chelsea's promotion party and annoy their trendy fans! So with much anticipation, after a much-needed greasy breakfast, we headed off to a Chelsea 'home' pub before the match to meet some mates who supported the other lot. No colours were worn, but with a couple of Yorkshire accents in our group that was enough to worry about, especially as we would be walking to and from the ground without safety in numbers! The beers didn't go down too easily due to the previous evening but we managed a few, grabbed a hot dog and headed off to the ground.

Although we had nothing to play for, as usual we had a big and noisy contingent in the away end. The atmosphere was building up nicely and our impressive and friendly support impressed their owner (can't remember his name) so much, that he walked along the pitch to applaud us. I can't remember if this was before the match or at half-time, but I do recall that we were less than appreciative of his gesture and responded with verbal abuse and the chucking of various objects in his direction!

Photo courtesy of Craig Gill

So far so good, but then the match started and Messrs Dixon, Nevin and Speedie took us apart and the match was over as a contest well before half-time. Understandably with nothing to interest us on the pitch, we looked around for something to entertain us and lo and behold, someone had left what looked much like a railway sleeper (well, there was a train line behind the away end), lying around at the back of the open terrace. A few hardy souls picked it up and started restyling the shiny new scoreboard, which I understand was the pride and joy of the jovial chap who had applauded us earlier. I think he got the message this time!

Photo courtesy of Craig Gill

Photo courtesy of Craig Gill

No doubt slightly annoyed by this, the home fans decided to invade the pitch on several occasions and although there were plenty of plod and horses around and we had a good following, at times the sheer numbers and their proximity to us became a slight concern. The scoreboard wrecking, pitch invasions and the match (0–5 if anyone is interested), finally came to an end and unsurprisingly the plod decided to keep us locked in the ground for what seemed like an eternity. Unfortunately the Chelsea hordes were happy to carry on celebrating in the ground and streets and decided to hang around awaiting our exit.

Our big problem was that, unlike the majority of our fans, we were trying to get back to Putney for a few beers, before heading into central London and the best route seemed to be heading directly into the awaiting hordes. Our lack of numbers, blue colours and the Yorkshire accents issue made this a fairly risky venture, so we decided to head off to the tube station with the bulk of our fans.

After spending what seemed like an hour in a seriously over-crowded, sweaty, pi**y, stationary train, we finally arrived at Kings Cross where the plod tried to escort us onto the Leeds bound train. After protracted discussions with them where we tried to point out that we did not have tickets (as if a collector would have dared to board), did not live in Leeds and were in fact staying in Putney that night, we finally managed to slip away after some of our fellow fans distracted them by behaving badly.

As time was ticking away we decided to bypass the Putney beers and head off to the Marquis of Anglesey (Covent Garden) to catch up with more mates and for a few well-earned beers. (The Young's bitter in there is second to none). Happy days!

95

ANDY JOHNSON RECOLLECTIONS – BIRMINGHAM AWAY – 11 MAY 1985 AND MORE!

It was the last match of the season and with Birmingham already up; it was always going to be party time for them. Having a slight chance of promotion if results fell for us, meant everyone was just going to turn out for this one! Two coach loads of lads hit the pub late morning just inside Birmingham where we had a three and a half hour lager session. It was all good-natured, loud but no trouble. As usual for the Kippax Branch, as you couldn't get everyone out of the pub, we got to the ground late and realised then just what a following we'd brought over for this match.

I only saw two or three turnstiles open at tops that day and with pay on the gate, that meant hundreds trying to force their way to the front at 2.55 pm trying to get in before kick-off. I'm in the queue with all the surges and pushing and was getting quite near, but then someone stands on the back of my shoe and off it comes! Next thing someone's picked it up and it's being thrown around in the air, it's going up and down in the crowd and getting thrown all over with people cheering as they throw it. "F**k this", everyone's standing on my feet in the surge so I think, "I've no chance here..., just get out of it". I retreat from the crowd and try and watch my shoe as it gets thrown all over. Suddenly everyone's going through and up and over the turnstiles, as it becomes clear the operators have abandoned their posts and everyone's jumping through into the ground for free. As the crowd thins out I find my crumpled shoe, put it back on and make my way over the turnstile into the ground.

Photo courtesy of Craig Gill

Photo courtesy of Craig Gill

Climbing up into the stands, it's packed and I can't see a thing of the match, which is already 15 minutes in. Pushing my way forward, I see a mate perched on the canteen refreshments roof with others and they obviously have a cracking view of the match. They give me a lift up and I can see just how many we have around the ground... thousands! I watch the match a bit but it doesn't last long before the police are in, little things are kicking off all around us and the police cause their own problems amongst our contingent... antagonising. They make it clear we are nicked unless we get off the roof 'NOW!'

At that point just before half-time Birmingham score and that is the fuse for all the simmering resentment to explode. Birmingham are jubilant and invade the pitch, goading and that's all our

Photo courtesy of Craig Gill

Photo courtesy of Craig Gill

own support needed to erupt. Everyone's suddenly going mental. The canteen roof we were sat on gets broken into and the entire contents of it, cutlery, kettles, and pots are thrown all over while Leeds fans from two sides are invading the pitch in response to Birmingham's own pitch invasion. Birmingham in turn responds to Leeds and the police try and form two lines on the pitch to contain it all. Everything then becomes a battle with the police for half an hour as the second half is delayed.

If I'm honest, at the time I loved every bit of it and like hundreds of others my age joined in and got carried away with the moments. That's what it was like following Leeds away in the '80s and every away match back then; it seemed that something was always likely to happen.

The riot went on for ages, Birmingham from one end and Leeds from the other. Not one set of fans actually got to each other and it became fans against police, "Keystone Kop" stuff, only far more serious.

From my vantage point in the top right hand corner behind the goal I can see mates I've travelled down with from the Kippax Branch; now on the pitch themselves – met with applause from some and boos by others, they're trying to calm things down behind the goal and prevent further trouble. They start to clear some of the debris off the pitch, throwing them back behind the goal area to clear the goalmouth*

(Later these actions nearly backfire, as the police investigation into the riot in the coming weeks and the photographic evidence they've taken, puts our lads in the frame as offenders.

Whilst attending a LUSC meeting at Fullerton Park, investigating officers attend with incriminating pictures of the riot and are asking for help identifying suspects; thankfully the Supporters club Exec back our lad's actions – we by chance are in attendance at the meeting and the police accept their actions for what they were).

Eventually after pleas from both team's managers and the referee, control is gained and the match continues. I don't remember a single football incident from that second half; such was the football non-event after that, all everyone wanted around me, was the final whistle so it could all kick off again.

The antagonism and confrontation between fans and police who are now organised, is there for the whole of the second half and at full-time the police are proactive. As we're coming out, there's a surge behind us and we all scatter. West Midlands Police are up behind us… aggressive… looking for arrests and revenge and to crack heads.

Eventually we get back to the bus; one or two mention a wall collapsing but most are unaware of it, or its tragic consequences. As we make our way back home, all talk is of how Leeds will finally be getting kicked out of the League and how the FA will finally make the ultimate example of us, this is one riot too many and as we all agree, by far the worse.

Suddenly one or two are talking over their transistor radios about a fire in Bradford and possible fatalities. We get the coach driver to beam the radio on and listen out for the bulletins. The whole atmosphere on the coach changes into disbelief and silence as the horrific toll of what's happened at Bradford begins to sink in.

Photo courtesy of Craig Gill

Photo courtesy of Craig Gill

First there are reports of eight dead then 20, by the time we were back in Leeds it's 40. We clamour round the TV in The Madhouse Taproom for the Nine o'clock News and watch in numbed horror at the broadcasted scenes.

The Sunday papers next day understandably have wall to wall coverage of the events at Valley Parade with only small segments in most papers reporting the equally tragic death of a young fan and the wall collapse at Birmingham, in what was and still is one the biggest most violent Football riots in British Football History.

The consensus of opinion from most Leeds fans in attendance that day is the events of Bradford deflected from what would have been unprecedented sanctions and repercussions against LUFC. Considering their recent history for trouble at that time, the £5,000 FA fine and an order to make our away matches all ticket was seen as loose change and a get off.

In the aftermath of both the Bradford and Birmingham disasters, the Government commissioned an enquiry led by Mr Justice Popplewell of which part of it focused on the behaviour and self-policing by football fans in grounds. Because of the actions of some of the Kippax lads in trying to prevent the trouble at Birmingham, some of our members were called on to give their views to Popplewell himself. Their evidence then formed part of his final enquiry presented to Thatcher's Government. It was during this period that the Football Sociologist John Williams from Leicester University, followed the Kippax to a number of matches and submitted his own findings to Popplewell, something that didn't go down well amongst many of the Kippax members, but that's another story for a different time.

In the mid '80s The Kippax used to produce its own fanzine given out
free on away trips called The Kippax Journal, part of John Williams
report presented to Justice Popplewell is reproduced here

THE KIPPAX AT BIRMINGHAM 85

We watched a recent home match from the Leeds' Kop terraces with
a number of Kippax members. During the first half, a number of
Leeds fans from Brighouse began throwing objects at the opposing
goalkeeper as he was stepping closer to the crowd for his 'run up'
at goal kicks. Despite a number of warnings from within the crowd
the throwing persisted and, eventually the'Kippax' surged down to
the place where the objects were being thrown from and dealt some
summary 'justice' to those involved. The injured parties quickly
left, the throwing stopped, and supporters nearby were clearly in
assent with the manner and the effect of the intervention, especially as it came from a recognised 'legitimate' source within the
end. (Which is not to say,of course, that on occasions, rivalries
do not emerge within ends and the interventions of the kind we
have described here are not , sometimes, more vigorously contested)
In this case the incident was soon forgotten and a potentially dam-
aging episode for the Leeds club – suppose, for example, one of
the small bottles had struck the goalkeeper on the head – was quickly stifled. Intervention which involve the informal use of violence or intimidation to prevent hooligan incidents developing are
by no means unusual on football terraces. The 'Kippax' themselves
have used such strategies on previous occasions to significant effect. Other Leeds fans we spoke to confirmed, for example, that, at
Oxford United, it was the Kippax members who were involved in phy-
sically halting the destruction of a television gantry on the Leeds
terraces which threatened to move that match towards abandonment.
In addition, and as we have already described in this report, it
was members of the Kippax branch that began moves at St Andrews, on
this occasion, with the pitch littered with missiles and the occas-
ional bricks and lumps of wood still flying from the Leeds terrace
at Birmingham fans and the police, 'Collar' a miner now in his 30's
but still acknowledged and recognised as a respected leader,in their
travelling end, by the Leeds' fans, walked onto the pitch between
the lines of police officers and the Leeds Terraces and began to

clear the pitch of missiles. Other members of the 'Kippax' crew
followed, and within a matter of seconds around 50 Leeds fans were
involved in the clearance. Other members of the 'Kippax' manned
the open gates at the fence at the Leeds end of the ground to see
that this peaceful gesture was not misinterpreted by others as the
sign for an aggressive pitch invasion. 'Scouse' another Kippax fan
involved, shook hands with a police officer who thanked him and told
him that Leeds fans had 'done their best' but that they should now
clear the field before they were arrested.
We should say at the outset that the fact that large groups of Leeds
fans arrive early in pubs when travelling to away matches is not,
in itself, a problem. Many do so with no violent or disruptive in-
tent. Indeed, the 'Kippax' with whom we are familiar have such an
arrangement. Most of the group responsible for the clearance of the
missiles at Birmingham had been drinking heavily while at least
some of those involved in the throwing of missiles had not.

* *

It has to be noted that, after the publication of this report, one
of the authors, John Williams, arrived at Leeds to find out what
the reaction would be from the 'Kippax'. He was confronted by many
angry 'Kippax' members who took exception to the branch being named
and certain members being named in the report. He was asked in no
uncertain terms to leave. He has never been back.

* * * * * * * * * * *

WEST BROMWICH ALBION (WBA) 1986

This day is forever etched in my mind – 6 December 1986. We went down on a double decker Yorkshire Rider bus with the Kippax and stopped at Cannock, for what was always in those days a good drink. We pulled in at West Brom singing like you do, piled off the bus and started walking up to the ground. That's when West Midland's finest steamed into us looking for easy arrests, lifted a couple aggressively for nothing and got the reaction they were looking for, it kicked off a bit. The end result was that they came in at us team handed with 13 of us nicked from a 70 seater bus; **there were only 21 arrested at the whole of match that day (I know because I bought the papers next day!)**

One of our lot who was in the police van with me, slipped his cuffs and did a runner whilst they were doing their stop and arrests on the way to the WBA underground holding cells. It was funny as f**k watching their faces seeing a pair of dangling handcuffs still cuffed to the transit seat with no one in them. They gave me a kicking alright for laughing at that one... and if that twat PC H is still alive today and I ever get the chance to meet him, I would kick him from LS12 back to f*****g Oldbury Magistrates Court for the liberties he took with me and the lies he got away with in court at my trial

One of our lot who was in the police van with me, slipped his cuffs and did a runner whilst they were doing their stop and arrests on the way to the WBA underground holding cells. It was funny as f**k watching their faces seeing a pair of dangling handcuffs still cuffed to the transit seat with no one in them. **For laughing at that one, the copper who arrested me went to the duty Police Sergeant and pressed for an assault charge as well as the normal Section Five.** I tried to defend it in Court but no chance, Magistrates Courts were always Police Courts in those days and you had next to no chance, their clever prosecutors in those days would tear you to bits even with a decent brief. I got a £300 fine and a six-month Jail Sentence suspended for six months. My brief said he thought we'd got a result!

CHEERS MR BRIEF....

They'd kept us in the cells underneath the stand after they'd nicked us, then smoke started coming through down below from a workman's hut that had gone up in flames (I think it was about half-time) and then they had to remove us to a proper Police Station instead. They weren't happy about having to do that either before the match had finished, probably weren't happy with their head count for the day.

Big John was the first one lifted, he didn't do anything wrong, three of them took him down and he went down with a right crack. Big John wasn't any kind of fighter, there was no need and that's what incensed the rest of us!

Later on when they bailed us, they did it one at a time at 30-minute intervals. They tried to f**k us off from the Police Station and split us up, so that we would have to go back into

Birmingham on our own. We stood our ground and made a nuisance of ourselves and waited for each other. Suddenly they didn't want us going back into Birmingham 13 handed; they got us a minibus back to Leeds from the Police Station. Thankfully – Big John one of the committee lads, had a big wedge of money on him from the coach takings and used it to pay for the minibus from Birmingham back to Leeds. When we answered bail two weeks later, we booked a minibus and made a day out of it.

Heidi's comments; I agree Big John didn't do anything wrong as we were all just walking along after getting off the coaches, some singing as you say. It had all kicked off behind me and the first I saw of it was when I turned round when I heard all the commotion. The Kippax asked if I'd seen anything, as they knew I'd be a credible witness, but unfortunately I didn't see it happen.

FA CUP SEMI-FINAL – HILLSBOROUGH 1987

I remember how well policed the 1987 FA Cup semi-final was. Licensing laws were stricter then; because it was us and in order to attempt to stop mass drunkenness and disorder, the FA ordered a Sunday dinnertime kick-off, which at the time every Leeds fan condemned as another victimisation against us and the club.

Sunday football was unheard of back then, but we'd already had two of them in the cup run that season – Telford, Wigan and now Coventry. In hindsight though it was the correct decision, as who knows what might have happened if it had been on a Saturday with a 3.00 pm kick-off? Plenty of older fans will remember the bedlam of the Elland Road car park when the few thousand remaining tickets left for the general public went on sale for that semi-final tie, our first in 10 years! Can you imagine how many ticketless Leeds fans would have turned up on a warm spring Saturday afternoon, like they did in Bournemouth three years later?

One thing that sticks in my mind that day was walking down the hill towards Leppings Lane and every 50 yards or so, cordons of police were across the road checking tickets and filtering fans through to the turnstiles without too much congestion. A total difference to the crowd control novice in charge two years later in '89 when tragedy struck.

We were in the upper Leppings Lane seats and I'm so glad we were. The middle standing pens were dangerously packed, with fans climbing up into the top tier to escape the crush. I have old archive footage of the match and you can see when Keith Edwards scores, just how crammed it is in those pens.

Before we entered the ground prior to the match, all our banners and flags were confiscated by police, mine included. We could pick them up afterwards from a Church Hall just outside the ground where the police were holding them; afterwards I found mine easy enough. Little did I know at the time, that the same hall would be used as a temporary mortuary for the Hillsborough victims two years later.

THE KIPPAX

Gary Edwards in recent years has penned his recollections of The Kippax Branch in his popular books series. They are a good read but believe you me, they are a watered down version of some of the things that happened on those trips. Football Hooligan books are a popular genre these days and I know that what went down on some of those away days could just as easily have been written as one, had that been the persuasion of the author's pen.

Gary has chosen to make his books a light-hearted account of some of the stuff that happened – and that's fair play to him – but the Kippax in those early days of the late '70s and early '80s were making their presence felt around Football Grounds ages before it became the 'Designer' '80s thing to do.

From the first match I went with them, I knew I'd found my way of following Leeds. It was a lad's only coach – and although an official branch of the Supporters Club – flew close to the wind. There were elements on the 'Top Table' within the Supporters Club that didn't like the 'Pirate' attitude of the branch and would frequently look for ways to censure or get us kicked out – they eventually got their way in 1995. This though was 1980–81 and I was one of the youngest on there at 20. All the other lads were mid to late 20s – I travelled with them for 10 years and had the best times of my life ever following Leeds.

We were doing things then that I don't think any other supporters club group in the country were doing at the time or even maybe since. That coach with the band of lads we had back then, were as tight and together as any around at the time. Although originally started in Kippax, it evolved into a Town Centre based set up that drew support from across the City and beyond. We had a regular 100 that would always travel out of a membership of around 250 and for the bigger matches, we would fill four coaches. The older lot were ex Skins or Suedes from the Boot Boy era or old Soul lads from the Twisted Wheel and Blackpool Mecca days. By the early '80s a younger casual mob mixed in as well, making us a game old mob on its day.

We had characters like Collar, Brod, John West, Gary Edwards, big John Martin, Pete Dillon and loads of others who could all develop and organise the way we wanted to travel and get to matches. We always had a pub stop sorted beforehand, seemingly at any hour of the day or night, which in those times was groundbreaking and not the norm – considering the licensing laws of the day! The regular stop offs at Chatteris in Cambridgeshire was a great example, the Landlord – a Leeds Fan and ex Three Legs regular called Dick, would open at four in the morning when we were setting off at Midnight to – for example – the South Coast or London. He'd then stay open until whatever time we wanted when on our way back home afterwards. Collar always seemed to know someone from somewhere that could get us a pub stop before or after a match – John Martin once said, "He could talk the knickers off a nun!"

In those days the coach would pick up from the Marquis of Granby Hotel at the bottom of Eastgate. In later years The Nags, Mucky Duck, Mad House, Scotsman, Vine or Whip would all become regular pick up and drop off points for the coach – these were our regular watering holes.

The state of the coaches that the various coach companies would provide us with were a joke. They were more like sheds and how we managed to get to and from some of the matches in the wrecks we travelled on were astounding! Breakdowns were an occupational hazard, but you couldn't really blame the coach firms for giving us all their old c**p, when you saw the state the coaches were frequently left in afterwards. We would groom the drivers by having a healthy whip round, once we'd got them on board we made sure we kept them on board and asked for the same ones every time. In return, they would give us a free rein of the coach to go and do what we wanted. In the early '80s taking beer on the coaches wasn't really an issue and for our lot it was a pre-requisite anyway. These coaches in those days had no toilet facilities so we had a massive Jerry can placed at the front of the coach where we would all queue up to have a p**s. Once full the driver would pull onto the hard shoulder slow down and open the doors whilst one of the lads teamed five gallons of the steaming stuff onto Britain's motorways, held and supported by two lads so he didn't fall off! It was quite a skill and the looks we got from passing motorists were classic.

1980 to 1983 were the seasons that defined our away support into what it is now. Previous to that we would take thousands to the likes of say, Norwich and Brighton who were miles away but considered 'easy', but only a few hundred hard core would venture to the big north-west teams that were on our door step and even less to the London matches in the late '70s where our support was always sparse and disjointed. We were never together and were easy pickings for the blade carrying Scouse, Mancs and Cockney Gangs. Scum especially could be pretty much a no show. One night match in particular in March '78 when we won 1–0 thanks to Sniffer, stands out as one of the most intimidating. I was only 17 and we had no more than a couple of hundred behind the goal in the Scoreboard out of a 48,000 crowd. When Clarke's goal hit the back of the net, muted cheers went up and were promptly dispatched in seconds at the realisation Scum were in amongst us and surging through our pathetic ranks, we were a hunted and endangered species that night alright.

Things started to improve though by the beginning of the '80s, our numbers were still relatively small at the more dangerous grounds, but we stayed together more, became more compact and got to know each other better. Then it just seemed to explode from '81 onwards – aged 17 to 22, a whole new team of cocky young twat's from all over the country brought up on Don's team, just seemed to burst on to the scene and all come of age together. We took it right back to them on their own doorsteps in our thousands – and our support away from Elland Road would never take a backwards step again. This new breed, indignant and belligerent at the way

105

we had been cheated and were nationally hated throughout our glory years, emerged into our existing hardcore away support which of course had also gained a few lunatics from afar, who had jumped on the bandwagon after the rioting at Paris in '75. We soon had a massive and often violent away following.

I myself turned 21 in 1981 and just loved the sudden impact of the new away days and the mass of Leeds fans that suddenly turned up from all over the country. Previously, it had always just been the usual Wally Arnold stuff. Now, almost grenade like, it was going off all over the place; the explosion of lads from afar and coaches with all the different place names in the back windows, all from around the different Shires in the Country is something I'll always remember. As we got more into the '80s, it was kicking off more and every other week.

Scum, Spurs, Arsenal, Boro, Barnsley, Oldham, Huddersfield, Pompey, Man City, Oxford, Brighton… God, the list went on culminating in the mayhem at Birmingham in 1985. It made following Leeds the maddest days ever in our history and became embroiled in the story of 1980s Football Hooliganism.

Our reputation became more maligned with every passing match, alcohol was deemed to be one of the main reasons for trouble at matches and soon you couldn't get a pint in the grounds any more. Further pressure was put on coach companies to enforce alcohol bans on football supporters travelling on their coaches. But for a coach like ours, this just increased the drunkenness that had always been likely to occur on away trips. The measured units of tinned beers like Harp, Long Life and Skol, were now getting replaced by half bottles of Bacardi, Whisky or Vodka poured into pop bottle mixers. Shared around the coach and mixed together with whatever else we'd smuggled on, they became lethal concoctions. Some brought home made wine and one lad, an ambulance driver, would regularly bring a bag of oranges laced liberally with Vodka injected in by the syringes he got from work. Then of course there were the other 'stimulants' that had started to come into play around this time. By the time we actually got to the match we were paralytic. This alcohol ban on coaches actually increased the potential for hooliganism rather than preventing it!

It soon became the norm after long away trips to stop off at some small sleepy town or village on the Saturday night, but nine times out of ten they turned out not to be so sleepy though and by throwing out time at 11.00 pm we were usually fighting in lumps with the locals. Lifelong friendships were forged in some of these places; initially we would all hit the first pub together, a few of us would even take a change of top or T-shirt and get a scrub up in the bogs nice and fresh for the local talent… but within half an hour we'd be splitting up into groups of fours and fives… either going on the piss or pull – or for a bite to eat. Word would go around and local lads would soon be ganging together trying to pick us off, you had to stick together – Chesterfield, Berwick, Loughborough and Alsager were just some of the towns where it came on top at some stage or other when you were least expecting it. It became the continuous cycle of our travels throughout whole decade.

Leeds fans were subsequently banned from three away matches at Carlisle, Wimbledon and Hull because of trouble that happened at the Millwall match. 1985 was the first time we played Millwall when they had just come up. The trouble was mainly with the police with both sets of fans having it with them mainly after the match. Nobody left the ground, it was almost as if they were waiting for the other to make the first move after the final whistle, with both mobs psyching each other out, nobody moved. It was the first and last time I've ever seen that at a ground! It was also the first time opposing supporters had dared to go in their seating area! The Halifax lot and others were in the seats next to the standing area where most of us were. The Supporters Club exec members were also sat in the seats where we had at least 200 tickets. This was the first time we had played them in years, they had just come up and both mobs were coming up against each other on the backdrop of trouble that had happened the previous season when they were at Luton and we were at Brum. As the police stepped in to clear the ground before it went off, both mobs kicked off with the old bill, especially underneath and outside when we came out. The service lot had a massive presence and I don't think Millwall had ever seen a bigger mob at theirs from a non-London club. The ban ended up being lifted before we played Hull because it was unworkable. Most Leeds fans had already got their tickets for the Hull sections though, which resulted in trouble when we scored as we were in their seats behind the goal.

RAY ASHWORTH – MEMORIES, BILLY LEEDS – DON REVIE'S TESTIMONIAL AND 5 MAY 1990 – BOURNEMOUTH BY DAISY

RAY ASHWORTH

A week following the Hillsborough disaster, Leeds were away to Chelsea on 22 April 1989. This was the season Howard Wilkinson joined the club and despite a spirited run we hadn't done enough to secure a Play-off spot. Chelsea had already sealed promotion and were I think already Champions of the old Division Two. As I was doing the London Marathon the next day I travelled solo to this match and stayed in London Friday, Saturday and Sunday night. For the record (nothing to do with the story) I was staying near Oxford Street. On the day of the match and with the next day in mind, instead of my usual pre-match session of alcohol I decided to do a bit of shopping at Harvey Nicholls and Harrods then walk to the match from there. I left the shops sometime after 1.30 pm and set off to walk to the ground. Even getting close to the ground, although the traffic was snarled up, there were very many fans walking with me.

There was, however, a Leeds supporters' coach (and here my memory fails me but I think it was a Halifax, Dewsbury or Heavy Woollen flag in the back window). As it passed a pub on the road I was suddenly surrounded by a large group of snarling Chelsea fans whose opening gambit was to throw their empty beer glasses at the coach. The fans on the Leeds coach retaliated with coins coming out of the sunroof windows of the coach. I quickly realised that if any of these Chelsea fans found out I was Leeds I was in for a real kicking and reasoned the best way not to draw attention to myself, was to stay within the group rather than slip away and perhaps be noticed. I'll be honest I was totally bricking it yet bizarrely as the two sets of fans traded missiles and insults I had this urge to give the Leeds salute to the coach to let them know I was there. I never did and know had I done so would have been sussed immediately. I stayed within the group for what seemed an age but was probably at the most 10 minutes, until we reached the ground and a line of police made it a 'Leeds only' zone on the other side of them. I showed my ticket and was allowed through and can always remember hearing a Chelsea fan saying 'F**k me, did he walk to the ground with us?' I was too shook up and I freely admit to being truly frightened I didn't even have the bottle to turn and face them after that.

For the record a minute's silence was held before the match for the Liverpool fans that had died the week earlier. This was impeccably observed for 20 or 30 seconds and broken by a voice from the Chelsea Shed who shouted "f**k off you northern bastards"; as you can imagine it then descended rapidly into sections of both support trading insults whilst some asked for silence and others respectfully stayed silent for the remainder of the minute. Chelsea won the match 1–0, Howard Wilkinson and the team came to the fans after the match and I think we were allowed out before the Chelsea team did a lap of honour. I also remember after the match getting the tube from Fulham Broadway with all the Leeds supporters and we had to change lines somewhere so I slipped out of the main body to get back to my hotel. There were some Chelsea fans there who had heard the Leeds fans singing all desperately hiding their colours, so I had a little chuckle to myself. As for the marathon the next day I got round I reckon in under three hours 45 minutes, one of my better marathons.

Although the next part was from the '70s, and not the '80s, it was the time that I was scared the most at a football match, which was at Tottenham in 1976. In those days it was very hit and miss as to how many Leeds fans went to away matches. In London we always seemed to take a lot to QPR, Arsenal and Fulham but the support at Tottenham, Chelsea and West Ham was in my experience, very poor until the early '80s. I travelled down by coach as we used to do in those days.

We'd catch the Wallace Arnold coach in Normanton, it would then pick up in Castleford then either Barnsley or Leeds dependent upon numbers. There were occasions we'd fill a coach on our own from Normanton but on this day it was myself and two other regulars and I would guess the coach picked up in Castleford and then filled up in Leeds. I cannot remember how many coaches travelled but when we arrived (and even in those days we parked some way from the ground) there were a few Leeds fans hanging around trying to get everyone to stick together. Eventually around 100 of us started to walk towards the ground. We stopped for some refreshments in a pub (can't remember the name) but it was really rough and clearly hostile. One of the Leeds fans who was from Hull grabbed a pool cue and distributed the balls amongst some of his close friends as he said, "so we're ready, just in case".

After two pints we continued our walk to the ground although our numbers had diminished to 50 or 60 and we were being followed by a large group of Tottenham fans. To this day I don't know why they didn't attack us there and then; no police and they had a clear majority numbers wise. It seemed obvious that at some point they would, although it's possible they were wary as we were chanting and singing Leeds songs and on the face of it not fazed by them (although I most definitely was). Finally we got on a road that led to the ground and we got some security as a police escort of sorts appeared and moved us to the away turnstiles.

We pointed at the large group of Tottenham fans that had followed us and told the police not to let them in as they were not Leeds, but within minutes they were inside the ground and mingling and separating us into ones and twos. I was soon isolated and couldn't see either of the friends I had travelled with and was confronted by a Tottenham fan. He said to me "You'll know to never come in the Park Lane End again, if you get home that is" and quickly flashed a knife across my line of vision. I hope to this day my face didn't give away the fear I felt and will readily admit up to that point of having heard but not fully understood the term "to s**t yourself", but my bowels did move. I was in the corner at the top of the terrace with a bar behind and when he looked away I ducked under this bar and moved onto the concourse below. I was really concerned and bumped into two guys who had what seemed to be the old Leeds United yellow away scarves on; little did I know that Tottenham fans also wore a similar scarf. I warned them to hide their colours as there were Tottenham thugs with knives looking for Leeds supporters. When I found out they were Tottenham once again I thought I was in for a beating or perhaps even worse. However, to be fair, they showed me a turnstile where for an additional 10p I could transfer into a paddock terrace that ran down the side of the pitch. It was the opposite side to the notorious Shelf. I was through there very quickly. There were already a few of our fans through and one by one others drifted through and I was re-united with my friends. We also had the comfort of the presence of a few policemen who were noticeable by their absence in the allocated away end.

However, during the first half the Tottenham fans once again started to group to the side of us although at least this time we were better able to stay solid as a group and stick together. Things were clearly going to come to a head at the end of the match. A police sergeant had a quiet word with the guy from Hull who was really our leader. Apparently the offer on the table was that with 30 minutes of the match left, they would open a gate and allow us to leave the ground and would hold the Tottenham fans in the ground for a further 10 minutes, or we were on our own. I never like to admit to running away, but we were unanimous in deciding we'd have the 10 minute start. We were allowed out, certainly no Tottenham fans were allowed to follow us initially and we went back to the coaches where there were already a large number of Leeds supporters who'd either been chased out of the ground or in some cases not even got there in the first place. As for how the match ended – I only know we lost 1–0, the remaining Leeds fans returned to the coaches but it was noticeable they were all coming in ones and twos.

One final incident I remember is as the coaches were leaving London, we didn't get the formal escort that happens these days and we were abused by a lone Tottenham fan who was across the road. The coaches were moving albeit slowly whilst in the outer lane the traffic was static. A Leeds fan jumped out of one of the cars, ran across the road and confronted and then punched the Tottenham fan, I think he regretted "bigging himself up". I will confess, I don't think I've been as scared as I was that day at Tottenham and people who travel away with Leeds now cannot possibly relate to what it was like then.

Sadly a few years later a Leeds fan was killed in an unprovoked attack at White Hart Lane (I recall he was punched and his head hit the kerb when he fell) and the Tottenham fan was jailed for 18 months. The court case for this was widely reported in the *Yorkshire Evening Post* in the weeks prior to us going there in the FA Cup in 1982. We took around 10,000 fans to this Cup match and the trouble outside before and after was really, really bad and we've always seemed to take good support there since. However, whether it is due to the incident above, I am always wary and on my guard there and it didn't seem much better when we visited there in the Cup in 2010.

BILLY LEEDS – DON REVIE'S TESTIMONIAL

As this was all so long ago, it's difficult to remember exactly how this transpired. It was after the match and fans were milling around the old West Stand entrance, waiting for the players and celebrities to emerge. I suddenly noticed the great man in his wheelchair, blanket over his legs and all alone in the old foyer. If I hadn't seen him pitch side during the match, I would never have recognised him. This frail shadow of what was once a big bloke – who I'd met many times whilst watching the first team train on Fullerton Park as a kid, was shocking to see.

Whilst the security men were dealing with the fans trying to get players' autographs, I snuck into the foyer. Not without some trepidation, I approached The Don. He was pale, to the point of greyness and his eyes, once so full of life and humour and even fire, were sunken into his once handsome face.

"Good evening Mr Revie," I said. He tried to turn his head but couldn't. I squatted down in front of him so he could see me. He was confused and just looked at me. "I just wanted to thank you for taking Leeds United to the top and for giving so much pride to the Leeds fans. I'm just here to thank you and shake the hand of one of my heroes". I held out my hand as he tried to raise his arm – and couldn't. I picked up his hand in mine as tears flooded down my face. It was

Photo courtesy of Heidi Haigh

Elland Road 1988 photo courtesy Heidi Haigh

as light as a feather, like a baby's hand. I just held it. Suddenly he slurred out softly "Don't cry for me, ye big Jessie," and I swear he tried to give me his famous wink! He couldn't, but I felt it. He drifted off into his thoughts and I gently lowered his hand.

Then a hand on my shoulder as Big Jack whispered in my ear, "let him rest lad – we're all crying tonight lad"... and led me outside.

5 MAY 1990 – BOURNEMOUTH BY DAISY

When the fixture list came out at the start of the season, the first thing we did was decide that we would go down to Bournemouth for the last match of the season and make a weekend of it. It was to be a Bank Holiday weekend, a seaside trip and the chance to have a good time. There were 11 of us, so we booked our digs for the Friday and Saturday night well in advance with the plan to return home on Sunday. At the time of booking it though we had no idea that Leeds United would be going up on that last day. As the season went on and it became more obvious that this could occur, so many other Leeds fans decided they would go for the weekend too. Luckily for us, we had booked our digs early so we had no problems getting our accommodation sorted.

It came to that weekend and it was going to be a crunch one, after beating Leicester the week before it meant that Leeds only needed a draw to go up. None of us had tickets for the match as we set off on Friday morning in three cars with me driving one of them. We arrived at Bournemouth at approximately 1.30pm and it was absolutely boiling which was a good omen for having a good weekend. As we drove into Bournemouth it was obvious all the pubs were packed with Leeds United fans and I think Bournemouth were totally unprepared for the amount of Leeds fans who turned up on Friday.

We parked up and checked into our digs without any problems and headed for our first stop, the pub! We found the main pub right in the middle of town near the front where the bother first started. By the time we got there at 2.30–3.00 pm the pub was rammed with Leeds fans, it was boiling and we started getting drunk with the rest of them. To this day I still don't know what sparked the trouble around mid-evening 5.00–6.00 pm. Everybody was drunk as the coppers or landlord tried to shut the pub as it was getting rowdier and rowdier and then it erupted! It started with someone trying to pull the cigarette machine off the wall, then someone kicked off in the pub and it spilled outside. A motorbike got knocked over in the car park and was torched but I've no idea how it happened. There were approximately 400 to 500 Leeds fans with the local coppers trying to sort it out as the pub was smashed up. All over Bournemouth it was kicking off everywhere you went. It was bedlam with everything getting trashed as the fans ran amok with only local cops in attendance. Finally we returned to our digs for the night.

We got up the next morning to another red-hot day and walked into town. The first thing we came across, was the local Sainsbury's where there was a conveyor belt of Leeds fans walking to the booze aisle and straight out of the other door but not paying for it. The copper tried stopping it but then decided to let them carry on so all 11 of us joined in. We got tanked up with our beer and down to the beach we headed. When we got down to the beach early on the Saturday morning, what a sight was to be seen as it was absolutely rammed with Leeds fans and they were all you could see. There must have been at least 10,000 on the beach. At some stage someone had the idea to walk to the ground so there was a mass exodus of Leeds fans off the beach; most of us had no tickets for the match. As we headed towards the ground, any Off Licence en route to Dean Court was raided for booze. One tried shutting his doors but had the door burst open and was left with the shutters hanging off. In the end the cops said to leave them to it as it was better to have half of them paying for it than none at all.

When we arrived at the ground, any Leeds fan without a ticket headed to a big grass area near where the coaches were parked and camped there. As it was still a red-hot day everyone had been drinking heavily all morning. Because of all the bother the previous night, the consequences were that the local coppers had called in reinforcements from London, Gloucester, Bristol and everywhere. I do think that was a catalyst for the trouble, because all we saw between the ground and us was a wall of coppers in riot gear. I could never work out what the spark was, but seeing the riot coppers there was like a red rag to a bull. It was then running battles between ticketless Leeds fans and a wall of coppers 800–900 in riot gear. The build up to the match from 1.00–2.00 pm and during the match was a constant running battle between us. Within the context

Photo courtesy of Craig Gill

of that, bottles and bricks were getting thrown as I picked up one of my two wine bottles from Sainsbury's and it was thrown into the coppers. Leeds fans charged the riot coppers, they'd back off then charge back at the Leeds fans and it carried on going backwards and forwards with running battles. Things calmed down as the second half kicked off and an uneasy truce occurred with line after line of riot coppers and Leeds fans listening to the match going on. Finally when Leeds got the winner, some of those outside managed to get into the ground.

After the match, which Leeds had won and gone up, we went back into town, but Bournemouth had learnt its lesson from the night before and all the pubs were shut on Saturday night. We got taxis to Poole to get drinks and on Sunday morning made our way home.

What I didn't know was that I had been caught on camera when I threw the bottle. I knew on Bank Holiday Monday after the match that there was a problem and the trouble I could be in, as there was a photo on the front page of the *Yorkshire Evening Post* of both me and my brother. I got a bit nervous, as I knew it was only a matter of time, but didn't know when. Around July, a lad I know who is a painter and decorator walked into the Black Bull in South Milford and said to me he had a contact at West Yorkshire Police in Wakefield. He had just seen my face on a photo board so I knew they would be coming for me.

An appeal was put out in July to identify fans and eventually two months after the event I was picked up. They had finally worked out who I was and along with three or four others, we all got dawn raided. On the morning they came, there were two coppers from Selby and one CID from

Bournemouth. Unfortunately they got the wrong address and instead of going to 2 Beech Close, Sherburn went to 2 Beechwood Close. As they knocked on the latter's door they realised it was not me. After realising their mistake with the wrong address, they got to my house and found I had already gone to work. My brother was in though, who phoned me at work to say that they were on the way to arrest me there. It was pointless running off, so I sat there and waited for them to come into work and they took me to Selby cop station. There they showed me still photo evidence and CCTV which is how they got me.

I was bang to rights and knew I had a problem. When I told Paul Hines, my solicitor in Leeds what had gone on, he advised me to plead guilty with mitigating circumstances and asked me to get as many references as possible. He said I would get a lesser sentence by pleading guilty. There were so many court cases going on with 30 going down with me. As some of them were pleading not guilty, it took 17 months before it came to court so the final trial wasn't until December 1991. My solicitor had to get a barrister to represent me in court and used the references I got and it worked. The author of this book had also given me a character reference as I had never caused any problems whatsoever whilst travelling with her to away matches. Basically going down to Crown Court I got six months but at least I knew I would be okay as I would only serve three

Photo courtesy of Craig Gill

Photo courtesy of Craig Gill

months. It was a good job I got the lighter sentence too, as this meant that I kept my job. Work knew it had happened as I owned up and told them what I had done. I did a deal with them and agreed that if I got six months or less that I wouldn't take any holidays until the court case, which kept my job open. It's also the place that I still work at.

We weren't thinking in October the previous year that there would be any trouble that weekend. It was the last match to go to anyway, a Bank Holiday and we just wanted a good

Photo courtesy of Craig Gill

Photo courtesy of Craig Gill

weekend. I still don't think anyone thought we'd go up. As it was, it happened to kick off in the first pub we were in!

One other memory I have is when we stopped at Grantham on our way back from Peterborough I think. Ben our driver had told us to be back on the coach for 11.00 pm. When half of the lads hadn't returned to the coach on time, Ben set off back up the A1 leaving half of the lads still in the pub. When the old bill came to the pub as it was getting funny with the locals, they wanted to know what we were doing there and where our coach was. We told them it should have been in the car park but was probably half way up the A1. We had to stay there till it came back for us!

INTERVIEWS WITH LEEDS FANS

BY ANDREW

ANDY PETERSON

How long have you supported Leeds?

I have supported Leeds since the early '80s.

First match you went to?

Leeds v Chelsea – 19 Feb 1983.

What was it like supporting the Whites in the 1980s?

I've never watched anyone else, so it's hard to make comparisons with anything. There was of course a perpetual sense of unrequited ambition, although I never saw Leeds in the First Division until 1990. There's a lot of myth perpetuation around the era, but some of those are true; the atmosphere was different, more hostile and more partisan than now. But there was a sense of naivety about the whole thing as well; people still using football as an escape from their lives. There was also a difference in money and therefore a more level playing field for smaller clubs – the likes of Oxford, Shrewsbury, Oldham and Wimbledon were all successful on tiny playing budgets but honing spirit, discipline and organisation. Somehow, it felt like less of an obligation than it does now – I can't explain why. It's probably easiest to say that times – and people – change.

Favourite player in the 1980s?

John Sheridan and Gordon Strachan, polar opposites in many ways, with the latter replacing the former, both were as iconic. With Sheridan everything was off the cuff (it had to be – training wasn't his strong suit) a player who could be brilliant one minute and then abysmal the next. He was probably lucky to play in a side in which by comparison he was a maestro, one Bremner built around him and that came so close to success in 1987. Strachan's era was captured via television, and his achievements dwarf Sheridan's in relative terms, but he prospered with higher quality players around him and although comparisons are futile it's still the latter who for me is held in higher esteem.

Best moment in the 1980s?

Brendan Ormsby's goal against QPR in the 1987 FA Cup tie.

Worst moment supporting Leeds in the 1980s?

Losing at Birmingham and the tragic death of a fan there in 1985, probably football's worst year with the Bradford and Heysel disasters.

Did you see any of the hooliganism live?

I saw quite a bit between 1983–85 but after that, things began to improve. As now, Leeds were a target for the day hooligans, people who will fight with anyone around their home town on a Saturday night and for whom a visit from us is Christmas and birthdays all wrapped into one. The thing to remember is that as now, there was a good deal more talking about hooliganism than it actually taking place.

Best match in the 1980s?

Easy to pick the Hull 4–3 in the promotion season (or Sunderland, or Newcastle from 1989) but I always feel that represents a different era. Probably any home match from that late run to the play offs in 1986–87 – a classic case of hitting form at the right time.

Worst match in the 1980s?

So many terrible experiences but of the matches I was actually at, losing at home to Chester in the league cup (they were 92nd at the time) stands out.

What was the atmosphere like following Leeds in the 1980s?

Slightly anarchic, sporadically charged and lots of fun!

What affect did Howard Wilkinson have on the club?

Total. Out went almost everything that had gone before it; Wilkinson killed the sacred cows and enabled people to jettison the baggage. Did we play 'worse' or 'better' football? It's hardly relevant now. We owe him a huge debt.

Most important signing in the 1980s?

Gordon Strachan.

Favourite season supporting Leeds in the 1980s?

1986–87 – Play-off Final, FA Cup semi-final. Sheridan, Baird, Edwards, then heartbreak arriving right on cue.

Least favourite season supporting Leeds in the 1980s?

1983–84. We were never in the hunt at any point and by the end were playing in front of crowds of below 10,000. I did get to see Eddie Gray's last match though.

CHRIS PAYNE

How long have you supported Leeds?

As long as I can remember – my older brother has been a fan all his life, so supporting anyone else simply wasn't an option.

First match you went to?

My brother took me to watch, I remember it was '79 the last match of the season – we beat man utd 2-0. Don't remember much about the match if I was honest, it was the first time I had been inside Elland Road and the first time I climbed the steps and saw the pitch I was hooked... standing in the old Lowfields Road stand.

What was it like supporting the Whites in the 1980s?

I was a teenager in the '80s, so hadn't really seen the Revie team in all its glory, so my expectations were a lot less. Politics of club ownership never really came into question. I was very fortunate that my parents were employed by LUFC at the time, and I was able to get tickets to most matches. The matches themselves were very much like we see today – never comfortable on a lead, with the ability to let a 2/3 goal lead slip easily.

Favourite player in the 1980s?

I had a number of favourite players – the usual 1988–89 gang of Strachan, Fairclough, the unsubtle defending of Noel Blake, the complete 100% effort that both Baird and Davison put in, plus the direct straight line running of Neil Aspin – but my favourite had to be John Sheridan. I remember him warming up in front of the Kop to the chant of "On the Piss" as he had probably been in trouble the night before in Leeds. He just had the ability to change a match and score from free kicks!

Best moment in the 1980s?

Like most – the 1987 Cup run is high on the list – but both my best and worst are the Play-off Final. I had attended the match at Elland Road to watch Ormsby scramble over an already goalbound shot, and also Keith Edwards nearly win it with an overhead kick!! I hadn't been to many away matches, so a trip to St Andrews was a must. We must have had two thirds of the ground and you could virtually count their supporters by comparison. Although we lost to two goals by a bl***y centre-half, the banter and togetherness of the fans was brilliant. Sheridan's cheeky free kick was equally as good.

Worst moment supporting Leeds in the 1980s?
Downside was the career ending injury to Brendan Ormsby. After dreaming about Anfield and Old Trafford, it was a big bump back to earth to contemplate going back to the likes of Hull, Shrewsbury and Walsall.

Did you see any of the hooliganism live?
I didn't really see much hooliganism, as my main experiences were at Elland Road. That said, I remember the likes of Millwall and Chelsea coming to Elland Road and the atmosphere was very different to some of the other matches. I remember speaking to fans who had attended Millwall away and had been told about the bricks and stones thrown at coaches by fans who lined the road to the 'Den'.

Best match in the 1980s?
There are two, Boro at home in '89 that contained the 'Revie Bounce' as I called it. I remember standing in the South Stand and watching the back pass simply bounce over the goalie's shoulder. It was like slow motion, I think everyone had already turned their attention up field for the goal-kick and I seem to remember it took a few seconds before the Kop realised we had scored. The other, again from the South Stand was watching one of the best goals I had seen up to then – from Vinnie Jones, he just connected perfectly, the goalie didn't really move and it hit the

Lowfields Road photo courtesy Craig Gill

back of the net. I remember looking at Vinnie and it was pretty funny – I don't think neither the fans nor Vinnie knew what to do for a few seconds; it was like everyone just stood and admired it including Vinnie. I personally think that match was where he started to turn into a very competent midfielder.

Worst match in the 1980s?

There are a couple that immediately spring to mind - Crystal Palace in 1988–89. I remember we had to queue to get in and therefore there were already 10 minutes on the clock when we got in and we were already losing. Wright and Bright tore us to shreds that night, simple over the top balls caused panic in the defence, losing 2–1. Also there was the match against Millwall, with Cascarino and Sherringham terrorising us and finishing any lingering interest in the Play-offs that season.

What was the atmosphere like following Leeds in the 1980s?

Following Leeds in the '80s was a bit like famine and feast. There were matches where right up to five minutes before the start, you could sit on the Kop and there would be lots of space around you. Bearing in mind, it was standing at that time and we struggled to get 15,000 fans for home matches – and other matches, Crystal Palace and Aston Villa in the Cup it would feel like a sell-out. With certain teams there was a definite undercurrent in terms of potential violence, although as I said, I didn't really experience any, especially when the likes of Millwall, and Chelsea came to town. I seem to remember that the fans were more forgiving – and saw genuine effort as a reason for applause. Players like Aspin, Haddock and McDonald, whilst not gifted with outstanding talent did put a shift in and this was appreciated more than I think it would be now. That said, we still had players that could and maybe should have achieved more, John Stiles, had some ability but could be frustrating, Vince Hilaire simply didn't live up to the expectations I had of him, although I do remember a blinding goal he scored direct from a cross-wind assist.... into the Kop end!

What affect did Howard Wilkinson have on the club?

I believe that Howard built to a certain extent on what Billy Bremner started, he had the vision – and not to mention a substantial transfer budget by the days standards, to add players of both ability and downright aggression. Mel Sterland, Strachan, Chapman and Vinnie. The signings he brought in made fans sit up and really get on board with what he was trying to do. When you look at the team sheet – leaders everywhere, one of seven or eight players in my view could have been made captain.

Most important signing in the 1980s?

The important signing for me has to be Gordon Strachan. This signing gave us the one player that was able to interpret Wilkinson's tactics onto the pitch. There are few players around now that had the ability to influence a match to such an extent that Strach was able to. Not bad for a player that some felt was passed his best and cost us 300k – less than we paid Wimbledon for Vinnie.

Favourite season supporting Leeds in the 1980s?

Most will say 1989–90 season and I agree. However for me, the first season I really attended a substantial number of matches has to win – 1986–87... Baird, Davison, Snodin, Ashurst and Aspin, even though we lost in the Cup and Play-offs.

Least favourite season supporting Leeds in the 1980s?

I don't really have one. It's always been a roller coaster ride and the '80s were no different. We couldn't defend, sometimes couldn't string two passes together and on other occasions gave the opposition a hammering. I've seen crowds of 30,000 and other weekends there would be less than 15,000 fans in attendance. Every season starts with the same 'glass half full' for me and no matter how badly we play – there's always next week!

DAN TORONCZAK

How long have you supported Leeds?

I have supported Leeds since 1982.

First match you went to?

Southampton in April 1982 – lost 3–1. My dad took me as he was a steward at Elland Road and still is to this day.

What was it like supporting the Whites in the 1980s?

As a child for me it was fantastic. It didn't matter that it was a poor era or the football was terrible, I was star struck by the players and used to wait for autographs for hours after the matches most weeks!

Favourite player in the 1980s?

A difficult question, but for me two players, Tommy Wright and Ian Baird!

Best moment in the 1980s?

It had to be the cup run in '87, the full house for the QPR match and the semi-final at Hillsborough, even though we lost!

Worst moment supporting Leeds in the 1980s?

It had to be sitting at home listening on the radio to the Play-off Final against Charlton, jumping around my bedroom when John Sheridan scored near the end of the match, only to be inconsolable minutes later when Peter Shirtliff got them two late goals for Charlton. I cried myself to sleep that night and it was my first major let down supporting LUFC.

Did you see any of the hooliganism live?

I don't recall too much hooliganism at Elland Road, the only time I remember it was at Huddersfield Town in both 1983 and 1984. I remember the game being stopped in both matches as LUFC fans were throwing the wooden seats from the main stand onto the pitch. Also at Bradford City in about 1988 outside the ground.

Best match in the 1980s?

It had to be the Play-off semi-final against Oldham when Keith Edwards scored in the last minute of both legs! Also the match against Sheffield Wednesday in 1982–83 when Andy Ritchie scored the equaliser with a blatant handball!! The match was also shown on *Match of the Day* that Saturday night!!

Worst match in the 1980s?

It had to be any meaningless end of season match. Brighton and Walsall spring to mind in '88, low crowds and no atmosphere! I think the Walsall match was Mark Aizlewood's infamous two-fingered salute to the Kop after scoring!!

What was the atmosphere like following Leeds in the 1980s?

The atmosphere was very much like today, average crowds, but for the big matches it was full, electrifying and very noisy! The way you got thrown about in the Kop or Lowfields Road terrace when a goal was scored was an experience!!

What affect did Howard Wilkinson have on the club?

Howard Wilkinson transformed the club from top to bottom when it looked like we were going nowhere again after the previously exciting Cup run and play-off season under Billy Bremner. Howard's appointment was certainly the next step up for the club that they needed.

Most important signing in the 1980s?

The deadline signings of Gordon Strachan and Chris Fairclough, then the season after Vinnie Jones were masterstrokes. It showed the intentions of the club. On a personal note the return of Ian Baird from Portsmouth!

Favourite season supporting Leeds in the 1980s?

1986–87, simply because of the Cup run and Play-off experience. Also the 1989 season because of promotion, but then it finished in 1990s it probably doesn't count!!

Least favourite season supporting Leeds in the 1980s?

I never had a least favourite season supporting LUFC because as a kid they were my life growing up. I couldn't wait for the next Saturday to come round when I could go to the next match. When all my mates at the time were supporting Liverpool or man utd I was extremely proud of who I was, win, lose or draw!

DARREN AVEYARD

How long have you supported Leeds?

I've been a Leeds United supporter since 1980. My interest in the game started as a small boy in the late seventies. Football on TV was rare at that time so I didn't support a team until my first trip to Elland Road as an eight-year-old. Then I was hooked!

First match you went to?

Brighton at Elland Road, November 1980. This was when a lifelong love affair began. My dad took me to my first match with a friend and his sons and we sat in the West Stand. The team at that time was mid-table in the old First Division and Allan Clarke was Manager. We won the match 1–0 through a Carl Harris goal and I loved it!

What was it like supporting the Whites in the 1980s?

Personally I found it exciting as it was a new experience for me. Even though the club was in the doldrums I loved going to matches and it was the highlight of my week as a kid. I was too young to have seen Don Revie's great side, so the '80s players were my heroes. During the school holidays I and my Leeds supporting friends would catch a bus to Elland Road to watch the players train on the old Fullerton Park training pitch. We would get autographs from the players as they came across the West Stand car park after training and pop in to the old club shop before getting another bus home. The club was my life and I remember those times with great fondness.

As you grow up you have other responsibilities to think about and I think this is why I look back at the eighties with such affection. Your childhood is a wonderful time in your life and Leeds United was my childhood.

Favourite player in the 1980s?

Ian Snodin, closely followed by John Sheridan. Two classy midfielders. Shez was the cult hero of the fans and he was a terrific player. He scored some wonderful free-kicks, including one against Derby where he flicked the ball up and then volleyed it in to the top corner. He was with us pretty much throughout the eighties and I always thought it was a shame that he left the club and couldn't be part of the team that finally got us promoted. Ian wasn't with the club very long but I liked him straight away when he joined us from Doncaster. Midfield players have always been my favourites and I think that was part of it, plus he had long hair, which made him stand out! I was gutted when he left the club in 1987, but he got a great move to Everton who were a great side at that time and went on to win the League that season.

Best moment in the 1980s?

The 1987 Play-off home matches versus Oldham and Charlton – late goals in both matches and incredible atmospheres. The potential of the club was shown in those matches. Sell-out crowds and a buzz around the city that I hadn't experienced before.

Odsal 1986 photo courtesy Craig Gill

Worst moment supporting Leeds in the 1980s?

Losing in the Play-off Final replay, the same season. The Final was played over two legs back then rather than at Wembley. As the scores were level a replay had to be played at the neutral venue of St Andrews. The match went in to extra time and when we took the lead through a John Sheridan free-kick it appeared promotion would be ours. Then, in true Leeds United fashion, we conceded two late goals and missed out. It was absolutely heart breaking!

Did you see any of the hooliganism live?

I was at Odsal in 1986 when the infamous chip fan fire took place. I was 14 and my Dad took me to the match. Bradford City were playing their home matches at the Rugby ground following the tragic fire at Valley Parade in 1985. Odsal wasn't the best stadium by any means, but it was big and around 9,000 Leeds fans turned up that day. I'm pretty sure it was pay on the gate. Our fans had filled a massive terrace running down the side of the pitch. My Dad and I were stood towards the back of that terrace, just above a concourse area where a van was selling chips, plus other food and drinks. On the pitch, we didn't play well and were losing 2–0 when the trouble started. The main thing I remember is fans rocking the chip van. It didn't take long for my Dad to get me away from the trouble and we left before the fire started. The reputation of our fans was already tarnished, but the events of that day were terrible bearing in mind what had happened at Bradford just a year earlier.

Best match in the 1980s?

The 2–1 win versus QPR in the FA Cup, 1986–87. As with the Play-off matches later in the same season, this match gave us a taste of the big time again. QPR were a Division above us, and a packed house saw a terrific match. Fans who hadn't managed to get in to the ground had found other vantage points, including the Peacock roof on Elland Road and I'm sure a fan climbed up one of the old floodlight pylons as well! We secured our place in the quarter-finals with a late header from Brendan Ormsby in front of the Kop and the noise was incredible.

Worst match in the 1980s?

Losing to Chester in the League Cup, 1983–84. I always remember this match as a low point because Chester were bottom of the old Fourth Division at that time. It was an awful match in front of a very low crowd and we lost 1–0. The ties were played over two legs in those days and I think we won the second leg comfortably to go through but that home leg was awful.

GRAHAM WATSON

How long have you supported Leeds?

I have supported Leeds for 43 years.

First match you went to?

My first match was QPR in the old First Division. It was a Friday, 4 May 1979. My first memory was those floodlights as the bus approached the ground. I paid the princely sum of 50p to stand on the Kop and soon found my voice as I learnt the songs. A classic see-saw match saw Leeds win 4–3 and I was hooked.

What was it like supporting the Whites in the 1980s?

Supporting Leeds was hard work for most of the '80s. We were awful for a lot of it. Relegation and average managers and players made sometimes going a chore, but still we went. We had some great days; some of the matches against Newcastle for instance, had atmospheres that still make me tingle today just thinking about them. Sometimes the away following was better than home matches. I remember, again on a Friday, being in an 8,000 crowd at home to Cambridge.

Favourite player in the 1980s?

The early '80s saw us still have a decent side. Eddie Gray, Arthur Graham, Carl Harris and Brian Flynn were still class acts, supplemented by precocious youngsters like Terry Connor and Aidan Butterworth. As these left, people like Kenny Burns and Frank Worthington arrived and we drifted into Second Division anonymity. Second-rate strikers like George McCluskey, Derek Parlane and Jim Melrose failed to inspire and we drifted along. The likes of Ian Baird, not skilful but who gave 100% every time he pulled on the white shirt and the skilful John Sheridan gave us hope but it wasn't until Sgt Wilko arrived with the likes of Strachan, Jones, Haddock, Fairclough, Chapman and the emergence of Batty and Speed that hopes were raised. Overall my favourites of the '80s were Sheridan and Baird. Beauty and the Beast!

Best moment in the 1980s?

It was undoubtedly winning the Second Division and going back to the big time. There were false dawns here and there, some good cup runs but really it was a massive barren spell.

Worst moment supporting Leeds in the 1980s?

Relegation was a defining moment, but for me it was the depressive seasons rather than one defining moment with hopes raised then dashed and promising players sold. It was as if there was a black cloud hanging over the club. A succession of crap managers not good enough or over the hill players came and went. The '80s were a tough time to be a Leeds fan.

Odsal 1986 both photos courtesy Craig Gill

Did you see any of the hooliganism live?

Following Leeds away everybody saw fighting. When you were Leeds you were a target, a big scalp. Go to Blackburn and thugs from Wigan, Bury, Stockport and Manchester would team up to have a go at you and anywhere you went you would face a battle. Everyone knows about Stamford Bridge, Upton Park and such, but I found there were worse grounds such as Ayresome Park (Middlesbrough) which was a nightmare and Fratton Park (Portsmouth) was bad too. We were Leeds, everyone hated us and everyone wanted a pop. I've seen and been involved in running battles at Derby, Brighton, Arsenal, Everton, both Manchester clubs and Liverpool. Virtually everywhere, wherever we went we expected and got trouble.

129

Sometimes the police were worse than the fans, Wolves being a classic example. The Wolverhampton police loved a ruck! Birmingham away in 1985 saw our coach drive in slow moving traffic past The Bull Ring; the road was lined four or five deep with black lads looking for Leeds fans. Every window went through, people were fighting hand to hand and our driver saved us when he went on the wrong side of the road at great speed! A cold ride home mind! The good thing was we travelled in massive numbers, we stuck together – we were Leeds!

Best match in the 1980s?

Manchester City at Maine Road in a top of the table clash springs to mind. We went one down after about 85 minutes then scored in the 88th and 90th minutes to win it. It was mayhem inside and outside though after! Beating Newcastle 3–1 at home in a supercharged atmosphere was another. The referee took the teams off after missiles were thrown. QPR in the Cup at home was brilliant with Brendan Ormsby heading home the winner with minutes left. This was my first match after my banning order so I went disguised in a hat and Burberry scarf around my face, only my eyes could be seen. I thought I was unrecognisable until a copper came past and said "behave today Watson!" Most matches were pretty poor, scratching wins here and there. Under Howard Wilkinson, Leicester at home was superb.

Worst match in the 1980s?

Cambridge at home on a Friday night saw me in a crowd of just over 8,000. The place was empty, soulless and I thought it can't get worse than this. In 1982 we went six matches without even scoring! Losing 6–2 at Stoke was a bad day too. I couldn't really pinpoint one defining moment. The '80s, or most of them, were a depressing time to follow Leeds.

Least favourite season supporting Leeds in the 1980s?

So many to choose from but I'll plump for 1985–86. We were simply rubbish, we finished 14th in Division Two with an average crowd of under 13,000. Ian Baird was top scorer with a huge 14 goals and we only scored 56 goals in 42 matches. Heavy defeats at Stoke 6–2 and Manchester City 6–1 summed the season up. The last match was Norwich away in the sun. They stuffed us 4–0 and lifted the championship. We drove home in silence thinking why can't that ever be us?

KAY FOX

How long have you supported Leeds?

Since watching the 1972 Cup Final on television.

First match you went to?

QPR – 4 October 1975, sat in the West Stand with my dad and David Essex who was playing in Leeds that evening was sat a few rows behind us.

What was it like supporting the Whites in the 1980s?

In a word tense, never knew what to expect from the team, the fans or security.

Favourite player in the 1980s?

David Batty or John Sheridan.

Best moment in the 1980s?

Having a teacher who let me take a radio in to school so I could listen to the Valletta match walking home.

Worst moment supporting Leeds in the 1980s?

Relegation.

Did you see any of the hooliganism live?

Bits and pieces, the closest personally was two lads fighting at a bus stop on Whitehall Road.

Best match in the 1980s?

Blackburn Rovers away on Boxing Day, doing a conga in the away end.

Worst match in the 1980s?

Newcastle away August 1989 felt like another season was over before it had begun.

What was the atmosphere like following Leeds in the 1980s?

Very similar to now, just after relegation there was disbelief that this could happen to us, followed by bouts of optimism and pessimism.

What affect did Howard Wilkinson have on the club?

The fact that he made it clear that the club's history had to be put behind us and needed to look forward took some getting used to, but in the long run was exactly what we needed.

Most important signing in the 1980s?

Gordon Strachan, gave us belief that Wilko could get good players to sign for Leeds.

Favourite season supporting Leeds in the 1980s?

Enjoyed the 1986–87 season with the FA Cup run.

Least favourite season supporting Leeds in the 1980s?

The relegation season of 1981–82.

KEITH INGHAM

How long have you supported Leeds?

I've been a Leeds United fan since the 1973–74 season.

First match you went to?

My first match was against Ipswich Town that season. A fantastic first visit, I fell in love there and then up in the Kop.

What was it like supporting the Whites in the 1980s?

Quite surreal, wherever we went we were feared, not the team but its fans. Some pretty hard lads followed the Whites way back then. Most didn't wear colours, instead chose sports gear that was popular around that time.

Favourite player in the 1980s?

My favourite players from that era were John Sheridan, Ian Snodin and Ian Baird. All these players had reputations of being 'lads' when they were out.

Best moment in the 1980s?

The FA Cup run in 1987, beating QPR and Wigan before the epic semi-final versus Coventry City when despite taking the lead and equalising in the last minute, a Bennett goal, I think won the match for City. I was heartbroken!

Worst moment supporting Leeds in the 1980s?

The Play-off final replay match in Birmingham in 1987 after we had played against Charlton twice without the promotion place decided. When 'Shez' scored I thought we'd done it, but two goals from Peter Shirtliff broke mine and Leeds United's hearts.

Did you see any of the hooliganism live?

I saw a few 'runs' at fans and it was quite hostile at Elland Road for visiting fans. I was a victim when I was 'jumped' by Newcastle United fans, they gave me a kicking and nicked my favourite Leeds scarf as a souvenir.

Best match in the 1980s?

Leeds v QPR FA Cup 1987, classic!

Worst match in the 1980s?

Leeds v Shrewsbury in Division Two, awful.

What was the atmosphere like following Leeds in the 1980s?

It was very intimidating if you weren't a Leeds fan. Gangs of fans would circle away fans and then attack them. There were some classic matches, but some games where you wondered why you still went. The South Stand was for the Supporters Clubs and where most of the singing was done in my opinion.

What affect did Howard Wilkinson have on the club?

Howard Wilkinson lifted the club with his presence and raised belief in the club. Also the signings he brought in were first class. A really great time to be a fan of the club, we'd been through a lot of hard times before his tenure.

Most important signing in the 1980s?

Gordon Strachan, a born leader of men.

Favourite season supporting Leeds in the 1980s?

1989–90 – Promotion, going back to Division One. An incredible season.

Least favourite season supporting Leeds in the 1980s?

The 1981–82 season. Relegation was like a dagger through my heart, honestly!

MEMORIES FROM THE EIGHTIES
BY IAN HALMSHAW

CHELSEA

A branch of the Leeds United Supporters Club was started up by me together with Wayne Cheetham and Dave Marsden. This was called The Pioneer based in Hunslet and it was predominantly a lad's coach. When some of the lads worked away, they sussed out the pubs in advance for the season so this meant we booked into pubs everywhere for a pre-match drink. On one occasion we went down to Chelsea and called in at our usual pub in North London that was just off the A1. We drank all the way down on the coach as you did in those days. I had collected all the cash for the tickets on the coach and had about £1,400 in my back pocket. We left the pub late so by the time we arrived at Chelsea it was only 15 minutes before kick-off. The coppers stopped the coach outside the ground which was right opposite the Chelsea pub and made everyone get off to go to the match. As we got off I said to one of the lads Steve Knowles, "I want a drink" and Steve said, "you can't go in a Chelsea pub!" "Just watch me," I said as I dragged Steve with me and a couple of others off the coach followed us in making four of us in total. As we went to the bar to order our beer, the Chelsea fans still left in the pub heard our northern accents and immediately turned round as an atmosphere occurred. Steve Knowles said to me, "have you still got the cash in your back pocket?" and as I said "yes", his face went white. As we were drinking at the end of the bar, a Chelsea fan picked up a bottle and threw it at us. At that point we finished our drinks quickly and decided to leave before it got worse and had a barrage of bottles thrown at us.

SWANSEA

We went to Swansea and took a coach that left The Pioneer at midnight on the first match of the season when they pummelled us. We drove through the night and when we got to the Severn Bridge, Steve Knowles and a few others decided they wanted to walk into Wales. We drove across and waited at the other side for them at five in the morning. Before they managed to walk to the other side though, they were picked up by the coppers and dropped off at the coach. We got to Swansea at seven in the morning and as one lad had brought a ball with him, it meant that there were 50 lads playing football on the beach! There was no trouble, just everyone having some good fun. The coppers turned up and asked what we were doing there and who was in charge. I went with Wayne and told them that we were not here for trouble but just here for the football and a good day out. They told us that we wouldn't get in any pubs so we wandered about till 11.00 am.

We went into a pub and the landlord said it was a Swansea pub but was happy for us to give him a £100 bond as we told them we weren't there to cause any trouble, so he put us in one room. The other room was full of Swansea fans but we got talking to them, laughing and joking and mixing in the pub. There were approximately 300 of Leeds and Swansea fans in the pub till 2.30 pm and not a bit of bother, when the cops came to check all was okay and parked up outside. They came in then and closed the pub so we all had to go, we drank up and left and all walked together to the ground each singing Leeds and Swansea songs.

As we got to the ground, we shook hands and wished each other all the best, went our separate ways and they hammered us on the pitch 5–0. On the return fixture at Elland Road, we invited them to Leeds and 10 of them came to visit us and stayed in a hotel for the night. They came to the Pioneer and we are all still friends to this day!

WEST BROMWICH ALBION (WBA)

When we got relegated at WBA, we booked a 55-seater coach for the night match. Because of the demand to go to the match, 80 odd turned up for the coach, so when it arrived, some lads jumped into four or five cars instead. When we got to WBA we were crammed into the end and it was a very tense atmosphere, as we had to win to stay up. There were a lot more fans in the ground than there should have been with a fence in front of the stand. As the match went by we were losing 2-0, then Leeds fans started throwing things from the back. We had Steve Wood with us who was disabled and then the fans surged forward and we were pushed against the fence. Some were trying to get on the pitch and then the fence collapsed with them on it. We were crushed as the coppers got their truncheons out and waded into Leeds fans indiscriminately and not at the ones at the front causing trouble, but ones at the back. I was there with my then wife Carol. One of the coppers came very close to me and hit Steve, Carol and my brother Mark 14. Steve was on the floor as I got hold of him and I grabbed hold of the copper and was going to punch him, but another copper stopped me saying "don't, I've seen what's happened don't worry". He helped me to get Steve and the others up and got all four of us onto the pitch away from the crush. It was a sad day as we got relegated.

Another time we travelled to WBA after all meeting up in the Scarborough Taps in Leeds where we had a few pints, then set off with a full coach as usual. For a laugh, one of lads suggested that we should go in the WBA end when we got there. It was a stupid idea, but a group of 20 of us did it anyway! We went underneath the stand, had a few beers and kept ourselves to ourselves then 15 minutes before kick-off went onto the terrace behind the goal. All was fine until from the away end where the rest of the Leeds fans were congregated, they started singing *Marching on Together* and like idiots we followed them and joined in. Oh dear, that gave the game away; at that point the WBA fans charged us as most of the lads ran to the fence and climbed over it. I was with Gadge who later died of cancer in his mid-30s and Cockney Steve, but we got stuck behind one of the barriers. Fists flew until we eventually got underneath the barrier and climbed onto the fence. The fence though was five or six feet high and as we climbed over it Gadge slipped. His trousers caught on top of the barrier and ripped and he was left hanging upside down on the pitch side where we had got to safety, as the WBA fans were battering him from the other side. The coppers didn't have a clue what was going on when 20 fans came out of their end. We were on the pitch not at the side and when the Leeds fans in the away end started singing Leeds fans here, Leeds fans there, Leeds fans every f*****g where, we ran across the pitch to join them just as both teams came out.

SPURS IN THE CUP AFTER THE LEEDS LAD HAD GOT KILLED THERE THE YEAR BEFORE.

We took a coach down with Phil Binks, Cockney Steve and G from South Leeds. There was an atmosphere before you went as everyone was talking about trouble as soon as the names came out of the hat. On the way down I was talking to Cockney Steve and he was up for it with his demeanour. We stopped at a pub in St Albans then set off to the match and again the atmosphere on the coach was different with an aggression and loads I didn't know. We parked up and started walking up to the ground with the cops trying to escort us. Some were slipping away to walk on the other side of the road up Tottenham Court Road. A group of Spurs fans appeared 20 to 30 of them, all mouthing off and only a few cops around at the time as several Leeds fans ran at them and waded into them even though they were outnumbered. With that a couple of hundred in the cordon broke it and attacked the Spurs fans. Once it had all settled down and another 150 yards further down the road, we passed a pub full of their fans banging on the windows and chanting. A Leeds fan threw a brick that went straight through the window and shattered it. With that 150 Spurs fans came out of the pub and thought they would do the Leeds fans. Wrong, the Leeds fans turned and stood their ground and came out on top again.

We managed to get down to the ground with more Spurs fans and cops and it was kicking off left, right and centre. As we got to the White Hart pub, groups of Spurs fans charged us and had split us up into groups of 15 or 20 of us and there were 100 of them. They waded into us and a big full height glass window in the pub shattered as a Spurs fan hit one of the Leeds fans and he fell back into the window. This opened the pub up to the Spurs fans in there. We were in a corner sandwiched in the pub doorway where Spurs fans were coming in and out and we had to fight our way out of it. The Spurs fans couldn't believe what was happening and ran away. The cops came and arrested two Spurs fans but no Leeds fans. We went to the match, which I think we lost, where there was a massive cop presence and afterwards, they kept us in the ground for a while. We were escorted back to the coaches and set off back to Leeds, where we called off at a pub in Watford on our way back. We got talking to half a dozen Spurs fans who had been to the match, they were right lads and had no trouble with them. They did say that in all the years that any fans who had come to Spurs and stood their ground, West Ham, Millwall, Chelsea and Arsenal, nobody had stood out as well as Leeds had that day. It had been a tough day but we had no option but to stand and fight our way out!

MANCHESTER CITY

One time we went to Manchester City and because of the demand for tickets, we took a double decker bus. We stopped for pre-match drinks in the Junction pub in Bury and eventually got to the ground and parked outside the Kippax. The coppers wouldn't let any more Leeds fans in to the away end as they said the stand was full and there was no more access. Seven or eight of us managed to get away and get tickets in the seats at the other end of the ground. The match kicked off and there was no trouble as we just sat watching the football. After about 20 minutes, one of the lads said he thought something was kicking off behind us. As we looked around, there were approximately 30 black lads there as one pulled out a blade with no coppers around! One lad said f**k this I'm off as they charged us so we ran onto the pitch. The coppers got hold of us and kicked us out of the ground after 20 minutes. They made us go back to the double decker bus and eight of us had to stay upstairs with a copper till the end of the match so we couldn't go anywhere. There was loads of trouble in the ground as it kicked off and loads of Leeds fans were all kicked out. They ended up being put on our bus which they used as a holding pen.

In later years we went to another match at Manchester City with some old boys from the Station. With a full minibus from Salford Van hire, we called again at the Junction pub in Bury, which was a regular haunt for us. After leaving the pub we got caught up in traffic so were really late to the match. When we asked the cops where to park, they didn't want to know so we parked just across from the Kippax at the other side of road. We went to the match and had no trouble as Leeds won the match. We went back to the mini bus after being kept in by the cops for half an hour and there was a wooden stool smashed and embedded in the windscreen. Chris Ellis was driving so because it was a hire vehicle we reported it to the cops. They said it had to be reported at the local station and gave us directions to it. Chris turned the vehicle around and drove 200 yards to where we had to turn left. As we turned by a parade of shops loads of black guys came out and started to kick and rock the van. We were out of sight of the cops and in serious trouble. I said to Gadge, there is nothing to do here but fight our way out, so we opened the sliding door and ran out and ended up in a fight with several locals who I don't think had been to the match. One guy picked up a metal bin from outside a shop and threw it at the bus smashing some more windows, so Bobby Jones and a few others got out to help me. This seemed to go on for quite a while when eventually the cops turned up. Oh my God, the minibus was in a hell of a state with only one window left in it! We got back in the minibus and the cops escorted us to the local cop station where we did the relevant paperwork. We tried to get the cops to help us sort out a replacement minibus but got nowhere, so we had to drive back to Leeds with no windows including the windscreen over the M62 which was one long, cold and wet journey. As we got back to the Station I jumped in the car and followed Chris back to Salford Van hire and parked it up amongst the other vans and left it there. Chris Ellis got a phone call the next morning from them asking what had gone on? We all had to give statements and the cop incident number etc. I don't know why, but Chris was banned from hiring vehicles from Salford van hire for the next few years!

CARLISLE

The Pioneer started getting a reputation as trouble causers, but we weren't, we were a good set of lads out to have a good time and not out for trouble, but would stand our ground if anyone started on us. We had some from Wetherby who travelled with us, a great set of lads. We played Carlisle away and hadn't sorted out anywhere to stop so someone suggested Penrith. We set off early and parked in a car park between two pubs. I went with Wayne and asked if we could go in and put money in the pub but they wouldn't accept it and said no. We then went to the other pub and knocked on the door and an old lady came to the door who was doing the cleaning. She went and got the landlord out of bed who came down in his boxer shorts and said let me get dressed and no problem. We gave him a £100 bond and stopped there. They had a great turnover and did food as well using the cleaner and his daughter to help serve us all. We stayed till 2.00 pm and then went to the match. There were no issues and after the match as we got near Penrith the lads wanted to go back to the pub again. Fortunately we had the same driver every week who knew us all well, he was a great guy so agreed but we had to line his pocket. We all chipped in with a collection and managed to get 50 quid so he took us to the pub. We checked with the landlord again as there were a few locals in and he said he had a turn on at 8.30 pm but it was no problem. We stayed till closing time, had some great entertainment and a laugh and made some friends for life. The only problem was, the landlord took some stick as he supported scum. We returned to that pub the following season to repeat a great day out. Sadly Carlisle got relegated so we didn't go back there.

SHEFFIELD UNITED

The Pioneer folded in the late '80s for allegedly causing trouble. The club shut us down by no longer supplying tickets for the branch, but no one was arrested. Most lads went their own separate way. I started to go from the Station pub down Hunslet with lads who called themselves the Station Fossils, but the younger lads in the pub were known as the Station youth squad. They all played football together and the older end managed them, some great lads Popeye, Graham

A and Charlie Offord. Gadge and Mick Thompson (both died), Bobby Jones and Mick Dimmery (both passed away last year), Mickey Butterfield, Glen Butterfield and Squaddie. Micky had an accident on the M62 involving two wagons recently and was in a coma but had come out of it, but was not in a good way. Gary White, Kenny Morrell and many more, we used to hire a minibus or go in two or three cars to matches. One match comes into mind, which was the last time we won a trophy. We went to Sheffield United and won the league. It was a 12 o'clock kick off with some weird goals, but we managed to win and got back to the Station for last orders at 3.00 pm and said we would be back at 7.00 pm when it opened again and said it would be rowdy if man utd lost and we won! There were 50 guys and gals in there at 7.00 pm for opening time and what a night to remember down Hunslet. Every pub was full of Leeds fans as we went round several pubs and ended up in the Brass Moulders an old Tetley's pub no longer here. I don't know how, but John Rimmer had gone on the phone and had several telephone numbers for people in scum and every time they answered the phone, chants of 'Champions' and 'Marching on Together' meant they didn't stay on the phone very long! He kept putting the phone out to the crowd and kept ringing loads from the phone book. That night my wife Sharon was stood on one of the tables in the pub chanting away, unbeknown to us both that she was pregnant with our first child Keenan which we found out a week later. Back in those days pubs shut at 10.00 pm at night on a Sunday, but not in Hunslet, that night they stayed open till three or four in the morning!

BOURNEMOUTH

For Bournemouth we went down from the Station at midnight, four of us in a car and drove through the night to arrive at seven in the morning. As we drove into Bournemouth, we saw local people jogging, there were people walking dogs and fans with Leeds shirts on coming out of shops, on the beach, the promenade and everywhere we looked we saw Leeds fans wearing their Colours. We took shirts and ties with us so we could go out on the night and celebrate Leeds going up. We hadn't booked a hotel but found a bed and breakfast that wasn't booked up. The landlady and landlord weren't sure, but eventually agreed to take us in. We dropped our bags and left the car and went for a walk. As we came to the local supermarket that had only opened 20 minutes before, we found it was surrounded by cops. They had closed it to stop Leeds fans buying drink.

As the day went on, we ended up outside the ground where Leeds fans were in the park celebrating with a good atmosphere, playing football and partying. There were loads with no tickets but Chris Mabbutt's mum worked in the ticket office so we were lucky. As the match got closer and fans tried getting in the ground with no tickets the atmosphere started to turn and cops were turning fans away from the ground with or without tickets. Fortunately we were lucky enough to get to the turnstiles and get in the ground with our tickets as mayhem reigned outside.

Leeds won 1–0 when Chapman scored in the 78th minute and as all the Leeds fans went crazy, the lad next to me jumped up and landed on my foot, he must have weighed 18 stone! My foot hurt, but I didn't think much of it at the time, as we climbed onto the pitch at the end of the match as the players came out and celebrated with the fans. At the end we started walking back to the hotel and I was limping a lot.

We got back to the hotel and had a drink or two and a discussion with the landlord and landlady about the troubles that had been, they even considered kicking us out of the hotel as we were from Leeds, but didn't. We went and got changed into suits, shirts and ties and phoned for a taxi and went to Poole in Dorset where we tried to get into several pubs, but they all refused unless you had a local ID. My foot was getting worse and had started to swell up, so we jumped in a taxi and asked him to take us to a pub where we could have a drink. He took us to his local pub and came in with us and we stopped for two or three hours with some Bournemouth supporters and had a good night before we went back to the hotel. We set off next morning after breakfast for Leeds and my foot was that bad by then that I couldn't get my shoe on, so Chris Ellis had to drive back. We got back to the Station mid-afternoon and had a few more beers there. Sharon took me to Leeds General Infirmary to get my foot checked over and the whole of Accident and Emergency was full of Leeds supporters from Bournemouth, all with various injuries and I found I had broken a bone in my foot!

I stopped going to matches for a while and then started going again when Leeds got back into Europe and kept going.

PARTISAN BELGRADE

Leeds were due to play Partisan Belgrade which was to be played in Belgrade, but because of problems in Yugoslavia UEFA switched the tie. They cancelled the match on the Friday and it was now to be played on Tuesday in Herenveen in northern Holland. I had already booked to go for the day with the club, but the club got in touch with everybody and gave options of what they could do. We could pay an extra £100 and fly out with the players on their plane and stay in their hotel or go for nothing by coach but we would have to leave at 11.00 pm the day before the match. I opted to go by coach and we left on six coaches on Monday night at 11.00 pm from Elland Road and drove down to Dover, crossed over and drove up through France and Belgium to Herenveen. It was one long journey! When we got there, they parked the coaches up at the ground and the cops instructed us to go to the centre where a fans park had been set up. We got to a small square which had half a dozen restaurants and bars. The local authorities had set up a DJ, with music playing across the square and two mobile bars in the middle. There were 500–600 Leeds fans chanting away and everyone around them was doing their shopping and daily chores. There was a great atmosphere and no trouble at all. The authorities shut the bars and asked us to go to the ground but the Leeds fans persuaded the cops to keep the bars open for another half an hour, which they obliged. We all set off to the ground together singing *Marching on Together*! As we walked through the town by the canal which was lovely and quaint, all the shopkeepers stood astounded watching us all and a few Leeds fans broke away to dance with young girls outside the shops which was really funny. There was even a Marks and Spencers! There were 12,000 at the match with several thousand Leeds fans, 300 from Belgrade and the rest were locals. Again there was a great atmosphere with no trouble. After the match we set off back, drove through the night and crossed by ferry. We drove back up country and arrived at 11.00 pm on Wednesday and I went straight back to work the next day. It was not a very productive working day though!

LOCOMOTIV MOSCOW

When we played Locomotiv Moscow I went through the club to the match and flew from Leeds Bradford Airport. We had to be there at 4.00am and had to go to the arrivals baggage collection point where visas were being handed out, which had been set up by Leeds before we left. Once we'd got our visas we went through, got checked in and went to the lounge area ready for the day trip. It was rammed with Leeds fans and regular travellers going out to Spain who couldn't believe we were going for a day whilst they were going for 3–4 weeks. There was great banter with the old biddies though!

Once we got to Moscow we cleared the airport and they got us onto buses, old ones with windows that slid back, which were like going back in time! It was freezing cold. They took us to a hotel at the bottom of Red Square seven or eight coaches full of Leeds fans. I had worked with a lad who had been there three months before who had given me directions to an Irish pub. I wanted to do some sightseeing so went for a walk alone and found some Leeds fans with flags in Red Square. I wandered around and then found the Irish Bar ordering a pint of Guinness. Suddenly over my shoulder I heard someone say, "get me one" and turned round to find Tony from West Midlands who had gone for three days and turned up behind me. We ended up having a great laugh, sharing some good memories and a few beers before going back to where the others were at the hotel, which was rammed with Leeds fans drinking and eating. As we were going up in the lift laughing and joking to the next floor, I got a shock as they were full of ladies of the night and all doing a roaring trade as Leeds officials downstairs socialised with the rest of the fans. It was a great night and I think we won 3–0 with Bowyer, Kewell and Viduka scoring the goals.

NICK CONNOR

BARNSLEY, HUDDERSFIELD AND BIRMINGHAM – SEASON 1984–85

We were travelling to matches whilst the miners' strike of 1984–85 was taking place, which involved major industrial action that affected the coal industry. I thought this was a very nasty time for all concerned. During the strike we played both Barnsley and Huddersfield away on consecutive weeks in early October where the bitter months of the 1984 strike were yet to surface. A Leeds fan (Davy Jones) had died on the picket lines earlier that year so it was never going to be pleasant.

Anyway Barnsley away on 13 October 1984 was always going to be the most bitter of the two, seeing as many of the pits in that area were affected. We arrived to the usual reception of hundreds of the old bill and chants of 'Scargill' were very loud, which the old bill didn't like one bit! Chants of 'Davy Jones murdered' were loud too. On the way to the ground there were plenty of scuffles with the locals, but as usual the old bill left them to it. We got pushed into the ground, but I can't remember paying, as they wanted us in the ground as soon as possible. I can't remember much about the match but we lost 1–0. There were loads of scuffles on the way back to the station where sadly the miners' strike became very real with the tragic death of a policeman on a bridge. He tried to stop a fight but collapsed and died instantly. What was more shocking was that nobody tried to help him. A girl ran over to help and said she was a nurse but couldn't

Barnsley 1984 photo courtesy Craig Gill

Barnsley 1984 photo courtesy Craig Gill

save him; the fact she was told some nasty things when she went to help shocked me, such as, "they stood and watched Davy die, why should we help him?" It got really nasty then amid lots of chants of 1–0. More than 40 fans were arrested at this match according to a newspaper report out of a crowd of 16,199.

It was not nice at all at Huddersfield the following week on 20 October 1984, which ended in another 1–0 defeat. It was a good match but there was much more trouble. We arrived from Kings Cross station with Marion's group (RIP Marion Fudge) and about 300 of us were kept at the station with virtually very little problems or so I thought. We left the station on our way to the old Leeds Road ground, then out of nothing as we passed a pub on the left hand side, their fans started chucking bottles and glasses at us and they WEREN'T plastic either! What I didn't know, was that some Leeds fans had gone round the back of the pub to confront these fans. Our escort had got larger so I presumed that they had arrived after we left. This match made the national news when everybody was climbing up and rocking the fence and almost but not quite, pulling it down. The police made 63 arrests with two policemen and eight other fans taken to hospital out of a crowd of 15,257.

A newspaper report after the event had a police spokesman say that, "Our officers were showered with missiles, including ball bearings; chairs in the stand were smashed up and thrown on the pitch and windows in turnstile booths smashed". And this just seven days after the rampage in Barnsley in which even the handicapped were regarded as targets.

143

Karen, Kelly and Wayne at Barnsley 1984 article Yorkshire Evening Post

The actual match was better than Barnsley even though we lost 1–0 again. I can't remember anything bad on the way back to the centre and the station. It certainly didn't have the miners' feeling like Barnsley did, although there was more trouble from the Huddersfield fans than the Barnsley fans!

My last story from 1980s is totally different as you will see. WITHOUT A DOUBT 11 MAY 1985 IS THE WORST DAY I CAN EVER REMEMBER AT A FOOTBALL MATCH AND I HOPE NOBODY EVER HAS TO GO THROUGH IT AGAIN! The journey up to Birmingham was uneventful until we got to the ground. We arrived about 1.00 pm and once we arrived outside the ground we were told that if we didn't have tickets we were not getting in! We thought that was it then or maybe not, but anyway went to pub for a while. When we got back to the ground about 2.45 pm there were hundreds of Leeds fans outside without tickets, then out of nothing, some fans jumped the turnstiles as a massive ruck broke out over the road. Most fans joined in as the old bill on horseback told us to wait there. As if, lol, anyway loads then climbed over and I kid you not, someone passed the actual turnstile barrier out as well! I thought then that if they can do it so can I! With that, Mars bars went flying as we were in for free!

We had a massive following and there must have been 10,000 Leeds fans there; not only did we have the huge terrace behind the goal but seats at the side too. A sequence of incidents kicked off in a fairly quiet 1980s end of season match. I remember if results went our way, we could have gone up although this was very unlikely. Just before half time somebody said promotion rivals Manchester City were losing (they were in fact winning). Birmingham were already up anyway along with Oxford United and Manchester City was the last team to be promoted in the end. Gates scored for Birmingham and that was that (promotion wise). It all kicked off everywhere with the Birmingham Zulus massing at the other end of the pitch. West Midlands Police were doing their usual charging as seats were being ripped out. The second half was delayed for approximately 45 minutes until they managed to clear the pitch. The match ended with the Zulus running onto the pitch again and there were police horses in the centre preventing any real clashes between the rival fans. To be honest the more serious tragic events elsewhere that day which we were not aware of, probably saved us a lot of bad publicity in my opinion.

After about an hour we were finally allowed to leave with only a few clashes outside and in the City. We got to the station where all the London trains were going to Paddington station as Euston was closed. After fighting all day long, the old bill were dressed in riot gear and at New Street Station it became more like *RoboCop*! We were getting on the train, which had Arsenal fans sat at the back who were on their way back from West Bromwich Albion. I thought here we go again expecting trouble, although as it happened nothing did. We got on the train and the Arsenal lot were okay and then somebody said there had been trouble at Bradford. There were no mobiles of course so it was only hearsay. Anyway we asked the coppers on the train what had happened at Bradford. They weren't aware of the Birmingham incidents so were very friendly with us and they said they would ask their colleagues at the Reading changeover for more information. When we got to Reading the copper got off and came straight back on and took his helmet off. He said, "lads I don't know how to tell you this but 15 people have died". The whole carriage went silent and I don't think anybody spoke from Reading to London. Of course at that time we didn't know how bad the day was to end not only for Bradford, but for the 15-year-old Leeds fan from Northampton. RIP to the 57!

STUTTGART 1992

This story is from when I travelled to the Stuttgart match in Barcelona in October 1992. I arrived at Gatwick with the Chiltern branch in the afternoon to get our £99 return cheap flights to Barcelona. We got on the flight which was fairly normal apart from some of the lads having one or two vinos, which made them loud but nothing over the top. We were standing next to the late (and up to that point I thought great) ITV commentator Brian Moore, but when he said we made him ashamed to be English that made me very angry! Nothing happened at all on the flight and I was even backed up by a stewardess on that too, so that disappointed me! Anyway on with our tour with our first job to find bed and breakfast accommodation, which we did with no problem.

The match wasn't until the following evening so we had all day to visit Barcelona. My mate John and I took in the sights such as the Olympic Park which had just staged the 1992 Olympic Games, so we spent some time there. We then went to various historical sites including the one where the Catalans fought Franco's Republican Army during fascist Spain rule and there were some very moving stories to hear too. Before we did this we took a cable car ride; when we were at the bed and breakfast accommodation, we were told to take our passports and plane tickets with us, as they were the most likely things to get stolen for obvious reasons. So not thinking what I had in my pocket, I threw a load of rubbish out of the cable car into the water below. Now at that stage, I had no idea what (although I'm sure you can guess what though, as I'm not thinking at all at that stage about plane tickets!) We went down to the Nou Camp to get our match tickets and there were even LUFC ticket office staff telling us where to buy tickets in English, so there were no problems there. We carried on with our tour of Barcelona not thinking of anything really as the match wasn't till the next day. We decided to go and watch the Barcelona B team at the reserve match where a certain *Pep Guardiola* who is the current manager of Bundesliga club Bayern Munich, was sitting next to us, who was learning to coach, sadly NO cameras I'm afraid! Anyway the next day began with more sightseeing then on to the Nou Camp for the match; where ooh ahh Carl Shutt who replaced some moody Frenchman then scored the winner! I remember the headline so well the next day, "Super sub Carl sinks Germans" (I bet that wouldn't be printed now!)

After the match we went back to our accommodation and as we were catching an early flight (we had to be there at 5.00 am for a 6.00 am flight, we stayed up all night. Up to this point I hadn't looked for my ticket until we got to the airport at 5.00 am and suddenly found that I had NO plane ticket and I also had no money either of course! Now what we didn't know at this stage was, that it was a Spanish national holiday and everything was closed and unfortunately for us so were the banks which also had a 48-hour transaction delay. This meant that any money taken out abroad wouldn't be debited, so my mate used his LUFC MasterCard and brought me another ticket, as Iberia refused to let me on without buying another one, even though I had all the booking details. They said I would get a full refund from their London office on production of a ticket receipt, (which I did by the way!) We had yet another adventure to come with a Leeds fan in the same position as me who had also lost his ticket. He had no money to get back either and was distraught at that prospect. We didn't know the guy but he was a Leeds fan and the thought of leaving him there wasn't nice. He gave us 100% assurance he would pay back the money as soon as he got back home and although we still weren't sure, we couldn't leave the guy. He flew to Manchester as we flew to Heathrow.

We then had another adventure as my mate went to the loo and crashed out! The call came for the plane but he wasn't on it; they put three calls out but to no avail so they then took off! This was pre 9/11 so an empty seat on a plane from Barcelona to Heathrow in 1992 wasn't considered a security risk then, I suppose. I got home and crashed out but when I woke up my mate wasn't home. Just as I was getting frantic, he walked through the door of the house we then shared. I went straight to Iberia's office and got the money to repay my mate. The Leeds fan from Doncaster phoned up and paid the money straight onto his credit card via bank transfer. To this day, we have never met or known him, but what an honest fan he turned out to be, as he could have been the opposite!

MORE INTERVIEWS WITH LEEDS FANS

BY ANDREW

MARTIN TAYLOR

How long have you supported Leeds?

I've been a Leeds fan since around 1974.

First match you went to?

Middlesbrough 4–4 Leeds United (Bill Gates's Testimonial) August 1974.

What was it like supporting the Whites in the 1980s?

Following Leeds in the '80s was my favourite decade. The fans that went to Elland Road and away were the hard-core and loyal fans. The away support was fantastic as ever while the crowds at Elland Road dwindled to sometimes fewer than 10,000. The size of the ground with only a small crowd didn't look right which showed the sign of the times. We went through some bleak times in the aftermath of relegation in 1982 as the big names left and the youngsters came through. We were often poor on the pitch but we supported the club home and away, through thick and thin and with my mates and me, it often meant hitch hiking to matches in the early '80s as none of us could drive then.

Favourite player in the 1980s?

It has to be the one and only Ian Baird. From his first match till his last he never gave less than 100% effort. He was strong and aggressive, not a prolific goal scorer but the goals he did score were usually well earned. He often overstepped the mark in aggression and often gave the centre halves a torrid time; but would never back out of confrontation AND scored some great goals for Leeds, especially against QPR in the FA Cup and a fantastic hat-trick against Plymouth in 1987; he was as hard as nails!!!

Best moment in the 1980s?

It was probably the first time I went to Elland Road in 1981 against Spurs in a 0–0 draw, although the club was in decline and relegation loomed I was hooked.

Worst moment supporting Leeds in the 1980s?

Apart from relegation in 1982 and the FA Cup semi-final defeat, it was the Play-off Final against Charlton in 1987. After two 1–0 results we ended up at St Andrews on a Friday night for the replay, when John Sheridan gave us the lead. Three sides of the ground erupted with euphoria as we were nearly back in the big time, only for it to be cruelly taken away by Peter Shirtliff with two quick fire goals. I cried my eyes out at the end, it was a long way home and it seemed to take forever on the coach. I will never forget that night, plus on the Monday morning after the match I was sacked from my job, as I was due to work on the Friday night and was refused the time off. I was never going to miss the match, the things you do for your beloved Leeds United!!!

Did you see any of the hooliganism live?

I attended many away matches in the 1980s where there was crowd trouble. In the early '80s we went on the special trains from Leeds central station and you would often see mindless vandalism on them. One match was Man City away in 1985 at Easter; once we got to Manchester we were then put on special buses to and from Maine Road and suffice to say a lot of the windows were kicked out and a few seats as well, but nothing compared to being at St Andrews, Birmingham and Odsal, Bradford. The Birmingham match in 1985 was one big mass riot. Leeds fans raided a snack hut on the terrace then duly ripped up and threw anything they could get their hands on, with wood and concrete thrown at the police. At one point Eddie Gray came on to the pitch to ask for calm but to no avail as a missile narrowly missed him. The Birmingham fans rioted at the other end as the police struggled to gain control and unfortunately led to the death of a fan. It was all very harrowing and also the same day as the Bradford fire!!!

The Bradford match in 1986 was also harrowing and started when Leeds fans raided a chip van on the Odsal terracing and then decided to push it down the terracing whilst on fire. The away end was packed and in the end it meant fans had to go on to the pitch for their own safety while the players were on the pitch. I actually shook hands that day with John Sheridan and David Rennie, which in one way was great but also embarrassing due to the hooligans. I was also at Leicester Forest service station on the M1 on the opening day of the 1985–86 season when we were going to Fulham and Millwall were heading to Huddersfield. We entered the service station and headed to the shop where we were in the shop two minutes when two large bins hurtled through the windows from Millwall fans. The next ten to fifteen minutes was like a war zone and unarmed combat when everything was getting thrown at each other.

There were many other matches throughout the '80s with trouble especially at Barnsley and Huddersfield and another fire at West Brom. All this was part of the bad times following Leeds United in the '80s. One funny thing that did happen at an away match was when I went to Hull City v Leeds on 22 December 1985. With me coming from Middlesbrough I was giving stick to a Hull player called Billy Askew who used to play for the Boro. I was in the corner of the away end near the corner flag and he was taking a corner. I was calling him a ginger so and so and using all the verbals at him. He took the corner, they scored and he turned around and shouted F**k off and stuck two fingers up at me. I didn't know where to put myself... still mention it today with all my mates!

Best match in the 1980s?

Was 5 April 1986 against Portsmouth away. Portsmouth were going for promotion while Leeds were in a relegation fight. We went with the Harrogate Supporters club and the match didn't start well in blustery conditions with Portsmouth scoring early. We thought we were going to be hammered, but we got through to half-time losing 1–0. When the second half started we seemed transformed when two goals from Andy Ritchie and an Ian Baird goal put us into a 3–1 lead and the legendary Ronnie Robinson had his best match for the club. Portsmouth pulled one back but we held on for a 3–2 victory to put a dent in Pompey's promotion hopes and it went a long way in preserving our Division Two safety. Leeds fans were packed into a pen behind the goal and we couldn't believe the transformation in the second half. I remember Leeds scoring the second goal and just grabbing a random Leeds fan in euphoria as we all went mental. And it snowed on the way home!!!

Worst match in the 1980s?

It was 21 Dec 1986: The season before we lost 6–2 at Stoke City. This season we went to Stoke and lost 7–2! It was a disgraceful performance and you just couldn't believe what you were watching. Everything that could go wrong did go wrong. The players were very poor and they knew it, we were given a complete run around by a team we ended up finishing 10 points better off than at the end of the season.

What was the atmosphere like following Leeds in the 1980s?

The atmosphere in the '80s was up and down throughout the decade. In the early '80s the crowds had dwindled but the club still had its loyal following especially away from home, where they followed in large numbers and were always very vocal. The loyal fans at home were always very vocal and always got behind the team although results were poor. 1986–87 was probably the season we all got behind the team and the atmosphere was great with the Cup run and the Play-offs looming.

What affect did Howard Wilkinson have on the club?

When Howard Wilkinson took over in 1988 we knew we could be in for good times ahead and although he took over from our hero Billy Bremner who had taken us as far as we could go, Wilkinson breathed new life into the club. He took us away from the bottom of Division Two and guided us to a top ten finish. Two big signings in Gordon Strachan and Chris Fairclough and the signing of Carl Shutt, changed the atmosphere and left us with the possibility of something to look forward to the following season.

Most important signing in the 1980s?

The most important signing in the '80s would have to be Gordon Strachan. Although he signed at the back end of the decade, he was the catalyst of greater things to come in the seasons ahead and was far too good and superior for Division Two.

Favourite season supporting Leeds in the 1980s?

My favourite season following Leeds was 1986–87. That season we followed the club home and away and went to virtually every match. A fantastic FA Cup run ending with the semi-final against Coventry and a decent run in the league ending in fourth place and a Play-off spot. Beating Oldham Athletic over two matches and then that Charlton Athletic match! I still to this day watch the 'season to savour' video from time to time, great goals, great matches and so close to glory that season!

Least favourite season supporting Leeds in the 1980s?

Well to be truthful there really wasn't one; we were in Division Two and some seasons weren't as good as others, but I loved every match I attended and love following Leeds so would find it difficult to really choose one. If I had to, it would be my favourite season of 1986–87 and only because of the semi-final loss and Play-off Final loss.

PAUL BLANN

How long have you supported Leeds?

I was born in 1962 on the South Coast. I moved to Yorkshire in the early '80s (1983) but now live back on the coast. I started supporting Leeds in 1968.

First match you went to?

Chelsea (a) on 30 November 1968.

What was it like supporting the Whites in the 1980s?

It was fairly drab supporting Leeds in the '80s. There were a number of promises but nothing materialised until the end of the decade. The 1986–87 season stands out but the rest of it wasn't that good. That said, I was still as fanatical as ever.

Favourite player in the 1980s?

Paul Hart who shouldered great responsibility in a poor side. Ian Baird ended up as my favourite player of the '80s.

Best moment in the 1980s?

Best moment of the '80s was getting to the FA Cup semi-final v Coventry in 1986–87. We made the Play-offs that year too.

Worst moment supporting Leeds in the 1980s?

Worst moments were losing to Charlton at St Andrews in the Play-off replay and to Coventry in the semi-final (after extra time). However, it must not be forgotten that we lost to West Brom in the last match of the 1981–82 season which ended many glorious years of being in the top division.

Did you see any of the hooliganism live?

I did see hooliganism live on a number of occasions. Fortunately I wasn't at Odsal in 1986 or Birmingham in 1985. There was also the said match at West Brom in 1982. One match which stood out for me was Sunderland home in 1981. They brought their usual thousands with them. They were stood on the Lowfields terraces segregated from the Leeds fans. However, they kept breaching the segregated areas and got closer and closer to the Leeds fans. The police did a good job but things could have got quite serious.

Best match in the 1980s?

One of the best matches of the '80s was beating QPR at home in the fifth round of the FA Cup in 1987. Also beating Oldham at home in the first leg of the Play-off semi-final, also in 1987. However, the match that stands out for me is the final home match of the season in 1982. We were in a bad place (third from bottom) and just had to beat Brighton and Hove Albion, my local team. We were in the South Stand Upper and Leeds found themselves 0–1 down. Realising that things were getting serious, the Kop got everyone in the ground singing and the renditions of *Marching on Together* were amongst the best ever. Even the fans in the West Stand were giving it a good go. The passion transferred to the pitch and two goals in a minute from Hamson and Hird ensured a 2–1 victory. Unfortunately, the defeat at West Brom a few days later condemned us to Division Two. The singing was mentioned a few times in the report by the *Brighton Evening Argus* on the Monday after the match.

Worst match in the 1980s?

I think the worst matches of the '80s can be coupled with the worst moments. However, there were too many bad matches throughout the period to single any out.

What was the atmosphere like following Leeds in the 1980s?

The atmosphere in the '80s was in the main fairly poor. As the statistics will show, the crowds were generally low. With small crowds, fans are dotted around the ground and getting an atmosphere was difficult. People would save themselves for the big matches at which the atmosphere then would be much better. That said, the away support still held up very well.

What affect did Howard Wilkinson have on the club?

Howard Wilkinson had a huge effect on the club. He replaced Billy Bremner in 1988. His style of football was different but he got the team going. He came with a plan and slowly but surely resurrected the club. He brought an air of ambition to the club at a time when it really needed it. We were promoted back to Division One in his first full season.

Most important signing in the 1980s?

The best signing was undoubtedly Gordon Strachan in 1989. Vinnie Jones, Chris Fairclough and John Hendrie were also important signings. All of a sudden, Leeds were signing good players again.

Favourite season supporting Leeds in the 1980s?

Favourite seasons supporting Leeds in that decade were 1980–81 believe it or not, 1981–82 as I was so passionate (even though we went down), 1986–87 and 1988–89. I would have to settle on 1986–87 due to the Cup run and the Play-off matches.

Least favourite season supporting Leeds in the 1980s?

Least favourite season has to be 1983–84 as it was dull.

PETER DILLON

How long have you supported Leeds?

I have supported Leeds since 1962–63.

First match you went to?

I think it was at Easter in 1963 against Derby at Elland Road. We were at Filey in a caravan and my dad drove us back for the match, then back to Filey.

What was it like supporting the Whites in the 1980s?

Very interesting and very expensive. I went to virtually every match home, away, friendlies and European pre-seasons.

Favourite player in the 1980s?

David Batty, Ian Baird and Gordon Strachan.

Best moment in the 1980s?

Visiting Belfast against Glentoran on a Tuesday night in a minibus, we very nearly got hijacked in the city after the match, very memorable and very drunk.

Worst moment supporting Leeds in the 1980s?

West Brom away, relegation night has to be the worst. Although Don Revie passing away will stay with me forever. We took a transit van up to the funeral and ended up being seen on Calendar. Don Revie's secretary came over to us and said Mrs Revie has heard you have driven up in a van please come to the reception!! We were sitting in a lounge bar at the same table as Billy, Mick Jones, Mick Bates, Big Jack... they only told us it was a free bar for us! I still pinch myself that I was sat talking to Billy over a pint!

Did you see any of the hooliganism live?

I was one of the organisers of the (later banned) Kippax Supporter's club branch, along with Collar, Big John, John West and Gary Edwards. We had many scrapes which I could expand on in detail if you want later… obviously not too much detail though! We had a love/hate relationship with the service crew, we knew the older guys from the old special train days, but the younger ones hated us because we were not dressers like them. They grudgingly accepted us because they knew we could handle ourselves if we had to, but not go looking for it. At matches like Spurs away in the Cup etc. they were always glad we were around, I'm not glorifying it just telling you the truth.

Best match in the 1980s?

QPR in the cup is a strong candidate, but will go with man utd away when Brian Flynn scored.

Worst match in the 1980s?

Losing against Charlton in the Play-off replay Final, I drank a bottle of vodka on the bus going home, also losing by seven at Stoke one night.

What was the atmosphere like following Leeds in the 1980s?

Always lively, sometimes fun, sometimes terrible, but always challenging like getting tickets for banned matches. Wimbledon at Plough Lane (not only got in but got into the player's lounge).

What affect did Howard Wilkinson have on the club?

He totally resurrected the club, but maybe stayed a season too long.

Most important signing in the 1980s?

Gordon Strachan.

Favourite season supporting Leeds in the 1980s?

All of them, 1987 was both a high point and a low point.

Least favourite season supporting Leeds in the 1980s?

1982 the lack of atmosphere and the feeling of inevitability regarding relegation.

PHIL MASON

How long have you supported Leeds?

42 years!

First match you went to?

I started supporting Leeds in 1972. I grew up about 10 miles outside of Nottingham. My Dad was from Derby and Mum was from Manchester. My brother was 10 years older than me and supported man utd. My dad was one of those odd cases who just seemed to like football. I suppose deep down he was a Derby County supporter but he also followed West Ham as he was stationed there during the war, he also went to see both man utd and Manchester City because he lived in Manchester when he met my mum. I was actually bought a man utd kit and ball for my fifth birthday (for one moment I do not think I ever asked for this!) and my only memory of this is a photograph from my party. Whatever happened in the following year that resulted in me deciding to support Leeds I am not sure, but it was clearly the right decision!

My first match was in the 1973–1974 season, which was the year that Leeds won the old First Division. The match was a goalless draw against Derby at the old Baseball Ground. I don't have any memories of the match itself except standing on a milk crate at the front of the terraces near a corner flag. The front of the terraces were actually lower than pitch level so my head was only ankle height, which was an unusual experience for my first match. My first visit to Elland Road didn't take place until the 1979–80 season. This was a 2–0 victory over Southampton with goals from Paul Hart and Derek Parlane.

What was it like supporting the Whites in the 1980s?

The first few years of the decade I was still at school in Nottingham. When I joined the school there seemed to be a lot of Leeds fans around as the glory years had only just ended. However the late '70s and early '80s saw the emergence of Brian Clough's Nottingham Forest. Almost overnight this side went on to become First Division champions, double Champions of Europe and also winning a number of League Cup Finals at Wembley. Everyone at school and at the local park were wearing red and white and had a particular dislike of everything Leeds United because of our recent history and the infamous 44 days spell of Mr Clough. I was still haunted by an earlier 7–3 aggregate League Cup semi-final defeat to Forest in 1977–78. Forest totally outplayed Leeds over the two legs but I can still remember standing on the Bridgford End at the City Ground watching a screamer from Frankie Gray hit the back of the net in front of me and give hope that Leeds would overturn the 3–1 deficit from the first leg. I think the lead lasted about a minute!

I started work at 16 in 1982 at British Rail and with this job came my passport to start following Leeds properly. A perk of the job was that you got four free rail tickets per year. In those days the tickets were hand written passes and the Guards on the train never used to stamp them as they knew you were staff. The tickets were valid for three months so my travel to Leeds was sorted for the season. My weekly journey to follow Leeds initially involved a three-mile bike ride to my local station to catch a train to Derby. Then a train from Derby to Sheffield and another train to Leeds followed by the long walk from Leeds station to the ground. This travel pre-dates the fast intercity trains we all enjoy today and the train from Sheffield to Leeds used to take about an hour and a half and would stop at Rotherham and Barnsley and every point in between!

This period also coincided with the height of football violence during this decade and the preferred mode of travel for a football hooligan was British Rail. Looking back as a 16-year-old from a small village outside Nottingham, I was totally oblivious to the dangers of travelling week after week on trains wearing my Leeds United scarf. I witnessed many riots on a platform and saw more bricks go through train windows than I care to remember. On one occasion after a match versus West Ham, I was sat on the train at Leeds station reading all the days scores in the Football Green when a brick came through the window and landed on my lap! Thinking about it now following Leeds in the early '80s was all pretty depressing. Football violence was getting out of hand and Leeds fans were getting a reputation for being one of the worst offenders. I recall going to matches (against Blackburn Rovers and Shrewsbury I think?) when all the terraces were closed as a punishment for crowd violence and there would only have been around 10 or 11,000 fans in the ground.

The team were not particularly successful after relegation and a succession of former players tried to turn around our fortunes. The Allan Clarke era team was a mixture of youth and fading players who had taken the side down. I really enjoyed watching the Eddie Gray team which was built on some talented young players and played very attractive and open football. Unfortunately this did not deliver a successful team and Gray was then replaced by Billy Bremner and his workmanlike side that fell short in both the Play-off and the FA Cup semi-final. I probably watched Leeds more during the 1980s than any other decade but typically just as we got good again with the arrival of Howard Wilkinson, I met my future wife whilst working in Birmingham and my trips to Elland Road became less frequent. I actually got married on the day we won promotion at Bournemouth in May 1990!

Favourite player in the 1980s?

Ask me my favourite player from the '70s and that is easy, Lorimer. My favourite from the '90s is an even easier choice Batty and from recent times it is Delph (yes I know he only played a handful of matches in League One but he was something special for such a young age). However, the '80s is a much more difficult choice. It would be easy to go for one of the players from Wilko's successful side (Speed, Strachan, Batty again) but it is only appropriate to pick a player from a more under achieving side. I therefore have to go for John Sheridan. This selection is probably based entirely on the free kick he scored against Derby County when he flicked the ball with one foot and then volleyed it into the roof of the net with the other. That is probably not fair as he was a talisman for that team and by far the most gifted player we had during that era.

Best moment in the 1980s?

This is really difficult. At the start of the decade we were a fading Division One side, which were soon relegated. Whilst things improved after the arrival of Wilko, the promotion back up actually took place in 1990. In between was pretty rubbish. It therefore has to be the start of the 1989–90 season where for the first time in the decade we had a side capable of getting out of the league.

Worst moment supporting Leeds in the 1980s?

Relegation. Having beaten Brighton on the Saturday in our final home match, we went to West Brom needing just a point (I think?) to stay up and avoid relegation. I didn't go to the match but remembered listening to it on Radio Two. The 2–0 defeat which was marred by significant crowd trouble saw Leeds relegated from the top division for the first time in my lifetime. At the time it was incomprehensible as we were the mighty Leeds United. The FA Cup semi-final defeat in 1987 was also a major disappointment. Other than beating QPR at home, we had had a pretty easy run to the semi-final. There was real hope that Leeds would make it to Wembley for the first time in 14 years.

Did you see any of the hooliganism live?

Travelling to watch Leeds home and away on British Rail I witnessed lots of scraps and violence at the stations and on trains. I do not recall any particular violence at grounds but I think this is because most matches were a powder keg that could explode at any moment and often it did, so violence was just the norm. It was commonplace for the opposing fans to try and break into the home or away end for a quick scrap. Today all that gets thrown is a few insults and a bit of light hearted banter, whereas in the '80s it was permanently raining coins, bottles and concrete that had been broken away from the crumbling terraces. It was a normal occurrence for the opposing fans to try and break into each other's end for a scrap and often they were successful and the fight would go on for a few minutes before the police managed to break things up. This was of course all pre Hillsborough and the grounds, terraces, crowds etc. are nothing like the modern stadia and family atmosphere that we experience now.

Best match in the 1980s?

I probably didn't realise at the time how special it was, but I was at Old Trafford in February 1981 when Brian Flynn scored a late goal to beat man utd 1–0. Who would've thought it would've been a further 30 years before we won there again.

Worst match in the 1980s?

A 7–2 defeat at Stoke in the 1986–87 season is about as low as it got. There is another match that stands out for me which sort of encapsulates how far we had fallen. In 1984–85 we were beaten 5–2 at Oxford United in a match where we were leading either 2–0 or 2–1. Oxford United were a side going up the leagues from non-league and had limited if any pedigree as a football team. From memory, this match was shown on *Match of the Day* (for in those days they didn't just show matches from the top league), so the nation was able to witness our collapse in the second half. What was most depressing was that the Leeds fans behind the goal rioted with parts of the ground being ripped up and thrown onto the pitch. Oxford United were a small club, in a quaint ground attended by Dads and their young sons with the camera panning around showing them fearing for their safety. The commentary quite rightly was pretty scathing about Leeds as a club and in particular the fans and it was all very depressing. How the mighty falls aptly sums up that day.

What was the atmosphere like following Leeds in the 1980s?

In the final home match of the 1981–82 season against Brighton. We were deep in relegation trouble and after going a goal down we came back to win 2–1. I was sat in the South Stand to watch a Kevin Hird screamer at that end win the match late on for Leeds. At that time it was the best atmosphere I had ever witnessed at Elland Road. I think the results elsewhere had gone in our favour and everyone in the ground was convinced we would now stay up, with just a final away match to play at West Brom on the Tuesday.

What affect did Howard Wilkinson have on the club?

I was not overjoyed with the appointment of Wilkinson. Having grown up in Nottingham I had seen and watched his style of play since when he worked with Jimmy Sirrell at Notts County. His reputation for producing dour and unattractive sides had been reinforced at Sheffield Wednesday. However, looking back now at what he achieved and how he changed the culture of the club after a succession of managers, who had played under Don Revie, it was pretty incredible.

Most important signing in the 1980s?

This has to be Gordon Strachan. He only arrived late in 1988 but the banana eating Scottish genius singly inspired the team to promotion and the Championship a few years later. With all the managers we have had over recent times I am amazed that he has never got the job.

Favourite season supporting Leeds in the 1980s?

In a strange way it was the first season after relegation in Division Two, which was the 1982–83 season. This was because this was the first season that I first started watching Leeds home and away on a regular basis. This side still had players like Frank Worthington, Arthur Graham, Frank Gray and Kenny Burns. I used to deliver Burn's newspaper as a kid in Nottingham when he was playing for Forest and had just won the European Cup. Bizarrely some 20 years later I ended up playing a Sunday morning match of football in Derby against him. I was directly against Burns as we were both playing central midfield. At that time he was an overweight pub landlord and must have been near his 50th birthday. Nevertheless he still managed to control the whole match without moving from the centre circle! Another reason for picking this season is that we still had a core of popular players that had come through the system such as Terry Connor, Aidan Butterworth, Scott Sellars and John Sheridan.

Least favourite season supporting Leeds in the 1980s?

It has to be the relegation season in 1981–82. I think this needs no further explanation!

SOREN TRAPP

How long have you supported Leeds?

I have supported Leeds since 1972. I was six and my father and older brother were Arsenal fans, so I chose to support the players in white in the FA Cup Final that year. Even though Arsenal have had a lot more to cheer about in the last 40 years, I've never regretted that Leeds became my team.

First match you went to?

Leeds versus Bournemouth 3–2 on the 24 October 1987.

What was it like supporting the Whites in the 1980s?

It was frustrating and with a lot of poor football! I used to buy a lot of the matches on VHS (video) and then I received them a week or two later. But Leeds was and still is, the only club in the world for me!

Favourite player in the 1980s?

Ian Baird.

Best moment in the 1980s?

My first match at Elland Road in 1987.

Worst moment supporting Leeds in the 1980s?

The final match of the season in 1982 (when we were relegated).

Did you see any of the hooliganism live?

No, but I only attended two live matches in the 1980s. Up to this day I have never seen any real problems at Elland Road, but there were some nasty fights in an away match at Victoria Park in Hartlepool in 2009. The match was stopped at one point when the police moved in.

Best match in the 1980s?

Leeds versus Oldham in the first Play-off semi-final at Elland Road in 1987. We won 1–0 and hopes were high for promotion.

Worst match in the 1980s?

The 2–0 defeat at The Hawthorns against WBA on the final day of the 1981–82 season, they stayed up and we went down. In my deep frustration, I hurt myself by banging my head into a door! Also the Play-off Final replay in 1987 at St Andrews Stadium, where we lost 1–2 to Charlton Athletic after extra-time, was a terrible day. I also remember a 1–5 defeat to Shrewsbury in 1983 as a low point!

What was the atmosphere like following Leeds in the 1980s?

There wasn't any live coverage on Danish television and of course it was a long time before the Internet, so it was hard to keep up with the news. Therefore, I sent a letter to Leeds United and it was arranged that I bought the match day programme and it was sent to me after every home match. I also bought magazines like *Shoot!* and *Match* later on, but there weren't many Leeds supporters around in my hometown. The team weren't playing very well, so it wasn't exactly a joyride.

What affect did Howard Wilkinson have on the club?

Sergeant Wilko had a massive effect! Suddenly there was a lot of hope and belief surrounding the club.

Most important signing in the 1980s?

Gordon Strachan in 1989, he was a fantastic player and captain for us.

Favourite season supporting Leeds in the 1980s?

1989–90, it was a fantastic season! Great to return to the First Division.

Least favourite season supporting Leeds in the 1980s?

The relegation season 1981–82.

JAMES LYONS

How long have you supported Leeds?

I've been supporting Leeds for over 40 years.

First match you went to?

My first match was the season after we were Champions, I think against Leicester.

What was it like supporting the Whites in the 1980s?

Watching Leeds in the '80s was the best times in my view, I very rarely missed matches.

Favourite player in the 1980s?

John Sheridan.

Best moment in the 1980s?

Winning Promotion!

Worst moment supporting Leeds in the 1980s?

Losing to Coventry in 1987.

Did you see any of the hooliganism live?

I saw hooliganism at nearly every match… Odsal, Brum, Millwall, West Brom are the ones that I remember most and also Chelsea in 1984.

Best match in the 1980s?

The best match apart from Bournemouth away, I'd say QPR in the cup in 1987.

Worst match in the 1980s?

Too many to mention Stoke 6–2 and 7–2 were particularly bad. Shrewsbury 5–1 was also bad.

What was the atmosphere like following Leeds in the 1980s?

The atmosphere especially away, was always intimidating.

What affect did Howard Wilkinson have on the club?

Wilkinson was given money and made some excellent signings with Strachan, Fairclough and Zico etc.

Most important signing in the 1980s?

Strachan.

Favourite season supporting Leeds in the 1980s?

Promotion season in 1989.

Least favourite season supporting Leeds in the 1980s?

1982 relegation.

HEIDI HAIGH

How long have you supported Leeds?

I have supported Leeds for 50 years ever since seeing them for the first time on television with the FA Cup Final against Liverpool in 1965.

First match you went to?

I can't remember who we played but it was in 1967 when I was aged 12. My friend's dad took me along with another friend called Fiona for my friend Sue's 12th birthday present. We stood on Lowfields Road terracing and were overjoyed at half-time when they played a request for us all over the Tannoy, saying all our names! This song sticks in my mind which is *Lily the* Pink by the Scaffold! Being at a live match was fantastic and ensured I was a Leeds United supporter for life!

What was it like supporting the Whites in the 1980s?

I stopped going to away matches for the first two seasons of the decade after having my first two children Jamie and Michelle. I still went to all the home matches though and the crowds dwindled very much due to the football that was being played at the time. I was pregnant with Michelle in 1982 and stood at the top of the Kop with Jamie and my friends. This would have been unheard of in the seventies when you had to be in the Kop by 1.00 pm to get to the top due to it being packed. After enduring dire football under Jimmy Adamson's management it was a terrible time to watch Leeds but loyalty as a supporter wouldn't stop you going. When he resigned early in 1980 after taking over in 1978, Allan Clarke was installed as manager. There was real hope that change was around the corner and his first season wasn't too bad. Unfortunately in his second season with us, we got off to a bad start at Swansea and never really recovered. We thought we had escaped relegation though when we played Brighton in our last home match when we won 2–1. Unfortunately a few days later after defeat at West Bromwich Albion this ended our First Division status with our relegation to Division Two.

Somehow this galvanised our support to stick with them through thick and thin. I had started going back to sporadic away matches then I became secretary of the Leeds United Supporters Club Selby Branch organising transport and tickets to away matches. I then had another seven years without missing a match home or away. To miss a match wasn't an option; I would be there regardless of how Leeds were playing. The football or lack of it more often than not, got in the way of a good day out!

Favourite player in the 1980s?

Billy Bremner always was and always will be my hero. To then take on a favourite player after him was never going to be easy. I liked a player who tried hard and was competitive so people like David Batty, Ian Baird, John Sheridan and Vinnie Jones were favourites at the time.

Best moment in the 1980s?

Finishing the end of the era by being promoted back to the First Division. That was a euphoric moment to know we had done it!

Worst moment supporting Leeds in the 1980s?

Although relegation was hard to accept, I feel the 1986–87 season was worse. Being so near yet so far with both the FA Cup semi-final defeat against Coventry and the Play-off defeat against Charlton were gut wrenching. Billy Bremner my hero was also managing the club at that time, so the feelings were doubly felt as he had nearly steered us back to the big time!

*Michelle and Jamie with Lee Chapman
photo courtesy Heidi Haigh*

*Michelle with Gary Speed photo
courtesy Heidi Haigh*

*Selby Whites
Voyager International
photo Dave Morris*

*Selby Whites on Tour 1988-1989
photo courtesy Mark Dovey*

*Selby Whites on way to Barnsley 1988
photo Steve Waterhouse*

Dave Morris, Heidi Haigh and Shaun Livsey at Maine Road 1987-1988 photo Dave Morris

Selby Whites lads photo courtesy Dave Morris

Heidi asking for directions on way to Crystal Palace 1989 photo Steve Waterhouse

Selby Whites Port Vale away - photo courtesy Dave Morris

Did you see any of the hooliganism live?

I wasn't at West Bromwich Albion when we were relegated but was at all the other matches in the eighties where there was trouble. Birmingham will always stick out for me in 1985. It was 11 May, my friend Karen's birthday and is a date I will never forget. The trouble started when Birmingham fans invaded the pitch (we were told later that there were some Chelsea fans amongst them). There wasn't much fighting on the pitch as the two sets of supporters were kept apart by the police with dogs and horses although mayhem reigned throughout the match. What annoyed me afterwards was that every time they showed the rioting on the television, they would show the Birmingham fans on the pitch but always said it was us when it wasn't.

The worst thing was finding out at the end of the match that a Leeds fan had died when a wall collapsed. The Leeds fans had been forced into an area when the police decided they wanted to clear the ground and the wall gave way under the pressure of the fans. Ian Hambridge attending his first ever match from Northampton died that day and I will always feel for his family. He was 15 years old and his parents said in a newspaper interview that he is the forgotten victim and I tend to agree. The events at Birmingham were overshadowed by the tragic fire at Bradford on the same day where 56 people died. Recently Danny Priestley a Leeds fan and others have raised money for the 56+1, 30 years after the event.

Best match in the 1980s?

Bournemouth away on 5 May 1990 securing promotion. Actually being there to savour the moment was a special time especially when Chapman headed home the winner!

Worst match in the 1980s?

Probably the defeats at Stoke. I think the 7–2 defeat was the worst but the gallows humour from the Leeds fans doing congas made you forget about the football. The fans are what kept you going to the matches regardless of the lack of football. The comradeship is something that is still evident to this day and something that means a lot to me.

What was the atmosphere like following Leeds in the 1980s?

Although the crowds were down, the Leeds fans at Elland Road ensured there was a very intimidating atmosphere. Leeds fans congregated in both the South Stand and the Kop which were behind both goals and the atmosphere was fantastic. The fans have always been passionate about supporting their club and it is always something that I savoured as I loved the singing and chanting.

What affect did Howard Wilkinson have on the club?

I didn't like the fact that he wanted rid of all our history by taking all the photos of my heroes down from the walls. What he did do though was bring a vision with him by organising our Academy to bring the young players through for the future. He also brought the good times back to Leeds by getting us promoted to the First Division then winning the First Division Title in 1992 ensuring Leeds were the last proper Champions!

Most important signing in the 1980s?

Vinnie Jones and Gordon Strachan. By ensuring we had some steel in our midfield with Jones, together with the creative flair from Strachan, it gave us the required depth we needed to move forward. Although Jones came with a reputation as a bit of a bad boy after a picture emerged of him holding Gascoigne by the b***s, I can honestly say that he was a brilliant ambassador for Leeds United. He is still held in high esteem with Leeds fans.

Favourite season supporting Leeds in the 1980s?

Although the 1986–87 season was a favourite despite the outcome, I would say the promotion season of 1989–90 as there was a genuine feeling of optimism in the air. There was a fantastic buzz about the place and the Leeds fans were in full voice everywhere!

Least favourite season supporting Leeds in the 1980s?

1981–82 with the ups and downs of emotions thinking we could stave off relegation, to finally succumbing to this in the end!

G FROM SOUTH LEEDS, POPEYE, MARK DOVEY AND KBEES

G FROM SOUTH LEEDS

I was brought up in Belle Isle, Leeds 10, which was a very tough place with a passionate Leeds support. It was quite a deprived area with very little going for it. Playing football on the local field against different estates was a regular thing with many times it ending up with a massive brawl at the end. Most of us left school in the late '70s early '80s. The vast majority gaining apprenticeships and for the first time in our lives, having some money in our pockets. The football casual scene was just taking off. A unique and different style of clothing, which took off in a big way in Leeds. I remember as a youth going to matches and just staring at the opposition fans, eyeing up what clobber they were wearing. The football was dreadful and secondary, but football violence was a massive part of our lives. They used to say it was a minority who caused trouble. Maybe that is correct, but it was a big minority. We were decent hardworking people who got wrapped up in the bug that was football violence.

Match day used to always be an early start catching the bus into Leeds, either for a shopping spree or if it was a big match, to wait for visiting fans to arrive on the service train or football special. Coming to Leeds back then must have been daunting for an away fan. The Black Lion and Prince of Wales used to be packed out with lads. You would get little pockets of fans going for a walk to try and sniff out any visiting fans. I can also remember regular faces who would work alone. They were not part of a group but would just walk up to the opposition fans and have a go. The biggest and best turnout at home for me was Millwall in the mid '80s. We won the match 3–1 I think with Peter Swan scoring! We were playing poor at the time, but the crowd for this match which was 15,000 was about 5,000 up on the last match. In town before the match, I have never seen so many lads in casual gear. It ran into thousands not hundreds. Millwall even back then had a poor away following numbers wise, but always brought handy lads. They had a virtual empty section standing and some in the Lowfields's seats. During the match a few Leeds who had infiltrated their end stood at the front and offered all the Millwall fans out. A few punches were thrown and the Leeds lot were marched out to massive cheers from the mass ranks of lads in the South Stand and Lowfields's standing.

The casual scene was taking off all over the country. The main areas that took the lead initially were the Cockneys, Mancs and Scousers, with the rest following. Leeds was not blessed with that many shops back then to get your gear. My favourite was a shop called No Sweat in Chapel Allerton. A Fila or Ellesse tracksuit could set you back £100, which back then was a lot of money. I once bought a yellow diamond Pringle jumper from Terry Cooper

Sports one Saturday morning and had it ripped in a fight with Boro fans on Wesley Street the same day!

Leeds United are quite a unique football club. We are despised all over the country. Clubs who we do not really care about sing the *We all hate Leeds Scum* song. Would we ever sing about them? Do we class them as rivals? The two main factors as to why clubs love us to be their rival is because on the pitch, the Revie team in the '60s/'70s dominated with a swagger and arrogance unknown to the English game. Following that, the volatile reputation of our fans in the '80s, meant that over three decades on and off the pitch we were the top dogs. During our Second Division days we did not always get the recognition we deserved. Many authors who brought out books were very blinkered in their accounts of trouble at matches. Pennant from West Ham and Cowans from Sheffield United always claimed they never got done, when in reality every mob came unstuck at some stage.

Pennant mentioned Leeds and how they came in the South Stand early claiming a fantastic result. The reality was that they were escorted to the ground early and paid in via the West Stand ticket office around 12.30 pm, hardly a result eh? During the match they were as quiet as mice in the small section they had, top right facing the pitch. He conveniently forgot about when Leeds scattered the invincible Inter City Firm of West Ham hooligans (ICF) at the market at their place. Cowans mentioned that in '85 they beat Leeds on points over the two matches that season as if it had been a boxing match! Probably the biggest bullsh****r in the history of booksellers! They brought a mob to Leeds and got wrapped up; they were like scared rabbits approaching Elland Road. At their place we had a mob in with them and absolutely battered them outside the ground. How he got a win on points beggared belief!! The best book for me with a proper honest account was *The Guvnor's* by Man City. We got very high praise indeed!

Our bitter rivals always were man utd (scum). We played them in the early '80s then had a gap until the Wilko era when we got promoted. They played us once at Elland Road around 1980 when they had a chance of winning the League, the last match of the season. It was estimated they brought well over 10,000 fans. I was a 17-year-old at the time and fascinated by the intense fighting before and after the match. Scum used to take over most grounds back then, but not that day. Every lunatic Leeds fans turned out and weighed in to any scum fan who was looking for it that day. Another year Leeds ambushed their escort at the top of Elland Road. Everyone gathered on the hill at the side of the church. It was like a scene from Zulu! The tightly packed scum escort came under attack from all angles. They took a serious beating that day. It took a long time for Leeds to get their act sorted at scum. When Flynn got the winner, we had all the Scoreboard and part of the Paddock. Also if you check out the winning goal on YouTube, we had loads in their seats. We had to wait until Beckford scored in the FA Cup on 3 January 2010 for our next win there! Some people say the rivalry is one way, absolute bull, they sing about Leeds all the time! One day we will be back competing against the team we love to hate.

All of the lads I used to go to matches with were all in good jobs and away from football would never really engage in breaking the law. The one thing we all had in common was the fact we were Leeds and defended the badge off the field at all costs. It was as equally important to me as the result of the match. Elland Road was very rarely full back in them days, but the atmosphere for big matches was very raw and hostile. If I had to pick out a few matches where the ground was a cauldron, it would be the following. Brighton the relegation season, QPR in the FA Cup and the Play-off matches versus Oldham and Charlton. Whenever you hear fans or players of other clubs talking about the worst ground to attend, Elland Road is always mentioned from back in the '80s. I would have hated to be a club who nobody really cares about. A nice friendly family club! The fans who followed Leeds back then helped shape our reputation which today is still intact. We are known as Dirty Leeds to everyone and we would not have it any other way!

Another memory for me from the '80s, was going down to Elland Road and watching the team train on Fullerton Park. The summer of 1989 was when Leeds started to rise again. We made some exciting signings and had a squad ready to compete again. I remember a session one hot day when there were a couple of thousand to watch a training session. I watched from the roof of the old Supporters Club, which was packed. Vinnie Jones and Gordon Strachan were just a couple of the players we had brought in. When the players had finished training it took them ages to get from the training pitch to the stadium with fans all wanting autographs. This was the start of something special, a season where Elland Road was a cauldron for almost every match. The Kop, Lowfields, and South Stand were packed with fanatical support. No prawn munchers at Elland Road that season! It was a great time being Leeds. We had our fun off the pitch, but now the famous Whites were on their way back on the pitch!

I think the main reason that Leeds got a fearsome reputation off the pitch was because the teenage lads in Leeds during the '80s will have had fathers who were brought up on the great Revie team. All my mates were Leeds fans. A kid who is 10 years of age today will not have seen Leeds in the top flight. Unless his father is very staunch they will not be getting the bug like we did. Football will never be like the '80s again. It was a unique time following football. I feel sorry for the youth element who tries to recreate them days gone by. Leeds still does have casuals, but to throw a punch now at a football match can mean a charge of affray and a 12-month jail sentence. A loss of family and job means too much to lose.

As a young lad I always used to love travelling to London. You had to be on your guard always against the Cockneys. We once went to Millwall on a Saturday morning at 2.30am after coming out of the nightclub! We went by coach for a dinnertime kick off. Everyone was absolutely steaming. One lad called Macca from East End Park was talking to me in a kebab shop before we set off. I told him what we were doing and he then said, "I'm coming, is there any room?" I said, "ain't your lass expecting you home?" He said, "she'll be asleep, I'll deal with her when I get back!"

Millwall is in a very tough neighbourhood and when Leeds played every lunatic from down there used to turn out. It was a daunting place, but Leeds were one of the few clubs who would take numbers to The Den. They would never admit it, but they will have respected us deep down. I always found Spurs and West Ham horrible places to visit. We took a right mob to Spurs in the Cup one year and it went off big time after the match. Also we took a massive mob to West Ham where Leeds did them at the market before the match. Cass Pennant paints a different picture in his fantasy book about the ICF! We played Arsenal at Highbury and all the Leeds fans were in the middle section of the Clock End and for some reason the police were letting Leeds fans in through the turnstiles to the left facing the pitch, but we had to cut through the home fans to get to the middle. Just before kick off the Service Crew charged the entire Arsenal into the side of the pitch with zero resistance. I got kicked out of the ground but just paid back in! Another day of fun and games was versus Chelsea last match of the season. One hundred and fifty got nicked before kick-off and Leeds fans smashed the scoreboard up. Chelsea invaded the pitch whilst the police kept the fans apart. The incidents that day made the national news. I hate Cockneys more than Mancs or Scousers. They think they're something else but most of the time they were all mouth, rarely returning the favour and travelling up north.

In January 1987 Leeds were drawn away to non-league Telford in the FA Cup. The match was to be played at West Bromwich Albion's ground The Hawthorns on a Sunday morning. The chosen venue was the ground where Leeds were relegated from Division One and where a riot took place. I can honestly say this was the coldest I have ever been at a football match. We went down on a double decker bus from Leeds centre. It was packed with young lads drinking ice cold cans of beer and you could not see through the windows because of the ice! The crowd was around 6,400 with half that from Leeds. Ian Baird scored both our goals in a 2–1 win. We scraped our way through with nobody thinking that season we would reach the semi-final. Leeds fans were throwing snowballs at each other all through the match. The loyalty of our support was tested that day. The early kick off and dreadful weather did not deter Leeds travelling in numbers. We had suffered for years, very similar to the last 10 years since we left the Premier League, but our away support is legendary and we were back then in the top five for the amount of fans that travelled away.

POPEYE

Leeds Utd v Charlton play-off replay – 1986–87. Any Leeds fan of a certain age (mid-forties to early fifties), too young to remember Don Revie's aces but old enough to remember relegation and the doldrum years of the mid-eighties, must look at this match as the most stomach wrenching disappointing defeat that any fan could take! As a young fan, I didn't witness the injustice of Paris '75 or indeed relegation in '82, but started going to matches on my own with pals in '83. Then

1986–87 'a season to savour' came along and as a fan turning from 17 to 18, it was a season full of hope and promise after the close season signing of the goal machine Keith Edwards! I thought the FA Cup semi-final defeat at Hillsborough that season was possibly the lowest I could ever feel being a Leeds fan. It was such a massive disappointment in front of the biggest crowd I had ever witnessed but how wrong I was!!!!!! After a 0–1 defeat at Selhurst Park courtesy of a late goal by Jim Melrose in the first leg and Leeds winning the second leg at Elland Road 1–0 in front of over 30,000 fans with a Bob Taylor/Brendan Ormsby goal, it was all down to a replay to be played at a neutral ground the home of Birmingham City, St Andrews. Our family holiday had been booked to North Wales in the Play-off Final week (yes I know, how mum and dad could have been so optimistic that we would go up automatically!) So as mum, dad and my sister travelled to Wales, I was on my way to Charlton and afterwards I was allowed to stay home alone in Leeds for the second leg on the Monday and then get the train to Wales on the Tuesday.

In a time of when the only way to communicate was a good old fashioned land line telephone, I spent most of Tuesday, Wednesday and Thursday lobbing 10 pence pieces into phone boxes at every given opportunity, frantically trying to secure my ticket for the replay on Friday in Birmingham. I eventually sorted my ticket and travel out, BUT I had to travel from Leeds, so after some serious nattering to mum and dad they agreed to cut our holiday short. On Friday morning we returned back to Leeds for around 1.30 pm and I was on a double decker bus on my way to Birmingham at 2.30 pm. After a few hours travel and a pub stop later, we arrived at St Andrews to a sea of yellow, white and blue everywhere I looked. There were just Leeds fans everywhere and a chorus of *'We're on the march with Billy's Army, we're not going to Wembley and we couldn't give a f**k, 'cos we know we're going up, 'cos Leeds are the greatest football team'* was ringing out and we were all on a wave of optimism.

After a first 45 minutes of cautious football and the only thing of note was what turned out to be a serious injury to captain Brendan Ormsby, surely the second half had to be better! A second half of few chances followed most notably a John Sheridan free-kick just skimming the top of the crossbar. The final whistle blew 0–0 so after two legs and 90 minutes of a replay unable to separate the two sides, it was all down to 30 minutes of extra-time and then possibly penalties!!!! Ten minutes into the first half of extra-time it's a free-kick for Leeds on the edge of the area in a position very similar to where Shez had skimmed the bar earlier in the match. Shez was stood four yards away from the ball pointing at the Charlton wall and in an almost casual way stroked the ball over the wall and past Bob Bolder into the back of the net; YYYYEEEEESSSSS went up the cry from 18,000 Leeds fans although the noise suggested there could have been at least 50,000 there! Everyone was going mental it really was absolute pandemonium. The whistle blew for the end of the first half of extra-time and we were almost up!!!!!!

The second half began and seemed to be the longest 15 minutes in my entire life. There were seven minutes left to play when Charlton somehow managed to finally have an attempt on the Leeds goal. Peter 'f*****g' Shirtliff (still to this day I cannot bring myself to say his name without swearing) a big daft defender somehow turned into a prolific goal machine, scored and then four minutes later scored again. Within a matter of a few minutes and before we know it we are 2–1 down with two minutes left to play. The three stands at St Andrews that had just erupted like Mount Vesuvius only moments ago stood silently in absolute disbelief and shock. The final whistle went, the season was over and as the Charlton players went to celebrate with their 300 fans in the small corner of St Andrews, the contingent of 18,000 Leeds fans slowly dusted themselves down and burst into the loudest and proudest 'MARCHING ON TOGETHER' that I have ever heard. King Billy and the players just stood and watched in awe and then came over throwing shirts, shorts, socks and boots into the fans then walking down the tunnel in nothing more than their underwear. Then in the silent procession back to the buses I and many others shed a tear or two. A few of the older guys on our bus consoled me and a few other younger fans and told me, "It's Leeds United pal, get used to it". The only thing about the whole episode is that it really is LEEDS UNITED AND I AM STILL GETTING USED TO IT! Popeye age 46 M.O.T!

MARK DOVEY

I remember travelling down to Wembley at midnight for the Mercantile Credit Football League Centenary Festival that took place over two days on Saturday and Sunday 16 and 17 April 1988. This was to celebrate the 100th Anniversary of the Football League and involved Leeds United. The other teams that were taking part were Wolves, Aston Villa, Nottingham Forest, Blackburn Rovers, Everton, Wigan, Liverpool, man utd, Sunderland, Newcastle, Sheffield Wednesday, Tranmere Rovers, Luton Town, Crystal Palace and Wimbledon, although I've no idea how the teams were chosen to take part!

The first match that Leeds were involved in, was the First Round with a 10.00 am kick-off. Turnstiles were opened at 9.00 am and tickets were priced at £6.00. We were soundly beaten 3–0 by Nottingham Forest and were knocked out of the competition pronto having played only one match! I think most of us from the Leeds United Supporter's Club Selby Branch went, as we had near enough a full coach because it was the first time some of us had seen Leeds at Wembley. The coach had been hired for two days though so even though we'd been knocked out, we were there for the duration. On Saturday night, we all slept on the coach!

The next day the turnstiles were opened at 11.00am in readiness for the first semi-final. I still have my tickets from both of these matches and the Sunday one says Turnstiles A, Entrance 23, East Upper Standing Enclosure. Again it was a £6.00 ticket but this time for a reserved standing place. The Leeds fans were located in their own area as were all the other clubs. We mingled with the Newcastle fans as they had brought loads with them too, filling our allocated section as did

Selby Whites at Mercantile Credit tournament Wembley 16 and 17 April 1988
photo Steve Waterhouse

Mercantile Tournament Tickets
photo Mark Dovey

the Geordies. Even though we were beaten we still had a great weekend with no trouble, just lots of boozing and having a laugh with the Geordies as we were all northern fans.

One time that is etched in my memory was the day I got John Sheridan's shirt when we played Birmingham away on a Friday night. At the end of the match when the team came to our end, he threw his shirt to me, which I caught. I was over the moon and when I showed it off on the coach, found out that someone else from our branch had got Neil Aspin's shorts! Later at a Supporter's club do, we had Glynn Snodin on our table so he got Shez to come over and sign this for me! I wore this shirt everywhere and was gutted when someone stole it off my washing line never to be seen again. Glynn Snodin remembered me in later years when he saw me and said, "hello Mark", which nearly floored my mate as he wanted to know how he knew me. I have kept every shirt since the 1980s Lion Cabinet one, which would fit a six or seven year old!

Another time at Birmingham just before we went to Wembley when Tony Yeboah scored, Leeds fans tried shaking the scaffolding, which had the TV box on top of it which was in the Leeds end. I can't remember who was commentating in the box but they had them panicking as we thought it was going to come down with them in it! There was some trouble as Birmingham fans invaded the pitch at the end.

I was also at Birmingham for the last match of the season too in 1985 when the wall came down. We had a remote chance of going up and took thousands of fans. When we got there, it was kicking off on the grass area at the back of the away end and we just got in the ground as there were cops and horses everywhere. There was trouble in the seats after the Birmingham fans invaded the pitch and tried coming to our end as our fans were trying to climb the fence at the front to get at them.

At the end of the match they brought the police horses over to the Leeds fans and then forced everyone back into the stand, with cops coming in too, launching at anyone with truncheons whether woman, kid or youth. Everyone got squashed in the back where the turnstiles were when the wall suddenly collapsed as we were coming out and that's when a brick hit me. I couldn't

175

avoid it but luckily only had one cut to my head but not massive. As we didn't know if anyone was under the collapsed wall or who, we tried to help but the cops came and shoved us away. We found out later that a lad had died under it and it hurt to know someone had needed our help and we could have tried to help him.

I used to travel with my mate Chris Foster to matches and there was lots of trouble in the eighties. I can remember going to Millwall for an early kick-off with them bricking our coaches from the railway bridge, many times we came back with no windows. We set off at approximately 2.00 am from Sherburn for this but we just did it! Millwall set fire to the seats in Lowfields the season they went up and won the League with Sheringham and Cascarino. Bradford at Odsal, I was in the queue waiting for some food when some Leeds fans started messing about, then what started as something harmless ended up being really serious and the chip van ended up in flames. After that it all kicked off and the Bradford fans came onto the pitch first from the seats and ran to the Leeds fans, so ours ran over to them and into the seats where they scattered. There had been fighting at the station on the way to the match too.

I was at Bournemouth when we got promoted, Bolton when we got relegated but was in their end not the Leeds end. When it came to the Play-offs with Carlisle in 2008, me and Danny my son, had been to every match home and away and didn't get a ticket, but luckily got four off a lad who did programmes from Crystal Records in London. It didn't seem right that there were fans there who had only been to one or two matches that season.

Later on when Leeds were in the Champions League I decided to go to Barcelona as I thought that we wouldn't get very far, but it went on and on and we kept beating the cream. We had a right team. Where we had been at Bristol Rovers on a Friday night match a few years ago, now I was in the Bernabau stadium in a stand that shook when we all sang; the world of Leeds United eh?

I travelled with the club on all the organised trips when we played in Milan, Rome and Munich and it cost thousands to follow them. My favourite one was Real Madrid where there were 15 planes lined up in a row for all the Leeds fans going, which was something else and I will never forget that sight for as long as I live. Causing mayhem in the middle of Madrid by altering the roadwork signs! Moscow, we flew there after a five-hour flight only to find out the match had been called off! Besiktas was the only place I wouldn't go to as I was not going back to Istanbul. After the murders of Christopher Loftus and Kevin Speight when Leeds played Galatasary on 5 April 2000, I will not return there.

Bristol Rovers when Beckford scored, I have never heard Elland Road as loud as it was that day apart from when Viduka got a hat-trick as Leeds beat Liverpool at Elland Road. I could just see the Play-offs coming after Gradel was sent off, then Howson's screamer came and it all changed that day! Finally, going to Fulham last season where unbelievably 5,000 Leeds fans turned up for a non-meaning match and the stick that McCormack got! No one else can touch us for loyalty! All great memories that cannot be taken away from us!

KBEES

It was at Derby away where I got my biggest hiding at a match. For some reason Leeds fans were allowed in the seats above their main singing area and also down the side standing. In the second half the Leeds fans started ripping wooden seats out which cleared the Derby end unsurprisingly. I was in the seats down the side above the Leeds fans, which was the home end. With about 15 minutes left, a load of Derby came in to have a go at a group of Leeds. Me and my mate joined in and it went on for a good 10 minutes. No police were about as they were dealing with some other trouble elsewhere in the ground. I got my foot stuck down the back of the seat and got battered. I managed to get away and ended up in the first aid room surrounded by Derby fans with cut heads! The final score was 3–3, a match we were comfortable with until pressing the self-destruct button as usual. I ended up seeing myself on Look North on the Monday as the trouble had made the headlines. Derby was always one of the grounds where trouble was guaranteed. We never had a real hatred for them and it's the same today. However, once again they are one of our one-way rivals, always singing we all f*****g hate Leeds all the time. That's what made following Leeds away in the '80s good because you knew every man and his dog would turn out for us.

PRE-SEASON 2015
BY HEIDI HAIGH

Looking back at how things were in the '80s; our fans took many a beating at away matches in the '70s but all of a sudden there were many lads of the same age, who grew up and started fighting back. If anything happened, most of them joined in and some got carried away with the moment. Many a time, they wouldn't start any trouble but some wouldn't run away and would always stand and fight if they were attacked. I actually felt safer in the '80s travelling and attending the matches and many times, it was good to have these fans there to protect you.

The media though would always portray Leeds fans in a bad light, admittedly sometimes it was deserved, but many times it wasn't! They always went into overdrive when Leeds fans were involved in anything. It wouldn't be so bad if other fans also received the same bad press for events involving them, but for some reason they never did! I can remember travelling to Crystal Palace and despite there being some trouble with their fans in the ground, the London papers were keen to report that Leeds fans had been involved. It had nothing to do with our fans, so I wrote to the paper to complain. I received a response saying that they had retracted their first report when they realised they had got it wrong! The trouble was, it was too late as people had already seen the first article and then they jump to conclusions! It also meant that we had a reputation regardless of whether we did anything or not.

I never liked trouble or condoned it, but trouble always followed me around. As I was so scared many times, I never wanted it anywhere near me. For some reason, the more scared I became, the more trouble appeared around me!

This brings me to the current time having just returned from the pre-season tour with Leeds to Austria and Norway in July 2015. Below is the blog I wrote about the tour that I posted on social media on my return:

DAY 1 – ON MONDAY 20 JULY 2015

I had an early morning start at 5.30 am with my husband dropping me off at the airport to fly to Salzburg, Austria on the first stage of our European tour. Following Leeds United on the pre-season tour to Austria and Norway was to be an early birthday present for me. My friend Sue was on Mick Hewitt's trip and I was travelling on Roy Schofield's trip. Everything was booked for me so all I had to do was turn up and meet the others in my group. Roy, Ray, Sue, John, Lyn, Doug and Pam were the people I travelled with.

Sue and I have been friends for 49 years, started supporting Leeds 50 years ago and are still dedicated followers of Leeds United to this day. We are both loyal supporters like many others.

My books *Follow Me and Leeds United* and *Once a Leeds fan, always a Leeds fan* were also going on the tour.

On arrival I got a map and was shown where the Old Town was, as that was where the Leeds fans who had got there early had been heading over the last two days. I had a pleasant walk alongside the river, before crossing the lock bridge. Here many people had locked padlocks on the bridge at both sides although as per usual I've already forgotten the reason why!

I walked further up on the other side of the river where I came across a square where some Leeds fans were congregated having drinks at an open-air bar. I went to say hello and saw it was Gary Edwards, Tony, Coke and others from the trip Mick Hewitt had organised. They immediately told me to sit down and join them and I was bought a drink of coke. It was a lovely warm evening with everyone in good spirits. Tony kept breaking into Leeds songs he had written and even got a round of applause from other people sat around the same bar area.

DAY 2 – TUESDAY 21 JULY 2015.

We had no idea where Eugendorf was, where the match was taking place and couldn't decide between taking the train or the bus. On our way to the station we asked a taxi how much it would cost for the five of us travelling together and once we were quoted five euros each we opted for that instead. We arrived at the ground to see my friends Sue, Keith and Danny get out of the taxi behind us. They'd been at the ground since 2.00 pm but as there was nothing to do down there they had opted to go into Eugendorf for a while.

It was a gloriously hot day and we were all looking forward to the match. Bumped into quite a few people who I knew as we went into the ground and there were so many familiar faces. Once we were searched on entry we went through to the refreshment area outside the ground where I saw Alan Green. I started as I meant to go on by taking photos of all and sundry. I posed beside the Berlin Whites flag that was hung on the fence by the entrance, as I thought my mum would be pleased to see it, as that is where she was born.

It was great meeting up with loads of people again and chatting to everyone left, right and centre. I met a man who was there with his daughter Jessica and he asked me if I would take a photo of her. She had brought a Teddy Bear with her who was travelling all over the world for charity. Teddy was having photos taken of him wherever he was in the world which would then be shared on *Twitter*. I was glad to help and obliged by having photos taken to show where Teddy was on his travels. The charity is Teddy's Travel and raising awareness into Thrombosis. He can be found on Twitter @TeddiesTravels.

More and more Leeds fans were arriving and many getting stuck straight into getting some beer. I headed up into the small seating area to join Sue, Keith and Danny on the front row so we had an excellent view. The match was being recorded live by Leeds United. Just before kick-off at

Photo courtesy of Heidi Haigh

6.15 pm I decided to head downstairs to the toilets before it started. When I reached the bottom of the steps I was stopped by Steve from Thames Valley Whites who told me not to go outside, as two firms of Frankfurt fans had turned up and were causing trouble outside the ground with the police holding them back. There were approximately 50 Frankfurt fans in with us in the seats and a few downstairs on the terrace at that time, who stayed there for the whole match without any issues and it was all friendly with some banter. Leeds fans had loads of flags hung up on the fence behind the left hand goal plus approximately half a dozen on the right including a massive Harehills flag and the Leeds Fans Utd flag.

I returned to my seat for the start of the match. I was told later that this stand should have been for the Frankfurt fans and we should have been on the opposite side of the ground with no facilities. Sandra Downer from Essex and her family had arrived early and ensured that Leeds fans were let into this side.

Not long after kick-off I could see that the two firms of Frankfurt fans were being let into the ground but were being sent to the far side. The next thing I saw was that two Leeds flags next to the Leeds Fans Utd flag were torn down from the fence by these fans. I couldn't believe my eyes and shouted that the b******s had got our flags, which was when I began to shake with fear once again. As it was, nothing else happened during the match as the Leeds fans drank their beer, enjoyed the sun and watched Leeds in their first foreign match. Some of the younger Leeds fans set off some flares although personally, I have no idea why they have a fixation with these flares as they smell horrible! The Harehills flag ended up being hung from the seating area where I was sat together with the Leeds Fans Utd flag and I heard that all the flags were recovered. One lad was told to hand over a flag that was thought to be stolen only to find out it actually belonged to the Leeds fan holding it! That created a laugh though but I don't think the lad holding it was impressed!

Again it was similar to the York and Harrogate pre-season matches in England that were played prior to this tour, where Leeds played a settled squad for a while before making changes. We played okay but once any changes were made we conceded very soon after. Leeds had taken the lead through Morison who took his goal well. Frankfurt eventually equalised, as we could not defend a set piece. Byram was making some good runs down the wing nearest to us in the first half as we watched to see how we would play. Eventually though, Frankfurt took the lead when we failed to clear from a corner. We didn't disgrace ourselves by any means, but our weak links in my opinion are the set pieces and corners, which we cannot defend. Silvestri made some excellent saves from shots but he cannot command his area.

As the match was nearing the end it was clear that all the Leeds fans on the terrace below were going to invade the pitch. As soon as the whistle blew they did do just that and the Leeds players were surrounded and were all having selfies taken with them and it was a carnival atmosphere. The same had happened whenever anyone was substituted; the players had to go through the

Photo courtesy of Heidi Haigh

Photo courtesy of Heidi Haigh

gauntlet of fans having their photos taken before being allowed to go to the dressing room.

All of a sudden I saw something thrown at the far side of the pitch as the Frankfurt fans climbed over the wall and ran at the Leeds fans. The Leeds fans on the pitch stood their ground and didn't run but I saw that some had been cornered and fighting began. It only took place over a few minutes, but then they ran away and as the police came over too they jumped back over the fence and ran across the field around the right side of the ground

We hung back in the ground for a while for obvious reasons and personally I didn't want to go anywhere for a while as I knew it was kicking off outside. When we did come out, the first thing we saw was a Leeds fan with his head heavily bandaged being loaded into the back of an ambulance. He looked in a very bad way and there was a pool of blood on the floor. The Frankfurt fans had been running towards the Leeds fans and as he looked round behind him, at that point he was hit hard and he fell to the floor. The Leeds fans around were going nuts at the police as it turned out that one had said he shouldn't have been there to get attacked! Unbelievable, all I know is that he was a 50–60-year-old, called Brian and worked for the UN and had headed out to catch a train. I haven't heard since that day of how he was so I really hope he is okay as many were saying he was in a bad way. Sheppy had stemmed the bleeding with his Leeds shirt whilst he was on the floor and well done to him! As we started walking a Leeds fan came up to me asking if I recognised him from years ago. He told me that one Leeds fan had had a bike chain wrapped around his head and suffered some really bad injuries!

At this moment we could see it was all kicking off at the crossroads up ahead so we walked very slowly. Eventually the Leeds fans came back who had chased them away up the road. News was trickling through that they had already caused trouble in both Salzburg and Eugendorf on the way to the ground and had weapons, as well as bike chains, belts with blades on them, were wearing balaclavas and masks and had their knuckles taped to prevent them breaking their fingers when hitting people! On a red hot day it was obvious they had come to cause trouble especially when we heard they stormed the security guards on arrival at kick-off and injured a couple, one security guard/copper was apparently stabbed. Why on earth they were let into the ground in the first place I will never know, plus how did they get the weapons in?

We had no idea where the train station was so carried on up the road as the police cars headed off past us. The policewoman at the crossroads tried sending us a different way to some other Leeds fans who were told to carry straight on! I've no idea where we would have ended up by going left as it was the opposite way to the station. As we walked further up I became very anxious as I was expecting the Frankfurt fans to come back and ambush us. When we saw some lads coming towards us I panicked until I saw some were wearing Leeds shirts. We couldn't go any further up ahead as the police were holding us all back. We stood there for absolutely ages before they let us through, approximately 100 Leeds fans. The police were all lined up to the left blocking the road as we were sent to the right. There were lads stood outside a pub but I wasn't

Photo courtesy of Heidi Haigh

Photo courtesy of Heidi Haigh

sure if they were local people or Frankfurt fans. The police were being very abrupt with our fans even though they had been stood there quietly waiting, not doing anything wrong.

I spoke German to one of them asking where the station was and if the Frankfurt fans had gone and he answered in English telling me yes and it was 10 minutes down the road. It was very quiet as we all walked down the street into the middle of nowhere. At the corner where the station was signposted to the left, that is when I noticed where the shortcut to the ground that we had been told about was over two fields. We got down to the station and went under the railway to the other side. The station consisted of two platforms with a small shelter on each side but was isolated. It wasn't long before we heard a train coming, but instead of stopping it went straight through the station at speed. I panicked a bit then thinking that they had told the trains not to stop here!

It was getting darker by the minute and was very eerie and I kept expecting the Frankfurt fans to appear out of nowhere and attack us. We got talking to a black lad who told us that he and his mate had arrived by bus. They were sat on the bus in Salzburg when about 50 Frankfurt fans arrived and jumped on the bus they were on. It got very hairy as they clocked that him and his mate were Leeds fans due to the LU badge on his mate's shirt. It was just going to kick off when luckily the police turned up and proceeded to kick them off the bus for non-payment. They gave a sigh of relief then as they came close to being attacked. That was when the Frankfurt fans proceeded to walk to the ground and was probably why they arrived at kick-off. When I heard this I was so glad that we hadn't gone for a bus!

Eventually we caught a train at 9.30 pm and we all caught this for free as no one turned up for payment. It was a relief to get back to the hotel in one piece I can tell you! I did not feel safe on the streets as I'd no idea where their fans were and what would happen next. As it was, I was glad that we had not gone out later in our Leeds things or headed to the Old Town, as we heard later that isolated Leeds fans were being targeted and attacked by some Frankfurt fans. It definitely wasn't safe to be out in our colours!

We got changed and then headed out for something to eat, it was a longer walk than we thought as Ray and Sue had said it was just up the road! In fact when we walked back it wasn't that far away but it was worth it, having an excellent meal. I spent the evening talking with David Watkins another author and his friend who I shared a table with. We were talking about the events of the day and what we had heard, but once again it was a case of Leeds fans getting attacked and standing up for themselves

On our return to our hotel we got talking to some other Leeds fans who had been very lucky after having a flare gun shot at them that had just missed the ear of one of them. He had just been talking to his wife on the phone and said, "I think I've got to go now!"

I went straight on to social media then and it was very disappointing to find out that we were trending around the world for all the wrong reasons. They were making out that our fans had been fighting and causing trouble when it couldn't have been further from the truth! As usual with the media, when it is Leeds United they go into over drive to report it but don't wait to find out the truth!

MY THOUGHTS

The above shows that whenever anything happens with Leeds fans, then they cannot wait to report it. Everyone was jumping to conclusions and blaming us for what had happened in Austria earlier in the day, when it couldn't be further from the truth! The fans who were there were dubbed the flip flop gang with their deer stalker hats! We had been enjoying the sun and having a great day out and no one was looking for any trouble. I also have a theory that those Frankfurt fans who jumped over the wall to attack our fans at the end of the match caused a diversion. My reasoning is because as other Leeds fans had already started to leave the ground, they were attacked outside whilst this was going on. The events of today were also reminiscent of the pre-season friendly tournament in Amsterdam in 1976 when something similar happened with the Ajax fans who all had weapons! The only thing is, that currently Sheppy and I haven't been able to find out how Brian is, the fan taken to hospital in the ambulance. He suffered some really bad injuries and I really hope that he has managed to get over them. I have contacted the club to ask for a message to be put on the Leeds United website for Brian to get in touch, although I have had no success. I have also put a message on all the Leeds United message boards and Facebook groups I am part of, to find out if anyone had any information on him. If anyone does know him, I would appreciate our concerns being passed on to him.

I thought football hooliganism and trouble at matches were a thing of the past, unfortunately I have seen this returning during the last year at home too. It has been prevalent amongst other fans as well for instance, some Leeds fans who were in the Blackpool stands due to a lack of tickets, ended up taking a beating. I certainly don't want to go back to the dark days of the past!

CURRENT AFFAIRS
BY HEIDI

At this moment in time, things seem to have settled down in the background with Adam Pearson's arrival. Having a positive pre-season with new signings seems to have re-kindled many fans' enthusiasm. With Uwe Rösler's appointment as coach, we will see how this appointment works although he does come across well when speaking to fan's groups. Uwe was actually born in Altenburg, in East Germany, which is not far from where my dad was born in Zeitz. It would be nice to have a conversation with him about this at some time!

I always live in hope at the start of the season and too many times in the past few years; I have found that it didn't take long before the season was already written off! I expect Leeds to at least put up a fight and challenge for promotion, so fingers crossed that this year we are heading in the right direction. Cellino is still in charge of the club despite all the off field matters going on in the background. There are still many court cases to come and the issue is whether or not they will have an impact on the club or not. I want stability and to be looking at what is going on with football on the pitch and not off field matters. Having seen the impact from the 'alleged sick note six' who didn't turn up at Charlton last season, to the way Redfearn and Thompson were treated when they certainly saved the club from relegation back to the Third Division, is something I don't want to see happen at our club ever again!

That said, the feel good factor can so easily come back again with the belief that we are united and moving in the same direction as a club with its supporters. The first match of the season Burnley at home was shown live on TV yet again, as the viewing figures they get are enormous! There was also a crowd of over 27,000 to witness the draw after going ahead with a spectacular goal from Antenucci before the sucker punch of Burnley equalising a few minutes later! Before the match we went into the Peacock beer garden to savour the beautiful weather, which always makes it feel a great start to a footballing day! The atmosphere in the ground as the teams came out was something to savour too! It was absolutely brilliant and it is lovely to have that back. By having Leeds fans once again behind both goals in the Kop and the South Stand I am hopeful we can bring the intimidating atmosphere back to Elland Road and boost the team on to win. We got our first win of the season yesterday at Derby with goals from Adeyemi and Wood with an absolute corker of a goal! Being part of our support celebrating the winner is what makes being a Leeds fan special!

Heidi's birthday card from Dani
photo courtesy Heidi Haigh

Having just celebrated my, 'I can't believe I'm 60 birthday', I couldn't help but laugh at one of the cards I received from my daughter Dani titled 'Do you know this troublemaker?' It was a tongue in cheek spoof card and was taken in the spirit it was meant! Looking back on all the trouble that has followed me around over the years, the card wasn't wrong in stating that I had been in the midst of it all, although it wasn't through choice! Despite all the trouble I've seen over the years, I still feel privileged to have had the chance to see the best team ever play football live. Don Revie and his team of players gave me the chance to follow them all over the world and have meant that I have met thousands of fans along the way. Many of these I am still friends with after all the years I have followed Leeds with some getting back in contact after 30–40 years!

Billy Bremner is my hero; he always will be, as he instilled in me the love and loyalty of supporting my team. I will always be here following Leeds United and look forward to successful times coming back once again during my lifetime!

THE FUTURE!

BY ANDREW

I am hoping for a quiet season on and off the pitch. There have been many key appointments over the summer and I think the main one has been Adam Pearson. When Massimo Cellino took over the club in April 2014, I think he underestimated the job in hand. However slowly but surely, you get the sense that things are calming down and in Uwe Rösler I feel that we have a manager, who will be able to get the best out of his players. He has made some astute signings to date, including Chris Wood and Stuart Dallas and if we can get some consistency, there is no reason why we can't be in and around the top 10. I feel if we can progress then the building blocks will be in place for a tilt at promotion over the next couple of seasons.

I remember being at the Reebok Stadium on Sunday 2 May 2004 (my 19th birthday) when Leeds were all but relegated from the Premier League and thinking it would only take 2–3 seasons to get back. Here we are after 12 seasons, still fighting to get back up to England's top table. The surrounding issue we are now faced with is that with the parachute payments handed out to relegated sides, it is making it even harder to win promotion unless you are spending silly money. I really hope that we can see the emergence of a new Leeds United side that can create more memories for the supporters that travel the breadth of the country.

A big thank you once again to all the fans who have contributed to this book. The stories shared have taken us back in time to a forgotten era. Both Heidi and I hope you have enjoyed reading about the rollercoaster of emotions that happened whilst following Leeds United during the '80s. One thing is for sure though; the Leeds fans are still as loyal now as they were all those years ago!

LUFC – *Marching on Together!*

BIBLIOGRAPHY

WEBSITES

http://www.ozwhitelufc.net.au/leeds_stats/leeds_united_match_details/Results_by_season/1980-81.php

http://www.ozwhitelufc.net.au/leeds_stats/leeds_united_match_details/Results_by_season/1981-82.php

http://www.ozwhitelufc.net.au/leeds_stats/leeds_united_match_details/Results_by_season/1982-83.php

http://www.ozwhitelufc.net.au/leeds_stats/leeds_united_match_details/Results_by_season/1983-84.php

http://www.ozwhitelufc.net.au/leeds_stats/leeds_united_match_details/Results_by_season/1984-85.php

http://www.ozwhitelufc.net.au/leeds_stats/leeds_united_match_details/Results_by_season/1985-86.php

http://www.ozwhitelufc.net.au/leeds_stats/leeds_united_match_details/Results_by_season/1986-87.php

http://www.ozwhitelufc.net.au/leeds_stats/leeds_united_match_details/Results_by_season/1987-88.php

http://www.ozwhitelufc.net.au/leeds_stats/leeds_united_match_details/Results_by_season/1988-89.php

http://www.ozwhitelufc.net.au/leeds_stats/leeds_united_match_details/Results_by_season/1989-90.php

www.waccoe.com

www.bbc.co.uk/sport

www.leedsunited.com

www.soccerbase.com

www.teamtak.com

www.statto.com

BOOKS

Leeds United Service Crew, By Caroline Gall, Milo Books, 2009

And Weve Had our Ups and Downs, by Gary Shepherd and David Saffer, Vertical Editions, 2005

Leeds United, The Complete Record, by Martin Jarred and Malcolm MacDonald, DB Publishing, 2012

All White, Leeds United's 100 Greatest Players, by Jon Howe and Andrew Dalton, Pitch Publishing, 2012

The Who's Who of Leeds United, by Malcolm MacDonald and Martin Jarred, Breedon Books Publishing, 2008.

Rothmans Football Yearbook, 1981-82, by Jack Rollin, Queen Anne Press, 1981

Rothmans Football Yearbook 1982-83 by Jack Rollin, Queen Anne Press, 1982

Rothmans Football Yearbook 1983-84 by Tony Williams, Queen Anne Press, 1983

Rothmans Football Yearbook 1984-85 by Peter Dunk, Queen Anne Press, 1984

Rothmans Football Yearbook 1985-86 by Peter Dunk, Queen Anne Press, 1985

Rothmans Football Yearbook 1986-87 by Peter Dunk, Queen Anne Press, 1986

Rothmans Football Yearbook 1987-88 by Peter Dunk, Queen Anne Press, 1987

Rothmans Football Yearbook 1988-89 by Jack Rollin, Queen Anne Press, 1988

Rothmans Football Yearbook 1989-90 by Jack Rollin, Queen Anne Press, 1989

Rothmans Football Yearbook 1990-91 by Jack Rollin, Queen Anne Press, 1990

PROGRAMMES

Leeds United v West Bromwich Albion, May 6th 1981

Leeds United v Brighton & Hove Albion, May 19th 1982

Leeds United v Charlton Athletic, November 6th 1982

Leeds United v Rotherham United, May 14th 1983

Leeds United v Charlton Athletic, May 2nd 1984

Leeds United v Shrewsbury Town, May 6th 1985

Leeds United v Carlisle United, April 26th 1986

Leeds United v Charlton Athletic, May 25th 1987

Leeds United v Crystal Palace, May 2nd 1988

Leeds United v Oldham Athletic, May 6th 1989

Leeds United v Leicester City, April 28th 1990

Leeds United v Manchester United, August 28th 1990.